SHELLEY MEMORIALS:

FROM AUTHENTIC SOURCES.

EDITED BY LADY SHELLEY.

TO WHICH IS ADDED

AN ESSAY ON CHRISTIANITY,

BY PERCY BYSSHE SHELLEY:

NOW FIRST PRINTED.

BOSTON:
TICKNOR AND FIELDS.
M.DCCC.LIX.

Republished, 1970
Scholarly Press, 22929 Industrial Drive East
St. Clair Shores, Michigan 48080

Library of Congress Catalog Card Number: 70-115269
Standard Book Number 403-00299-0

This edition is printed on a high-quality,
acid-free paper that meets specification
requirements for fine book paper referred
to as "300-year" paper

PREFACE BY THE EDITOR.

HAD it been left entirely to the uninfluenced wishes of Sir Percy Shelley and myself, we should have preferred that the publication of the materials for a life of Shelley which we possess should have been postponed to a later period of our lives; but as we had recently noticed, both in French and English magazines, many papers on Shelley, all taking for their text Captain Medwin's Life of the Poet, (a book full of errors,) and as other biographies had been issued, written by those who had no means of ascertaining the truth, we were anxious that the numerous misstatements which had gone forth should be corrected.

For this purpose, we placed the documents in our possession at the disposal of a gentleman whose literary habits and early knowledge of the poet seemed to point him out as the most fitting person for bringing them to the notice of the public. It was clearly understood, however, that our wishes and feelings should be consulted in all the details.

We saw the book for the first time when it was given to the world. It was impossible to imagine beforehand that from such materials a book could have been produced which has astonished and shocked those who have the greatest right to form an opinion on the character of Shelley; and it was with the most painful feelings of dismay that we perused what we could only look upon as a fantastic caricature, going forth to the public with my apparent sanction, for it was dedicated to myself.

Our feelings of duty to the memory of Shelley left us no other alternative than to withdraw the materials which we had originally intrusted to his early friend, and which we could not but consider had been strangely misused; and to take upon ourselves the task of laying them before the public, connected only by as slight a thread of narrative as might make them intelligible to the reader.

I have condensed as much as possible the details of the early period of Shelley's life, for I am aware that a great many of them have already appeared in print. The repetition of some, however, was considered advisable, since it is very probable that this volume will be read by many who have not seen, nor are likely to see, any other work giving an account of the writings and actions of Shelley.

I little expected that this task would devolve on me; and I am fully sensible how unequal I am to its proper fulfilment. To give a truthful statement of long-distorted facts, and to clear away the mist in which the misrepresentations of foes and professed friends have obscured the memory of Shelley, have been my only object. My labors have been greatly assisted by the help of an intimate and valued friend of Mr. Shelley, and by Mr. Edmund Ollier, whose father (the publisher of Shelley's works) at once freely offered me the use of some most interesting letters written to himself.

It is needless to say that the authenticity of all the documents contained in this volume is beyond question; but the public would do well to receive with the utmost caution all letters purporting to be by Shelley, which have not some indisputable warrant.*

The art of forging letters purporting to be relics of men of literary celebrity, and therefore apparently possessing a commercial value, has been brought to a rare perfection by those who have made Mr. Shelley's handwriting the object of their imitation. Within the last fourteen years, on no less than three occasions, have forged letters been presented to our family for purchase. In December, 1851, Sir Percy Shelley and the late Mr. Moxon bought several letters, all of which proved

---

* Those printed in the work to which allusion has already been made have never, for the most part, been seen by any other person than the author of that work; and the erasures which he has already made in them, together with the arrangement of their paragraphs, render them of doubtful value, however authentic may be the originals which that gentleman asserts he possesses.

to be forgeries, though, on the most careful inspection, we could scarcely detect any difference between these and the originals; for some were exact copies of documents in our possession. The watermark on the paper was generally, though not always, the mark appropriate to the date; and the amount of ingenuity exercised was most extraordinary. Mr. Moxon published what he had bought in a small volume, but recalled the work shortly afterwards, on discovering that some of the letters had been manufactured from articles in magazines and reviews, written long after Shelley's death.

The letter to Lord Ellenborough has never before been published; but I regard it as too extraordinary a production for a youth of eighteen to feel myself justified in suppressing it.

The fragmentary Essay on Christianity, published at the end of this volume, was found amongst Shelley's papers in the imperfect state in which it is now produced.

Boscombe, March 31, 1859

CONTENTS.

CHAP.		PAGE
I.	Early Life of Shelley	9
II.	First Love: Oxford: Expulsion	20
III.	First Marriage	28
IV.	Acquaintance with Godwin	32
V.	Literary Correspondence: 1812	47
VI.	Poetical Labors and Domestic Sorrows	60
VII.	England and Switzerland: Judgment of the Lord Chancellor: the "Revolt of Islam"	77
VIII.	Italy: 1818	100
IX.	"Prometheus Unbound:" the "Cenci"	121
X.	The Poet's Life at Pisa and Leghorn	144
XI.	Shelley and Byron at Pisa	161
XII.	The Bay of Spezzia	193
XIII.	Shelley's Death and Obsequies	210
XIV.	Mary Shelley	221
	Extracts from Mrs. Shelley's Private Journal	248
	Essay on Christianity	271

SHELLEY MEMORIALS.

CHAPTER I.

EARLY LIFE.

At the close of the last century, the family of the Shelleys had long held a high position among the large landholders of Sussex. Fortunate marriages in the two generations preceding the birth of the poet considerably increased the wealth and influence of the house, the head of which in 1806 was a stanch Whig, and on that ground obtained a baronetcy from the short-lived Whig Administration of that year. Fourteen years previously,—viz., on the 4th of August, 1792,—his illustrious grandson drew the first breath of life. Percy Bysshe Shelley was born on that day at Field Place, near Horsham, Sussex. He was the eldest son of Timothy Shelley, Esq., subsequently the second baronet; and was christened Bysshe after his grandfather. At six years of age, the boy was sent to a day-school near the residence of his parents, and at ten left home for the seminary of Dr. Greenlaw, at Brentford, Middlesex. Here he acquired the dead languages, seemingly by intuition; for, during school hours, he would gaze abstractedly at the passing clouds, or would scrawl in his school-books (a habit which he never lost) rude drawings of pines and cedars, in memory of those standing on the lawn of his native home.

He was regarded by his school-fellows as a strange, unsociable person. Never joining in their sports, he passed much of his leisure time in solitude, and on holidays would walk backwards and forwards along the southern wall of the playground, indulging in wild fancies and vague meditations. Still, though he seemingly neglected his tasks, he soon surpassed all his competitors; for his memory was so tenacious that he never forgot what he had once learned. He was very fond of reading, and eagerly perused all the books which were brought to school after the holidays. Stories of haunted castles, bandits, murderers, and various grim creations of fancy, were his favorites; and in after years he began his literary life by writing similar wild romances. When at Field Place during the vacations, his propensity to frolic, — always, however, unaccompanied by the infliction of pain on any living creature, — his partiality for moonlight walks, and his wonderfully exuberant imagination, came under the notice of his sister, who, in some spirited and graceful letters, has recorded a few of the incidents of this period.

"Bysshe," writes Miss Shelley, "would frequently come to the nursery, and was full of a peculiar kind of pranks. One piece of mischief, for which he was rebuked, was running a stick through the ceiling of a low passage, to find some new chamber which could be made effective for some flights of his vivid imagination. The tales to which we have sat and listened, evening after evening, seated on his knee, when we came to the dining-room for dessert, were anticipated with that pleasing dread which so excites the minds of children, and fastens so strongly and indelibly on the memory.

"There was a spacious garret under the roof of Field Place, and a room which had been closed for years, excepting an entrance made by the removal of a board in the garret floor. This unknown land was made the fancied habitation of an alchemist, old and gray, with a long beard. Books and a lamp, with all the attributes of a picturesque fancy, were poured into our listening ears. We were to go and see him 'some day,' but we were content to wait; and a cave was to be dug in the orchard for the accommodation of this Cornelius Agrippa.

"Bysshe was certainly fond of eccentric amusements; but they delighted us, as children, quite as much as if our minds had been naturally attuned to the same tastes; for we dressed ourselves in strange costumes to personate spirits or fiends, and Bysshe would take a fire-stove, and fill it with some inflammable liquid, and carry it flaming into the kitchen and to the back-door;

but discovery of this dangerous amusement soon put a stop to many repetitions.

"My brother was full of pleasant attention to children, though his mind was so far above theirs. He had a wish to educate some child, and often talked seriously of purchasing a little girl for that purpose. A tumbler, who came to the back-door to display her wonderful feats, attracted him, and he thought she would be a good subject for the purpose. But all these wild fancies came to nought. He would take his pony, and ride about the beautiful lanes and fields surrounding the house, and would *talk* of his intention; but he did not consider that board and lodging would be indispensable; and this difficulty, probably, was quite sufficient to prevent the talk from becoming reality."

In stature, Shelley was slightly yet elegantly formed; he had deep blue eyes, of a wild, strange beauty, and a high white forehead, overshadowed with a quantity of dark brown curling hair. His complexion was very fair; and, though his features were not positively handsome, the expression of his countenance was one of exceeding sweetness and sincerity. His look of youthfulness he retained to the end of his life, though his hair was beginning to get gray — the effect of intense study, and of the painful agitations of mind through which he had passed.

At the age of thirteen, Shelley went to Eton, and there began his earnest and life-long struggle with the world. When he entered the college, the practice of fagging flourished in all its vigor under the superintendence of Dr. Keate, the head-master. To the hightoned feelings of Shelley, this daily experience of unhappiness and tyranny was most revolting. Won by affection, but unconquered by blows, he was not the kind of youth likely to be happy at a public school. He refused to fag, and was treated by master and boys with the severity of passion and prejudice. But to all the devices of despotism he opposed a brave and dauntless spirit. At the same time, the purity, unselfishness, and generosity of his nature gained him friends among his school-fellows wherever there were any corresponding qualities to appreciate these signs of the nobility of his disposition. The power of fascination was, indeed, possessed by Shelley all through his existence.

Mr. Packe, one of his school-fellows at Eton, relates in a letter that the embryo poet's tutor "was one of the dullest men in the establishment;" that he did not understand his pupil in the least; that the boys made a point of constantly "goading Shelley into a rage," though they would run away, appalled, directly the storm they had provoked burst forth; that their victim would never deign to pursue them, but would generously assist their dulness when they came to him with petitions to help them in their tasks; and that he would not at any time submit to the trammels of the "gradus." His facility in making Latin verses is described by Mr. Packe as wonderful; but, not being in accordance with rule, these compositions were generally torn up. However, his greatest passion at Eton was for chemistry.

Often did he astonish the boys by his experiments, and once he accidentally set fire to some trees on the common. At that time he lodged at the house of his tutor, who, on a certain day, found Shelley in his room amusing himself by the production of a blue flame. Chemical experiments were prohibited in the boys' chambers; and the tutor (Mr. Bethel) somewhat angrily asked what the lad was doing. Shelley jocularly replied that he was raising the devil. Mr. Bethel seized hold of a mysterious implement on the table, and in an instant was thrown against the wall, having grasped a highly-charged electrical machine. Of course, the young experimentalist paid dearly for this unfortunate occurrence.

"Among my latest recollections of Shelley's life at Eton," concludes Mr. Packe, "is the publication of *Zastrozzi*,* for which I think he received 40*l*. With part of the proceeds he gave a most magnificent banquet to eight of his friends, among whom I was included. I cannot now call to mind the names of the other guests, excepting those of two or three who are not now living. Shelley was too peculiar in his genius and his habits to be 'the hare with many friends;' but the few who knew him loved him, and, if I may judge from myself, remember with affectionate regret that his schooldays were more adventurous than happy."

His opposition to fagging was not without some good effect for the time. He formed a conspiracy against the system, and succeeded in checking it — at any rate,

---

* A novel so called.

as far as regarded himself. But the fiery conflicts through which he had to pass impressed him with a sense of wretchedness which he afterwards described with passionate sweetness in the dedication of the *Revolt of Islam:* —

> "Thoughts of great deeds were mine, dear friend, when first
> The clouds which wrap this world from youth did pass.
> I do remember well the hour which burst
> My spirit's sleep: a fresh May dawn it was,
> When I walk'd forth upon the glittering grass,
> And wept, I knew not why; until there rose
> From the near school-room voices that, alas!
> Were but one echo from a world of woes —
> The harsh and grating strife of tyrants and of foes.
>
> "And then I clasp'd my hands, and look'd around;
> But none was near to mock my streaming eyes,
> Which pour'd their warm drops on the sunny ground:
> So, without shame, I spake: — 'I will be wise,
> And just, and free, and mild, if in me lies
> Such power; for I grow weary to behold
> The selfish and the strong still tyrannize
> Without reproach or check.' I then controll'd
> My tears; my heart grew calm; and I was meek and bold.
>
> "And from that hour did I, with earnest thought,
> Heap knowledge from forbidden mines of lore;
> Yet nothing that my tyrants knew or taught
> I cared to learn; but from that secret store
> Wrought linked armor for my soul, before
> It might walk forth, to war among mankind.
> Thus, power and hope were strengthen'd more and more
> Within me, till there came upon my mind
> A sense of loneliness, a thirst with which I pined."

The agony which Shelley thus endured, for the very

reason that he was more outspoken and truth-loving than other boys, is only one out of many painful examples of the frequent unfitness of schoolmasters and tutors for the duty which they seek to execute. However, we have improved since the early part of the present century; for those were the days when coercion was looked on as the only principle of school government, and when kindness was regarded as sentimentalism. With one exception, Shelley found his tutors men of rough, passionate, and hard natures, who claimed obedience merely because they possessed authority, without showing that they had any right to exercise their power by reason of superior discretion and serener wisdom; men who answered inquiries by cuffs, who sought to tame independence by violence, who exasperated the eccentricities of a wild but generous nature by the opposition of their own coarser minds, and who made religion distasteful by confounding it with dogmatism, and learning repulsive by allying it with pedantic formality. Had these instructors possessed half as much knowledge of human nature as of Greek roots and Latin "quantities," they might have developed and guided the mind of Shelley; but they thought not of this, and therefore only irritated a sensitive and ardent disposition.

The one exception to this narrow and unfortunate rule was Dr. Lind, an erudite scholar and amiable old man, much devoted to chemistry, at whose house Shelley passed the happiest of his Eton hours. He was a physician, and also one of the tutors. Mrs. Shelley relates that the Doctor often stood by to befriend and support the persecuted boy, and that her husband never, in after life, mentioned his name without love and veneration. The poet has introduced him into the *Revolt of Islam*, as the old hermit who liberates Laon from prison, and attends on him in sickness; and into *Prince Athanase*, as the wise and benignant Zonoras. In the former poem, (Canto IV.), he speaks of the hermit's heart having grown old without being corrupted, and adds: —

> " That hoary man had spent his livelong age
> In converse with the dead, who leave the stamp
> Of ever-burning thoughts on many a page
> When they are gone into the senseless damp
> Of graves. His spirit thus became a lamp
> Of splendor, like to those on which it fed.
> Through peopled haunts, the city and the camp,
> Deep thirst for knowledge had his footsteps led,
> And all the ways of men among mankind he read.
>
> " But custom maketh blind and obdurate
> The loftiest hearts. He had beheld the woe
> In which mankind was bound, but deem'd that fate,
> Which made them abject, would preserve them so."

For his strange pupil, whose scientific studies he directed, and whose pleasures he was eager to promote, Dr. Lind entertained a warm affection. When Shelley was seized with a dangerous fever, he hurried at a moment's notice to Field Place, and by his skill, and the soothing influence of his presence, saved his young friend from pressing danger. The incident in the *Revolt of Islam* is, therefore, a fact. The Doctor's kindness made on Shelley a deep and lasting impression; the more so as, from the indiscreet gossip of a servant, who had overheard some conversation between his father and the village doctor, Bysshe had come to the conviction that it was intended to remove him from the house to some distant asylum.

Shelley also felt an affectionate regard for his relations, particularly for his mother and sisters; and I have heard his eldest surviving sister relate that, during a supposed dangerous attack of gout under which his father was suffering, Bysshe would creep noiselessly to his room door, to watch and listen with tender anxiety.

The chemical experiments which the young student eagerly pursued at Eton were not discontinued when he was at home. His little sisters' frocks were often found stained with caustic; and Miss Shelley states in one of her letters:— "I confess my pleasure was entirely negatived by terror at the effects. Whenever he came to me with his piece of brown paper under his arm, and a bit of wire and a bottle (if I remember right), my heart would beat with fear at his approach; but shame kept me silent, and, with as many others as we could collect, we were placed hand in hand round the nursery table to be electrified; but when a suggestion was made that chilblains were to be cured by this means, my terror overwhelmed all other feelings, and the expression of it released me from all future annoyance. His own hands and clothes were constantly stained and corroded with acids, and it only seemed too probable that some day the house would be burnt down, or some serious mischief happen to himself or others from the explosion of combustibles. He used afterwards to speak himself with horror of having once swallowed by accident some arsenic at Eton, and feared he should never entirely recover from the shock it had inflicted on his constitution."

The boy Shelley now passes from our sight, and in the next chapter we shall have to speak of the poet in the first dawn of manhood.

CHAPTER II.

SHELLEY'S FIRST LOVE: OXFORD: EXPULSION.

In 1809, Shelley left Eton and returned home; and, being now of an age when it is not uncommon for people to have some touch of romance in them — a tendency which in him was developed to an unusual degree — his delight was to steal from the house, and to wander about by moonlight. His sister remarks that "the prosaic minds of ordinary mortals could not understand the pleasure to be derived from contemplating the stars, when he, probably, was repeating to himself lines which were soon to astonish those who looked upon him as a boy. The old servant of the family would follow him, and say that 'Master Bysshe only took a walk, and came back again.'" But (as in Mrs. Barbauld's excellent story of *Eyes and no Eyes*) the walk of one individual along a given road may be as different from that of another along the same path as a plenum is different from a vacuum. While the old servant, probably, saw little but the dust, and the monotonous hedges, and the figure of his young master walking on before, the undeveloped poet saw the infinite beauty of Nature spreading out in all its vastness and its minuteness, and was busied with speculations which gave an additional and still more solemn splendor to the mysterious loveliness of the world.

It was in the summer of this year that Bysshe fell desperately in love with his cousin, Harriet Grove, who, with her brother, was on a visit to Field Place. Elizabeth Shelley, who was then at home, always made one of the party in their moonlight strolls through the groves of Strood and the beautiful scenery of St. Leonard's; at which time the young lover had just reason to suppose that his attachment had met with sympathy. The whole party, with Bysshe's mother, went from Sussex to Mr. Grove's house in London; and the presence of the parents, inasmuch as it appeared to sanction the daily intercourse between the young couple, carried to Bysshe's mind a well-grounded expectation that his ardent affections and wandering sympathies had found at last a resting-place and a home. It was not, however, so to be. In the letters which passed between them after Miss Harriet Grove had returned to Wiltshire, the speculative doubts which were expressed on serious subjects alarmed the parents of the young lady for the future welfare of their daughter; and, on Shelley being expelled from Oxford, all intimacy was broken off, and Miss Grove soon made another choice. The blow fell on Bysshe with cruel force.

Shelley went to Oxford in 1810, in which year he became an undergraduate of University College. His secluded habits, and the ardor with which he threw all the energies of his mind into the acquisition of knowledge, were gratified by the customs and opportunities which he found when entering on this new mode of life. The forms of study at Oxford, then as now, were well adapted to exercise a beneficial influence on a mind somewhat prone, at the time, to mysticism, and to the neglect of practical results; and it must therefore be forever regretted that Shelley's academical career terminated so early.

Notwithstanding the extremely spiritual and romantic character of his genius, he applied himself to logic with ardor and success, and of course brought it to bear on all subjects, including theology. With his habitual disregard of consequences, he hastily wrote a pamphlet, in which the defective logic of the usual arguments in favor of the existence of a God was set forth; this he circulated among the authorities and members of his college. In point of fact, the pamphlet did not contain any positive assertion; it was merely a challenge to discussion, beginning with certain axioms, and finishing with a Q. E. D. The publication (consisting of only two pages) seemed rather to imply, on the part of the writer, a desire to obtain better reasoning on the side of the commonly received opinion, than any wish to overthrow with sudden violence the grounds of men's belief. In any case, however, had the heads of the college been men of candid and broad intellects, they would have recognized in the author of the obnoxious pamphlet an earnest love of truth, a noble passion for arriving at the nature of things, however painful the road. They might at least have sought, by argument and remonstrance, to set him in what they conceived to be the right path ; but either they had not the courage and the regard for truth necessary for such a course, or they were themselves the victims of a narrow education. At any rate, for this exercise of scholastic ingenuity, Shelley was expelled. A college friend of the poet (Mr. Hogg) shared the same fate for supporting his cause.

Mr. Hogg was the son of a gentleman in the north of England, whose acquaintance Shelley had made on his first arrival at Oxford, by sitting accidentally next to him at the hall dinner. To reason on any subject, at any time, with any one, was to Shelley an irresistible temptation. Discussion, and the clash of argument with another, by which he strove to render his own perception of any subject more clear and defined, delighted him. In Mr. Hogg he found a companion acute enough to be a worthy antagonist, and one who was always ready to place himself at his disposal for the combat of words. The two friends were inseparable. The bonds of sympathy between them were their literary tastes and their intellectual activity; and accordingly they walked, dined, and supped together, always discussing.

On Shelley receiving the sentence of expulsion, which was ready drawn up in due form, under the seal of the college, as if the act had been resolved on previously, he immediately withdrew, and ran, in a state of painful agitation, to Mr. Hogg's rooms. His friend, with a generosity not uncommon in youth, though too seldom retained in later life, speedily wrote a letter, remonstrating with the authorities for their act. He was at once sent for, and, after similar angry and ill-mannered questioning to that which had been pursued in Shelley's case, was sentenced to the same honorable expulsion already pronounced against his companion.

This unhappy event took place on Lady-Day, 1811. The friends quitted Oxford next morning for London.

So far as I can gather from some scanty records, I am inclined to think that, at this time, Shelley's father would have been satisfied with some very slight concessions on his son's part—in fact, with his promising a merely formal compliance with the ceremonies observed in most households. But, had he asked his native stream, the Arun, to run up to its source, he would have had as great a chance of obtaining his desire. Exasperated by his son's refusal to conform to the orthodox belief, he forbade him to appear at Field Place. On the sensitively affectionate feelings of the young controversialist and poet, this sentence of exclusion from his boyhood's home inflicted a bitter pang; yet he was determined to bear it, for the sake of what he believed to be right and true.

Conscious of high intellectual power, and of unsullied moral purity, he had been persecuted at Eton for the resistance he always offered to despotism. From Oxford he had been expelled, with great injustice, for a pamphlet which, if it had been given as a translation of the work of some old Greek, would have been regarded as a model of subtle metaphysical reasoning. He was excluded from his father's house for acting in accordance with the dictates of his conscience; and he found himself separated from the society of his equals in rank by his shyness, his sensitiveness, and his ascetic habits. Among his few acquaintances at this time whose names are known, there was not one who had the slightest affinity with him; and it is not easy to conceive a greater loneliness of the heart than that which he now experienced. Feeling himself thus isolated, his naturally high spirit rose higher still; and the young warrior for truth went forth into the world alone, but full of ardor. And it should be recollected that he made this sacrifice out of a purely abstract and intellectual love of truth; for to all sensual pleasures Shelley was a stranger. His usual food was bread, sometimes seasoned with a few raisins; his beverage was generally water; if he drank tea or coffee, he would take no sugar with it, because the produce of the cane was then obtained by slave labor; and the unanimous voice of those who knew him acquits him of any participation in the lax habits of life too common among young men. Yet, when less than nineteen, "fragile in health and frame; of the purest habits in morals; full of devoted generosity and universal kindness; glowing with ardor to attain wisdom; resolved, at every personal sacrifice, to do right; burning with a desire for affection and sympathy,—he was treated as a reprobate, cast forth as a criminal." *

On the other hand, the conduct of his father is susceptible of some excuse. Let those who utterly condemn him ask themselves how they would like the presence in

* Mrs. Shelley.

their houses of a disciple of Spinoza or of Calvin, whose enthusiasm never wanes, and whose voice is seldom silent; who, with the eloquence of conviction, obtrudes his doctrines at all times; who seeks the youngest daughter in the school-room, and the butler in his pantry, to make them converts, in the one case, to the moral excellence of materialism, — in the other, to the æsthetic comforts of eternal punishment by election; and, if they can conscientiously say they would like it, they may condemn the elder Mr. Shelley; but not unless. Still, it is to be regretted that a milder course was not pursued towards one who was peculiarly open to the teachings of love.

In the present day, when a brighter morn seems breaking on the future; when another spirit is breathing over us; when vengeance is departing from our laws, and love is gradually creeping in; when freedom of inquiry is becoming at once a social and a legal right; when the fierce voices of hatred, which burst in Shelley's time on the man bold enough to question the received notions of Church and State orthodoxy, have ceased, or are faintly heard; when a protecting hand is extended over the toil of women and children; when the claims of the uninstructed to their share of education are cordially admitted; when there is a growing conviction that all the inhabitants of the earth, whatever may be their creed, their color, or their clime, should enjoy a fair portion of the gifts of God, and that the chief duty of all is to gird themselves, as in one common brotherhood, for the struggle with the many moral and physical evils which are interwoven with our existence, — it is not difficult to understand the throbbing interest with which, in the distant colony and in the crowded street at home, the many turn to the Memorials of the life of him who, self-inspired and self-impelled, from the earliest dawn of manhood to his day of death, shrank from no sacrifice in his devotion to the cause of human welfare.

CHAPTER III.

SHELLEY'S FIRST MARRIAGE.

Up to the present period of Shelley's life, there has been little to chronicle with respect to his progress as an author. While at Oxford, he had published, in conjunction with Mr. Hogg, a little volume of burlesque verses, and, at a yet earlier date, when still at home, he had written a great many wild romances in prose, some of which have been printed, though they have never taken any place in literature, and are, in fact, the crude productions of an enthusiastic boy. It was not, however, till he had been drawn into the conflict of existence that he began that expression of his inner nature in immortal verse which has since astonished the world. But we must yet for a while follow the course of his private life.

Discarded by his father, Shelley was now left in a state of considerable pecuniary embarrassment, though this did not prevent his performing acts of munificence whenever he had any money at command. At one time he pawned his favorite solar microscope in order to relieve an urgent case of distress. He took lodgings in Poland Street, but was often without the means of meeting the current expenses of the day. His sisters, who were aware of this, saved their pocket-money, and, from time to time, sent secretly to their brother the fruits of their loving economy. This was the origin of a new phase in Shelley's existence. The Miss Shelleys were at that period at school at Brompton, and among the pupils was a very handsome girl named Harriet Westbrook. To her (as her parents resided in London) was consigned the task of conveying the little sums of money to Shelley, on whose susceptible fancy she dawned as a celestial being, illumining the dingy lodgings he inhabited. During the young lady's holidays, Shelley was a constant and welcome visitor at the house of her father; and, on Harriet's recovery from a slight indisposition, the young poet was chosen to escort her back to school. About the same time, he went for a few days to Field Place, and during this visit came to an amicable arrangement with his father. In consideration of a new settlement of the property, Sir Timothy agreed to make him an allowance of 200*l*. a year, and his son was to be at liberty to live where he pleased.

On leaving Field Place, he went to his cousin, Mr. T. Grove, who resided at a country house near Rhayader, in Radnorshire; whence, summoned by the pressing appeals of the Miss Westbrooks, he hastily returned to London, and eloped with Harriet.

From Shelley's own account, and from other sources of information which have since transpired, this unfortunate marriage seems to have been thus brought about:

To the wild eloquence of the enthusiast, who claimed it as his mission to regenerate the world, and to give it freedom from the shackles which had been too long endured, and which barred its progress to indefinite perfectibility, Harriet had in their many interviews in London bent a well-pleased ear; and when the day came for her return to her Brompton seminary, these new lights seemed to her mind to have a practical bearing on the forms and discipline of her boarding-school. She therefore petitioned her father to be allowed to remain at home. On his refusal, she wrote to Shelley; and, in a sad and evil hour for both, this girl, "who had thrown herself upon his protection," and "with whom he was not in love,"* became his wife.

From London, the young pair (whose united ages amounted to thirty-five years, Harriet being sixteen, and Shelley nineteen) went to Edinburgh, and thence to York. During their residence in the latter town, a new inmate was added to their circle in the person of the elder Miss Westbrook — a visitor whose presence was in many respects unfortunate. From strength of character and disparity of years (for she was much older than Harriet), she exercised a strong influence over her sister; and this influence was used without much discretion, and with little inclination to smooth the difficulties or promote the happiness of the young couple.

Keswick was the next resting-place to which the Shelleys were tempted by the beauty of the scenery and the cheapness of the necessaries of life, which gave some hope that their scanty income might suffice for their

* These expressions are quoted from some published letters of Shelley's, the authenticity of which I am not able to guarantee.

moderate wants. While residing here, the then Duke of Norfolk, who owned a large extent of land in the neighborhood, greatly interested himself in Shelley and his girl wife, introduced them to the neighboring gentry, directed his agents to furnish their house with necessary accommodations, and interceded (but in vain) with the elder Mr. Shelley. The young poet became speedily acquainted with Robert Southey, Thomas De Quincey, and other eminent writers then resident in the north. With Southey he was particularly intimate for a time, despite the diametrical opposition of their creeds. It was in the year 1811, also — but previous to his marriage — that Shelley sought and obtained the friendship of Leigh Hunt, whose noble-spirited political writings in the *Examiner* had moved the highest admiration of the youthful enthusiast. While the latter was yet unknown to the journalist, he had proposed to him, in a letter, a scheme for forming an association of Liberals, with a view to resisting the spread of despotic principles; and this was followed by Shelley's self-introduction. The friendship of the two writers was only broken by death.

CHAPTER IV.

SHELLEY'S ACQUAINTANCE WITH GODWIN.

WE now come to that period of Shelley's life when the poet became acquainted with William Godwin—a period fraught with important results, and one over which it will be necessary to linger.

An eminent place among the writers of the eighteenth century is due to the author of *Political Justice*. He came of a family which had long been connected with the Nonconformist ministry; for both his father and grandfather were Dissenting preachers in their generation, and the grandfather had enjoyed the intimate friendship of Dr. Watts, Neale, and Baker. William Godwin was born at Questwich, Norfolk, in 1756. He was educated at the Hoxton College by Dr. Kippis and Dr. Rees, and for some time followed the profession of his father at Stowmarket, Suffolk; but, in 1782, owing to a change in his religious opinions, he returned to London, and for ten years devoted himself with unwearied assiduity to historical and methaphysical inquiries. The result of this mental discipline was the publication, in 1793, of his *Political Justice*, the effect of which work on the public mind is sufficiently attested by the fact that three editions were sold in as many years. *Caleb Williams* and the *Enquirer* followed, and gave Godwin a reputation which he preserved unsullied through the whole of his long life.

From the commencement of his career in London, the philosopher lived in a small cottage, without any further attendance than that of a woman who came every morning to set the house in order for the day. Liberal overtures from the leaders of the Whig phalanx, who desired to enlist in their service so eminent and influential an author, were repeatedly made to him, and as often refused; for Godwin, like a second Andrew Marvell, disdained to be the slave of party. This stern independence of character, combined with the mild, unimpassioned manner with which he prosecuted his inquiries into subjects which most men at that time debated with the fierceness and acrimony of personal strife, soon gathered round him a small knot of disciples, who sat at his feet and gathered up his sayings as they might have done those of a sage of ancient Greece. He became, as it were, the recognized head of a small sect; and of this sect Shelley speedily regarded himself as a member. The poet wrote to the philosopher from Keswick, and, frankly stating his position, his marriage, and his prospects, proceeded to reveal his political, religious, and moral opinions, and to declare his long-cherished hope of being on some future day of use to his fellow-creatures. Towards this end, and for the better regulation of his pursuits and studies, he requested the aid of the author of *Political Justice*.

Godwin received this unexpected communication with great kindness, and a long and interesting correspondence ensued between the two writers. Some portions of this will be found in the present volume.

From Keswick, Shelley went to Dublin, and during this period the influence of his newly acquired friend and adviser was of incalculable benefit to him, in guarding him from the consequences which his own fearless impetuosity would have entailed, in his championship of Irish wrongs. Ireland was at that time a disgrace to England and to herself. A dominant caste — proud, resolute, and vindictive, opposed to all change, and certain, in the last resort, of the support of England's strength — misruled a population which was priest-ridden, ignorant, and adverse from labor. The priests themselves (with the exception of those who had been specially educated on the Continent, for the purpose of representing the interests and maintaining the dignity of their church in the more polished circles of Dublin) were scarcely more literate than the rabble over whom they possessed unbounded influence; and the Union had handed over to still meaner minds and yet more uncleanly hands the traditionary struggles for the perquisites of a delegated Court.

Loud was the cry of Irish patriotism when Shelley visited the sister island, where he flung himself, with his usual impulsive ardor, into the turbid stream of Hibernian politics. It was then that the value of Godwin's calm, experienced intellect became manifest; for there is no doubt that his letters supplied the necessary balance of prudence and mature thought to the youthful vehemence of Shelley's mind. This good effect was aided by an adventure which occurred to Bysshe during his advocacy of Irish grievances. On one occasion, at a meeting — probably a meeting of patriots — so much ill-will against the Protestants was shown, that Shelley was provoked to remark that the Protestants were fellow-Christians and fellow-subjects, and were therefore entitled to equal rights and equal toleration with the Papists. Of course, he was forthwith interrupted by savage yells. A fierce uproar ensued, and the denouncer of bigotry was compelled to be silent. At the same meeting, and afterwards, he was even threatened with personal violence, and the police suggested to him the propriety of quitting the country.

The philanthropic association which was to bestow Arcadian days on Ireland was accordingly abandoned, and, after a brief stay in the Isle of Man, and a residence of some duration in North Wales, Shelley and his wife sheltered themselves in a cottage at Lymouth, a place situated in a romantic part of North Devonshire. While here, Bysshe addressed a letter to Lord Ellenborough, touching the sentence passed by him on a man named Eaton, a London bookseller, for publishing the third part of Thomas Paine's *Age of Reason*. In a letter to Godwin he says: —

"What do you think of Eaton's trial and sentence? I mean not to insinuate that this poor bookseller has any characteristics in common with Socrates or Jesus Christ; still, the spirit which pillories and imprisons him is the same which brought them to an untimely end. Still, even in this enlightened age, the moralist and the reformer may expect coercion analogous to that used with the humble yet zealous imitator of their endeavors."

The larger part of the letter to Lord Ellenborough is appended below.* It is a composition of great eloquence and logical exactness of reasoning, and the truths which it contains on the subject of universal toleration are now generally admitted. At the time of writing this letter, Shelley was only nineteen years of age; and, from his earliest boyhood to his latest years, whatever varieties of opinion may have marked his intellectual course, he never for a moment swerved from the noble doctrine of unbounded liberty of thought and speech. To him, the rights of the intellect were sacred; and all kings, teachers, or priests, who sought to circumscribe the activity of discussion, and to check by force the full development of the reasoning powers, he regarded as enemies to the independence of man, who did their utmost to destroy the spiritual essence of our being.

"A LETTER to LORD ELLENBOROUGH, *occasioned by the Sentence which he passed on* Mr. D. J. EATON, *as publisher of the Third Part of Paine's* 'Age of Reason.'

"'Deorum offensa, Diis curæ.'

"'It is contrary to the mild spirit of the Christian religion; for no sanction can be found under that dispensation which will warrant a

---

* The omitted portions are the passages which Shelley introduced into the notes to *Queen Mab*, and which are printed in the collected edition of his works.

Government to impose disabilities and penalties upon any man on account of his religious opinions.' — MARQUIS WELLESLEY'S SPEECH. —*Globe*, July 2.

"ADVERTISEMENT. — I have waited impatiently for these last four months, in the hope that some pen fitter for the important task would have spared me the perilous pleasure of becoming the champion of an innocent man. This may serve as an excuse for delay to those who think that I have let pass the aptest opportunity; but it is not to be supposed that in four short months the public indignation raised by Mr. Eaton's unmerited suffering can have subsided.

"TO LORD ELLENBOROUGH.
"MY LORD,
"As the station to which you have been called by your country is important, so much the more awful is your responsibility; so much the more does it become you to watch lest you inadvertently punish the virtuous and reward the vicious.

"You preside over a Court which is instituted for the suppression of crime, and to whose authority the people submit on no other conditions than that its decrees should be conformable to justice.

"If it should be demonstrated that a judge had condemned an innocent man, the bare existence of laws in conformity to which the accused is punished would but little extenuate his offence. The inquisitor, when he burns an obstinate heretic, may set up a similar plea; yet few are sufficiently blinded by intolerance to acknowledge its validity. It will less avail such a judge to assert the policy of punishing one who has committed no crime. Policy and morality ought to be deemed synonymous in a court of justice; and he whose conduct has been regulated by the latter principle is not justly amenable to any penal law for a supposed violation of the former. It is true, my Lord, laws exist which suffice to screen you from the animadversion of any constituted power, in consequence of the unmerited sentence which you have passed upon Mr. Eaton; but there are no laws which screen you from the reproof of a nation's disgust — none which ward off the just judgment of posterity, if that posterity will deign to recollect you.

"By what right do you punish Mr. Eaton? What but antiquated precedents, gathered from times of priestly and tyrannical domination, can be adduced in palliation of an outrage so insulting to humanity and justice? Whom has he injured? What crime has he committed? Wherefore may he not walk abroad like other men, and follow his accustomed pursuits? What end is proposed in confining this man, charged with the commission of no dishonorable action? Wherefore did his aggressor avail himself of popular prejudice, and return no answer but one of commonplace contempt to a defence of plain and simple sincerity? Lastly, when the prejudices of the jury, as Christians, were strongly and unfairly inflamed * against this injured man, as a Deist, wherefore did not you, my Lord, check such unconstitutional pleading, and desire the jury to pronounce the accused innocent or criminal † without reference to the particular faith which he professed?

"In the name of justice, what answer is there to these questions? The answer which Heathen Athens made to Socrates is the same with which Christian England must attempt to silence the advocates of this injured man. 'He has questioned established opinions.' Alas! the crime of inquiry is one which religion never has forgiven. Implicit faith and fearless inquiry have in all ages been irreconcilable enemies. Unrestrained philosophy has in every age opposed itself to the reveries of credulity and fanaticism. The truths of astronomy demonstrated by Newton have superseded astrology; since the modern discoveries in chemistry, the philosopher's stone has no

---

* See the Attorney-General's speech.

† By Mr. Fox's Bill (1791) juries are, in cases of libel, judges both of the law and the fact.

longer been deemed attainable. Miracles of every kind have become rare in proportion to the hidden principles which those who study nature have developed. That which is false will ultimately be controverted by its own falsehood. That which is true needs but publicity to be acknowledged. . . .

"Wherefore, I repeat, is Mr. Eaton punished? Because he is a Deist. And what are you, my Lord? A Christian. Ha, then! the mask has fallen off. You persecute him because his faith differs from yours. You copy the persecutors of Christianity in your actions, and are an additional proof that your religion is as bloody, barbarous, and intolerant as theirs. If some Deistical bigot in power (supposing such a character for the sake of illustration) should, in dark and barbarous ages, have enacted a statute making the profession of Christianity criminal, if you, my Lord, were a Christian bookseller, and Mr. Eaton a judge, those arguments which you consider adequate to justify yourself for the sentence you have passed must likewise suffice, in the suppositionary case, to justify Mr. Eaton in sentencing you to Newgate and the pillory for being a Christian. Whence is any right derived, but that which power confers, for persecution? Do you think to convert Mr. Eaton to your religion by embittering his existence? You might force him by torture to profess your tenets, but he could not believe them except you should make them credible, which perhaps exceeds your power. Do you think to please the God you worship by this exhibition of your zeal? If so, the demon to whom some nations offer human hecatombs is less barbarous than the Deity of civilized society. . . . .

"If the law *de hæretico comburendo* has not been formally repealed, I conceive that, from the promise held out by your Lordship's zeal, we need not despair of beholding the flames of persecution rekindled in Smithfield. Even now the lash that drove Descartes and Voltaire from their native country, the chains which bound Galileo, the flames which burned Vanini, again resound. . . . Does the Christian God, whom his followers eulogize as the Deity of humility and peace — He, the regenerator of the world, the meek reformer — authorize one man to rise against another, and, because lictors are at his beck, to chain and torture him as an infidel?

"When the Apostles went abroad to convert the nations, were they enjoined to stab and poison all who disbelieved the divinity of Christ's mission? Assuredly, they would have been no more justifiable in this case than he is at present who puts into execution the law which inflicts pillory and imprisonment on the Deist.

"Has not Mr. Eaton an equal right to call your Lordship an infidel as you have to imprison him for promulgating a different doctrine from that which you profess? What do I say! Has he not even a stronger plea? The word infidel can only mean anything when applied to a person who professes that which he disbelieves. The test of truth is an undivided reliance on its inclusive powers; the test of conscious falsehood is the variety of the forms under which it presents itself, and its tendency towards employing whatever coercive means may be within its command, in order to procure the admission of what is unsusceptible of support from reason or persuasion. . . . .

"I hesitate not to affirm that the opinions which Mr. Eaton sustained, when undergoing that mockery of a trial, at which your Lordship presided, appear to me more true and good than those of his accuser; but, were they false as the visions of a Calvinist, it still would be the duty of those who love liberty and virtue to raise their voice indignantly against a reviving system of persecution — against the coercively repressing any opinion, which, if false, needs but the opposition of truth — which, if true, in spite of force must ultimately prevail.

"Mr. Eaton asserted that the Scriptures were, from beginning to end, a fable.* He did so; and the Attorney-General denied the proposition which he asserted, and asserted that which he denied. What singular conclusion is deducible from

* See the Attorney-General's speech.

this fact? None, but that the Attorney-General and Mr. Eaton sustained two opposite opinions. The Attorney-General puts some obsolete and tyrannical laws in force against Mr. Eaton, because he publishes a book tending to prove that certain supernatural events, which are supposed to have taken place eighteen centuries ago, in a remote corner of the world, did not actually take place. But how is the truth or falsehood of the facts in dispute relevant to the merit or demerit attachable to the advocates of the two opinions? No man is accountable for his belief, because no man is capable of directing it. Mr. Eaton is therefore totally blameless. What are we to think of the justice of a sentence which punishes an individual against whom it is not even attempted to attach the slightest stain of criminality?

"It is asserted that Mr. Eaton's opinions are calculated to subvert morality. How? What moral truth is spoken of with irreverence or ridicule in the book which he published? Morality, or the duty of a man and a citizen, is founded on the relations which arise from the association of human beings, and which vary with the circumstances produced by the different states of this association. This duty, in similar situations, must be precisely the same in all ages and nations. The opinion contrary to this has arisen from a supposition that the will of God is the source or criterion of morality. It is plain that the utmost exertion of Omnipotence could not cause that to be virtuous which actually is vicious. An all-powerful Demon might, indubitably, annex punishments to virtue and rewards to vice, but could not by these means effect the slightest change in their abstract and immutable natures. Omnipotence could vary, by a providential interposition, the relations of human society; in this latter case, what before was virtuous would become vicious, according to the necessary and natural result of the alteration; but the abstract natures of the opposite principles would have sustained not the slightest change. For instance, the punishment with which society restrains the robber, the assassin, and the ravisher, is just, laudable, and requisite. We admire and respect the institutions which curb those who would defeat the ends for which society was established; but, should a precisely similar coercion be exercised against one who merely expressed his disbelief of a system admitted by those intrusted with the executive power, using at the same time no methods of promulgation but those afforded by reason, certainly this coercion would be eminently inhuman and immoral; and the supposition that any revelation from an unknown Power avails to palliate a persecution so senseless, unprovoked, and indefensible, is at once to destroy the barrier which reason places between vice and virtue, and leave to unprincipled fanaticism a plea whereby it may excuse every act of frenzy which its own wild passions, not the inspirations of the Deity, have engendered.

"Moral qualities are such as only a human being can possess. To attribute them to the Spirit of the Universe, or to suppose that it is capable of altering them, is to degrade God into man, and to annex to this incomprehensible Being qualities incompatible with any possible definition of his nature.

"It may be here objected: Ought not the Creator to possess the perfections of the creature? No. To attribute to God the moral qualities of man, is to suppose him susceptible of passions, which, arising out of corporeal organization, it is plain that a pure Spirit cannot possess. . . . . But even suppose, with the vulgar, that God is a venerable old man, seated on a throne of clouds, his breast the theatre of various passions, analogous to those of humanity, his will changeable and uncertain as that of an earthly king; — still, goodness and justice are qualities seldom nominally denied him, and it will be admitted that he disapproves of any action incompatible with those qualities. Persecution for opinion is unjust. With what consistency, then, can the worshippers of a Deity whose benevolence they boast embitter the existence of their fellow being, because his ideas of that Deity are different from those which they entertain? Alas! there is no consistency in those persecutors who worship a benevolent Deity; those who worship a demon would alone act consonantly to these principles by imprisoning and torturing in his name.

"Persecution is the only name applicable to punishment inflicted on an individual in consequence of his opinions. What end is persecution designed to answer? Can it convince him whom it injures? Can it prove to the people the falsehood of his opinions? It may make *him* a hypocrite, and *them* cowards; but bad means can promote no good end. The unprejudiced mind looks with suspicion on a doctrine that needs the sustaining hand of power.

"Socrates was poisoned because he dared to combat the degrading superstitions in which his countrymen were educated. Not long after his death, Athens recognized the injustice of his sentence; his accuser, Melitus, was condemned, and Socrates became a demi-god. . . . .

"Man! the very existence of whose most cherished opinions depends from a thread so feeble, arises out of a source so equivocal,* learn at least humility; own at least that it is possible for thyself also to have been seduced by education and circumstance into the admission of tenets destitute of rational proof, and the truth of which has not yet been satisfactorily demonstrated. Acknowledge at least that the falsehood of thy brother's opinions is no sufficient reason for his meriting thy hatred. What! because a fellow being disputes the reasonableness of thy faith, wilt thou punish him with torture and imprisonment? If persecution for religious opinions were admitted by the moralist, how wide a door would not be opened by which convulsionists of every kind might make inroads on the peace of society! How many deeds of barbarism and blood would not receive a sanction! But I will demand, if that man is not rather entitled to the respect than the discountenance of society, who, by disputing a received doctrine

---

* He has just been indicating what he regards as the weak points in the proofs of the Christian religion.— ED.

either proves its falsehood and inutility (thereby aiming at the abolition of what is false and useless), or gives to its adherents an opportunity of establishing its excellence and truth. Surely this can be no crime. Surely the individual who devotes his time to fearless and unrestricted inquiry into the grand questions arising out of our moral nature ought rather to receive the patronage, than encounter the vengeance, of an enlightened legislature. I would have you to know, my Lord, that fetters of iron cannot bind or subdue the soul of virtue. From the damps and solitude of its dungeon it ascends, free and undaunted, whither thine, from the pompous seat of judgment, dare not soar. I do not warn you to beware lest your profession as a Christian should make you forget that you are a man; but I warn you against festinating that period which, under the present coercive system, is too rapidly maturing, when the seats of justice shall be the seats of venality and slavishness, and the cells of Newgate become the abodes of all that is honorable and true.

"I mean not to compare Mr. Eaton with Socrates or Jesus; he is a man of blameless and respectable character; he is a citizen unimpeached with crime; if, therefore, his rights as a citizen and a man have been infringed, they have been infringed by illegal and immoral violence. But I will assert that, should a second Jesus arise among men, should such a one as Socrates again enlighten the earth, lengthened imprisonment and infamous punishment (according to the regimen of persecution revived by your Lordship) would effect what hemlock and the cross have heretofore effected, and the stain on the national character, like that on Athens and Judea, would remain indelible, but by the destruction of the history in which it is recorded. . . . . .

"The horrible and wide-wasting enormities, which gleam like comets through the darkness of Gothic and superstitious ages, are regarded by the moralist as no more than the necessary effects of known causes; but, when an enlightened age and nation signalizes itself by a deed becoming none but bar-

barians and fanatics, philosophy itself is even induced to doubt whether human nature will ever emerge from the pettishness and imbecility of its childhood. The system of persecution, at whose new birth you, my Lord, are one of the presiding midwives, is not more impotent and wicked than inconsistent. The press is loaded with what are called (ironically, I should conceive) *proofs* of the Christian religion; these books are replete with invective and calumny against infidels; they presuppose that he who rejects Christianity must be utterly divested of reason and feeling; they advance the most unsupported assertions, and take as first principles the most revolting dogmas. The inferences drawn from these assumed premises are imposingly logical and correct; but if a foundation is weak, no architect is needed to foretell the instability of the superstructure. If the truth of Christianity is not disputable, for what purpose are these books written? If there are sufficient to prove it, what further need of controversy? . . . .

"Let us suppose that some half-witted philosopher should assert that the earth was the centre of the universe, or that ideas could enter the human mind independently of sensation or reflection. This man would assert what is demonstrably incorrect; he would promulgate a false opinion. Yet, would he therefore deserve pillory and imprisonment? By no means; probably few would discharge more correctly the duties of a citizen and a man. I admit that the case above stated is not precisely in point. The thinking part of the community has not received as indisputable the truth of Christianity, as they have that of the Newtonian system. A very large portion of society, and that powerfully and extensively connected, derives its sole emolument from the belief of Christianity as a popular faith.

"To torture and imprison the assertor of a dogma, however ridiculous and false, is highly barbarous and impolitic. How, then, does not the cruelty of persecution become aggravated when it is directed against the opposer of an opinion yet under dispute, and which men of unrivalled acquirements, penetrating genius, and stainless virtue, have spent, and at last sacrificed, their lives in combating!

"The time is rapidly approaching — I hope that you, my Lord, may live to behold its arrival — when the Mahometan, the Jew, the Christian, the Deist, and the Atheist, will live together in one community, equally sharing the benefits which arise from its association, and united in the bonds of charity and brotherly love. My Lord, you have condemned an innocent man; no crime was imputed to him, and you sentenced him to torture and imprisonment. I have not addressed this letter to you with the hope of convincing you that you have acted wrong. The most unprincipled and barbarous of men are not unprepared with sophisms to prove that they would have acted in no other manner, and to show that vice is virtue. But I raise my solitary voice, to express my disapprobation, so far as it goes, of the cruel and unjust sentence you passed upon Mr. Eaton — to assert, so far as I am capable of influencing, those rights of humanity which you have wantonly and unlawfully infringed.

"My Lord, yours," &c.

CHAPTER V.

LITERARY CORRESPONDENCE: 1812.

IN the solitude of Lymouth, Shelley read much, projected many works, and addressed several letters on literary and social topics to his friends. These letters will, for the most part, speak for themselves, and will unfold, to a certain extent in an autobiographical form, some of the ensuing phases of the poet's life. The first of them is addressed to Mr. Thomas Hookham, of Old Bond Street, a valued friend of Shelley, and runs as follows:—

"*Lymouth, Barnstaple, Aug.* 18*th*, 1812.

" DEAR SIR,

"YOUR parcel arrived last night, for which I am much obliged. Before I advert to any other topic, I will explain the contents of mine in which this is enclosed. In the first place, I send you fifty copies of the Letter [to Lord Ellenborough]. I send you a copy of a work which I have procured from America, and which I am exceedingly anxious should be published. It develops, as you will perceive by the most superficial reading, the actual state of republicanized Ireland, and appears to me, above all things, calculated to remove the prejudices which have too long been cherished of that oppressed country. I enclose also two pamphlets which I printed and distributed whilst in Ireland some months ago (no bookseller daring to publish them). They were on that account attended with only partial success, and I request your opinion as to the probable result of publishing them with the annexed suggestions in one pamphlet, with an explanatory preface, in *London*. They would find their way to Dublin.

"You confer on me an obligation, and involve a high compliment, by your advice. I shall, if possible, prepare a volume of essays, moral and *religious*, by November; but, all my MSS. now being in Dublin, and from peculiar circumstances not immediately obtainable, I do not know whether I can. I enclose also, by way of specimen, all that I have written of a little poem begun since my arrival in England. I conceive I have matter enough for six more cantos. You will perceive that I have not attempted to temper my constitutional enthusiasm in that poem. Indeed, a poem is safe; the iron-souled Attorney-General would scarcely dare to attack [it]. The Past, the Present, and the Future, are the grand and comprehensive topics of this poem. I have not yet half exhausted the second of them.*

"I shall take the liberty of retaining the two poems which you have sent me (Mr. Peacock's), and only regret that my powers are so circumscribed as to prevent me from becoming extensively useful to your friend. The poems abound with a genius, an information, the power and extent of which I admire, in proportion as I lament the object of their application. Mr. Peacock conceives that commerce is prosperity; that the glory of the British flag is the happiness of the British people; that George III., so far from having been a warrior and a tyrant, has been a patriot. To me it appears otherwise; and I have rigidly accustomed myself not to be seduced by the loveliest eloquence or the sweetest strains to regard with intellectual toleration that which ought not to be tolerated by those who love liberty, truth, and virtue. I mean not to say that Mr. Peacock does not love them; but I mean to say that he regards those means [as] intrumental to their progress, which I regard [as] instrumental to their destruction. (See

* The poem here alluded to is (I conceive) *Queen Mab.* — ED.

Genius of the Thames, pp. 24, 26, 28, 76, 98.) At the same time, I am free to say that the poem appears to be far beyond mediocrity in genius and versification, and the conclusion of *Palmyra* the finest piece of poetry I ever read. I have not had time to read the *Philosophy of Melancholy*, and of course am only half acquainted with that genius and those powers whose application I should consider myself rash and impertinent in criticizing, did I not conceive that frankness and justice demand it.

"I should esteem it as a favor if you would present the enclosed letter to the Chevalier Lawrence. I have read his *Empire of the Nairs;* nay, have it. Perfectly and decidedly do I subscribe to the truth of the principles which it is designed to establish.

"I hope you will excuse, nay and doubt not but you will, the frankness I have used. Characters of our liberality are so wondrous rare, that the sooner they know each other, and the fuller and more complete that knowledge is, the better.

"Dear Sir, permit me to remain
"Yours, very truly,
"PERCY B. SHELLEY."

"I am about translating an old French work, professedly by M. Mirabaud — not the famous one — *La Système de la Nature*. Do you know anything of it?

"*To T. Hookham, Esq., Bond Street, London.*"

Although by this time several letters had passed between Shelley and Godwin, they had never met. The former therefore addressed to the latter a warm invitation to pay him and his wife a rural visit at their cottage, where, in the perusal of ancient authors, and the interchange of discourse on high social themes, they might become personally acquainted. Godwin, however, did not go immediately to Lymouth; and, in a letter dated

July 7th, 1812, Shelley declines to press the invitation, because, as his wife suggested to him, their wished-for guest was at that time in delicate health, and their rooms " were complete servants' rooms." Allusion is made in the same letter to the Shelleys going up to London, and living with the Godwins. On the 18th of September, the author of *Political Justice* unexpectedly arrived at Lymouth — only to find that the young couple had left since August 31st. This must have been a great vexation to Godwin; for, in a communication to his wife, written from Bristol, previous to embarking for Devonshire, he speaks of Shelley as " the young man who has so greatly excited my curiosity." A subsequent letter to Mrs. Godwin gives the details of the misadventure.

" *Lymouth, Valley of Stones, Sept. 19th,* 1812.

" MY DEAR LOVE,

" THE Shelleys are gone! have been gone these three weeks. I hope you hear this first from me; I dread lest every day may have brought you a letter from them, conveying this strange intelligence. I know you would conjure up a thousand frightful ideas of my situation under this disappointment. I have myself a disposition to take quietly any evil, when it can no longer be avoided, when it ceases to be attended with uncertainty, and when I can already compute the amount of it. I heard this news instantly on my arrival at this place, and therefore walked immediately (that is, as soon as I had dined) to the Valley of Stones, that, if I could not have what was gone away, I might at least not fail to visit what remained.

" You advise me to return by sea. I thank you a thousand times for your kind and considerate motive in this; but certainly nothing more repulsive could be proposed to me at this moment than a return by sea. I left Bristol at one o'clock on Wednesday, and arrived here at four o'clock on Friday (yesterday), after a passage of fifty-one hours. We had fourteen passengers, and only four berths; therefore, I lay down only once for a few hours. We had very little wind, and accordingly regularly tided it for six hours, and lay at anchor for six, till we reached this place. This place is fifteen miles short of Ilfracombe. If the captain, after great entreaty from the mate and one of his passengers (for I cannot entreat for such things), [had not] lent me his own boat to put me ashore, I really think I should have died with *ennui*. We anchored, Wednesday night, somewhere within sight of the Holmes (small islands, so called, in the Bristol Channel). The next night we came within sight of Minehead; but the evening set in with an alarming congregation of black clouds, the sea rolled vehemently without a wind (a phenomenon, which is said to portend a storm), and the captain, in a fright, put over to Penarth, near Cardiff, on the coast of Wales, and even told us that he should put us ashore there for the night. At Penarth, he said, there was but one house; but it had a fine large barn annexed to it, capable of accommodating us all. This was a cruel reverse to me and my fellow passengers, who had never doubted that we should reach the end of our voyage some time in the second day. By the time, however, we had made the Welsh Coast, the frightful symptoms disappeared, the night became clear and serene, and I landed here happily — that is, without further accident — the next day. These are small events to persons accustomed to a seafaring life, but they were not small to me; and you will allow that they were not much mitigated by the elegant and agreeable accommodations of our crazed vessel. I was not decisively sea-sick; but had qualmish and discomforting sensations from the time we left the Bristol river, particularly after having lain down a few hours on Wednesday night.

"Since writing the above, I have been to the house where Shelley lodged, and I bring good news. I saw the woman of the house and I was delighted with her. She is a good creature, and quite loved the Shelleys. They lived here nine weeks and three days. They went away in a great hurry, and in debt to her and two more. They gave her a draft upon the Honorable Mr. Lawleys, brother to Lord Cloncurry, and they borrowed of her twenty-nine shillings, beside 3*l.* that she got for them from a neighbor, all of which they faithfully returned when they got to Ilfracombe, the people not choosing to change a bank-note which had been cut in half for safety in sending it by the post.* But the best news is, that the woman says they will be in London in a fortnight. This quite comforts my heart."

In the restlessness of his disposition, Shelley had proceeded to Tanyralt, Caernarvonshire, where he hired a cottage belonging to a Mr. Maddox. This gentleman had reclaimed several thousand acres from the sea; but the embankment proved insufficient during an unusually high tide. The poor cottagers living on this hazardous land were thrown into great distress by the incursions of the sea consequent on the breaches made in the earthworks; and Shelley now exhibited a remarkable proof of that noble munificence which was one of the most striking features of his character. He personally solicited subscriptions from the gentlemen of the neighborhood, and himself headed the list with a donation of 500*l.*, though his means, as the reader has seen, were small. But he did not allow his zeal to stop even here; for, accompanied by his wife, he hurried up to London, to obtain further succor. He was finally successful in his efforts; the embankment was repaired and strengthened, and the inhabitants were protected from future risk.

* They had received only the half. — ED.

During his visit to London, Shelley made the personal acquaintance of Godwin, with whom he lived for a time; and to the philosopher's daughter Fanny he addressed the subjoined letter, after having rather abruptly left their house: —

Dec. 10*th*, 1812.

" Dear Fanny,

"So you do not know whether it is *proper* to write to me? Now, one of the most conspicuous considerations that arise from such a topic is — who and what am I ? I am one of those formidable and long-clawed animals called a *man*, and it is not until I have assured you that I am one of the most inoffensive of my species, that I live on vegetable food, and never bit since I was born, that I venture to obtrude myself on your attention. But to be serious. I shall feel much satisfaction in replying, with as much explicitness as my nature is capable of, to any questions you may put to me. I know that I have in some degree forfeited a direct claim to your confidence and credit, and that of your inestimable circle; but, if you will believe me as much as you can, I will be as sincere as I can. I certainly am convinced that, with the exception of one or two isolated instances, I am so far from being an insincere man, that my plainness has occasionally given offence, and caused some to accuse me of being defective in that urbanity and toleration which is supposed to be due to society. Allow me, in the absence of the topics which are eventually to be discussed between us, to assume the privilege you have claimed, and ask a question. How is Harriet a fine lady ? You indirectly accuse her in your letter of this offence — to me the most unpardonable of all. The ease and simplicity of her habits, the unassuming plainness of her address, the uncalculated connection of her thought and speech, have ever formed, in my eyes, her greatest charms; and none of these are compatible with fashionable life, or the attempted assumption of its vulgar and noisy *éclat*. You have a prejudice to contend with in making me a convert to this last opinion of yours, which, so long as I have a living and daily witness to its futility before me, I fear will be insurmountable. The second accusation (the abruptness of our departure) has more foundation, though in its spirit it is not less false and futile than the first. It must indeed, I confess it, have appeared insensible and unfeeling; it must have appeared an ill return for all the kind greetings we had received at your house, to leave it in haste and coldness — to leave even the enlightened and zealous benevolence of Godwin ever [active] for good, and never deterred or discouraged in schemes for rectifying our perplexed affairs — to bid not one adieu to one of you; but, had you been placed in a situation where you might justly have balanced all our embarrassments, qualms, and fluctuations, had seen the opposite motives combating in our minds for mastery, had felt some tithe of the pain with which at length we submitted to a galling yet unappealable necessity, you would have sympathized rather than condemned, have pitied rather than criminated us unheard. Say the truth: did not a sense of the injustice of our supposed unkindness add some point to the sarcasms which we found occasionally in your last letter? . . .

"If all my laughs were not dreadful, Sardonic grins, disgraceful to the most hideous of Cheshire cats, I should certainly laugh at two things in your last letter. The one is, "not knowing whether it is proper to write to me," lest — God knows what might happen; and the other is, comparing our movement to that of a modern novel. Now, a novel (modern or ancient) never moves but as the reader moves, and I, being a reader, if I take up one of these similitudes of our progress, never can get beyond the third line in the second page; therefore, you ought rather to have compared a novel to a snail than to us.

"Now, my dear Fanny, do not be angry at either my laughs, my criticisms, or my queries. They proceed from levity, my proper view of things, and my desire of setting them before you in what I consider a right light.

"Your questions shall be answered with precision; and, if hope in my quality as a man be not too tremendous, I shall acquire from the result an interesting and valuable correspondent.

"With much esteem, your true friend,
"P. B. SHELLEY.
" To Miss Fanny Godwin."

The following letter of literary advice from Godwin to Shelley possesses great interest:—

"Dec. 10*th*, 1812.
"MY DEAR SHELLEY,

"I SIT down the sooner to answer your very kind and excellent letter, because, if you are really desirous to make an experiment of a plan of my recommending, it would be unfair and unjust in me to withhold the information you ask.

" The light in which I should wish every man, every young man in particular, to consider the study of history, is as a means of becoming acquainted with whatever of noble, useful, generous, and admirable, human nature is capable of designing and performing. To see all this illustrated by examples carrying it directly into act, is, perhaps, superior to all the theories and speculations that can possibly be formed. History, in its most comprehensive sense, is a detail of all that man has done in solitude or in society, so far as it can be rendered matter of record. It is our own fault, therefore, if we do not select and dwell upon the best. This is so much matter of feeling among all who read history, that it is universally agreed that, next to the history of our own country, the histories of Greece and Rome most deserve to be studied. Why? Because in them the achievements of the human species have been most admirable; in Rome, in high moral and social qualities; in Greece, both in them and also in literature and art.

" The just way of criticizing man, in my opinion, is analogous to the right way of criticizing works of literature and art. When you talk to me of Milton and Shakspeare, I should begin with saying: Let us set their faults out of our view; not that they are never to be considered, but that this makes no part of what is most peculiar in them. Faults are like paper and ink; no book can exist without them; but they have nothing to do, in the first instance, with deciding upon the merits of an author. Put a new book into my hands, and the first question I shall ask you, if I question you wisely, is: What are its excellencies? Does it exhibit any grand views? Does it contain any beautiful passages? Here all the good and all the honor lies. Just so is man. I am bound first to examine whether there were really great and high qualities in Cato, in Regulus, in Brutus, in Solon, in Themistocles; and when I have made my very heart familiar with the conception of these, I will then proceed, if you like, to the examination of those defects by which they were allied to the weakness and errors of our common nature. A true student is a man seated in his chair, and surrounded with a sort of intrenchment and breastwork of books. It is for boarding-school misses to read one book at a time. Particularly when I am sifting out facts, either of science or history, I must place myself in the situation of a man making a book, rather than reading books. When I have studied the Grecian history in Homer, in Herodotus, Thucydides, Xenophon, and Plutarch, together with those of the moderns that are most capable, or most elaborate, in unfolding or appreciating the materials the ancients have left us, I shall then begin to know what Greece was. I need not, of course, mention how superior is the information and representation of contemporaries to those who come afterwards and write their stories over again. The compilers are a sort of middle class between the real authors and the makers of dictionaries. True reading is investigation — not a passive reception of what our author gives us, but an active inquiry, appreciation, and digestion of his subject.

"Yet there is a certain difficulty in this. We ought first to take a comprehensive survey of every subject, and a private view of every author who, for his own merits, is worth our studying. Hence it follows that there are various processes to be successively performed by him who would master the history of any one country or memorable period; and hence it appears (what has been observed in various forms by many writers) that it is almost impossible for any man to get fully to the end of any subject. There is another rule, that, both from experience and reason, I should strongly recommend to any one desirous of becoming a student, and that is, to have three or four different studies for different parts of the day, or, if you will, to be taken up in a sort of rotation in each day. Such a plan adds wonderfully to the stimulus moving us, and to the progress actually made. I have for the greater part of my life read at least for one hour a day in some Greek, and for one hour in some Latin, author; and I am sure I have done twice as much as I should have done in any other way of proceeding.

"You ask me concerning some of our elder writers, and I will therefore very briefly mention a few. I observed to you that Shakspeare had many contemporary dramatists, any one of which would have done for almost the best man of any other age. Such were Ben Jonson, Beaumont and Fletcher, Webster, Ford, Dekker, Heywood, and Massinger. Then what illustrious poets had those times in Spenser, Drayton, and Daniel! not to mention the minor poets (I mean in quantity), such as Davies and Donne. Chapman's Homer has infinitely more fire than any other translation I have ever read. He was thoroughly invested and penetrated with the sacredness of the poetic character.

"To proceed from poetry to prose. Shakspeare, Bacon, and Milton are the three greatest contemplative characters that this island has produced. Therefore, as I put Shakspeare and Milton at the head of our poetry, I put Bacon and Milton at the head of our prose. Yet what astonishing prose writers had we in Sir Thomas Browne and Jeremy Taylor! not to mention two others, only inferior to them, Robert Burton and

Isaac Walton. Hobbes and Shelton, also, as prose translators may almost rank with Chapman in verse.

"Those were the times when authors thought. Every line is pregnant with sense, and the reader is inevitably put to the expense of thinking likewise. The writers were richly furnished with conception, imagination, and feeling; and out of the abundance of their hearts flowed the lucubrations they committed to paper. *You* have what appears to me a false taste in poetry. You love a perpetual sparkle and glittering, such as are to be found in Darwin, and Southey, and Scott, and Campbell."

Some light is thrown on the peculiar literary tastes and antipathies of Shelley by a letter which he wrote about this time to Mr. Hookham, commissioning that gentleman to purchase certain books for him. The disgust of history here confessed has probably been shared by all minds which have longed for a state of ideal perfection; but the young student resolved to follow the advice of his self-chosen guide, whose words the reader has just perused.

"*Tanyralt, Dec. 17th,* 1812.

"My dear Sir,

"You will receive the *Biblical Extracts* * in a day or two by the twopenny post. I confide them to the care of a person going to London. Would not Daniel J. Eaton publish them? Could the question be asked him in any manner?

"I am also preparing a volume of minor poems, respecting whose publication I shall request your judgment, both as publisher and friend. A very obvious question would be — Will they sell or not? Subjoined is a list of books which I wish you to send me very soon. I am determined to apply myself

* This work has never been published. — Ed.

to a study that is hateful and disgusting to my very soul, but which is, above all studies, necessary for him who would be listened to as a mender of antiquated abuses. I mean that record of crimes and miseries, History. You see that the metaphysical works to which my heart hankers are not numerous in this list. One thing will you take care of for me? that those standard and respectable works on history, &c., be of the cheapest possible editions. With respect to metaphysical works, I am less scrupulous.

"*Spinoza* you may or may not be able to obtain. Kant is translated into Latin by some Englishman. I would prefer that the Greek classics should have Latin or English versions printed opposite. If not to be obtained thus, they must be sent otherwise.

" Mrs. Shelley is attacking Latin with considerable resolution, and can already read many odes in Horace. She unites with her sister and myself in best wishes to yourself and brother.

" Your very sincere friend,
" P. B. SHELLEY.

"*T. Hookham, Esq.*,
 " *15 Bond Street, London.*"

CHAPTER VI.

POETICAL LABORS AND DOMESTIC SORROWS.

THE poetical element in Shelley's nature — that faculty by which we mainly know him, though he himself conceived it to be secondary to his love of logic and metaphysics — was now beginning to develop itself more fully and systematically than it had yet done. That he must have felt an intense pleasure in the gradual unfolding of that gorgeous imagination which afterwards produced so many images of almost supernatural loveliness, cannot be doubted; but, at the same time, his keen, critical perceptions detected with remarkable accuracy the faults of his early productions. In writing to Mr. Hookham, during the January of 1813, he says: "My poems will, I fear, little stand the criticism even of friendship. Some of the later ones" (it should be recollected that these "later ones" must now be regarded as among the early fruit) " have the merit of conveying a meaning in every word, and all are faithful pictures of my feelings at the time of writing them; but they are in a great measure obscure. One fault they are indisputably exempt from — that of being a volume of *fashionable literature*. I doubt not but your friendly hand will clip the wings of my Pegasus considerably."

The early poems of Shelley, however, showed nothing more than the faults incidental to all young writers; and from the midst of their greatest obscurities issued a golden dawn of promise.

But the pursuits of art were always cheerfully abandoned by the poet when any occasion arose for the exercise of his philanthropy, or whenever he conceived himself called upon to vindicate and support an oppressed fellow-struggler for liberty and justice. In the year 1813, one of a series of government prosecutions of the *Examiner* newspaper, for speaking with more freedom on political topics than rulers at that time would tolerate, ended in the conviction of Messrs. John and Leigh Hunt, who were sentenced to two years' imprisonment, and condemned to pay a fine of 1,000*l*. Hereupon Shelley wrote from Tanyralt, as follows, to Mr. Hookham:—

"*February*, 1813.

"My dear Sir,

"I am boiling with indignation at the horrible injustice and tyranny of the sentence pronounced on Hunt and his brother; and it is on this subject that I write to you. Surely the seal of abjectness and slavery is indelibly stamped upon the character of England.

"Although I do not retract in the slightest degree my wish for a subscription for the widows and children of those poor men hung at York, yet this 1,000*l*. which the Hunts are sentenced to pay is an affair of more consequence. Hunt is a brave, a good, and an enlightened man. Surely the public, for whom Hunt has done so much, will repay in part the great debt of obligation which they owe the champion of their liberties and virtues; or are they dead, cold, stone-hearted, and insensible — brutalized by centuries of unremitting bondage? However that may be, they surely may be excited into some slight acknowledgment of his merits. Whilst hundreds of thousands are sent to the tyrants of Russia, he pines in a dungeon, far from all that can make life desired.

"Well, I am rather poor at present; but I have 20*l.* which is not immediately wanted. Pray, begin a subscription for the Hunts; put down my name for that sum, and, when I hear that you have complied with my request, I will send it you.* Now, if there are any difficulties in the way of this scheme of ours, for the love of liberty and virtue, overcome them. O, that I might wallow for one night in the Bank of England!

"*Queen Mab* is finished and transcribed. I am now preparing the notes, which shall be long and philosophical. You will receive it with the other poems. I think that the whole should form one volume; but of that we can speak hereafter.

"As to the French *Encyclopédie*, it is a book which I am desirous — very desirous — of possessing; and, if you could get me a few months' credit (being at present rather low in cash), I should very much desire to have it.

"My dear sir, excuse the earnestness of the first part of my letter. I feel warmly on this subject, and I flatter myself that, so long as your own independence and liberty remain uncompromised, you are inclined to second my desires.

"Your very sincere friend,

"P. B. SHELLEY.

"P. S. — If no other way can be devised for this subscription, will you take the trouble on yourself of writing an appropriate advertisement for the papers, inserting, by way of stimulant, my subscription?

"On second thoughts, I enclose the 20*l.*"

---

* The Hunts, with a noble magnanimity, for which they long suffered in a worldly point of view, however great might have been the reward of their own consciences, refused to accept any subscription, public or private, and paid the fine entirely out of their own pockets. — ED.

According to Mrs. Shelley, in the collected edition of her husband's works, and to the poet himself, as we shall shortly see, the latter was eighteen when he wrote *Queen Mab;* but it would appear from the foregoing that it was at least not completed before he was in his twenty-first year. He never published it (though at first he designed to do so), but distributed copies amongst his friends. In 1821, however, when Shelley was in Italy, an edition was surreptitiously issued; on which its author applied to Chancery for an injunction to restrain the sale. In addressing the *Examiner* (under date June 22d) on the subject, he thus spoke of the chief composition of his youth: —

"A poem, entitled *Queen Mab,* was written by me at the age of eighteen — I dare say, in a sufficiently intemperate spirit. I have not seen this production for several years; I doubt not but that it is perfectly worthless in point of literary composition, and that, in all that concerns moral and political speculation, as well as in the subtiler discriminations of metaphysical and religious doctrine, it is still more crude and immature. I am a devoted enemy to religious, political, and domestic oppression; and I regret this publication, not so much from literary vanity, as because I fear it is better fitted to injure than to serve the sacred cause of freedom." And in a letter to his publisher, Mr. Ollier, dated June 11th, 1821, he uses almost the same words, and speaks of the poem as "villanous trash" — in which sweeping condemnation, however, many readers will disagree with him. He continues: —

"In the name of poetry, and as you are a bookseller

(you observe the strength of these conjurations), pray, give all manner of publicity to my disapprobation of this publication; in fact, protest for me in an advertisement in the strongest terms. I ought to say, however, that I am obliged to this piratical fellow in one respect; that he has omitted, with a delicacy for which I thank him heartily, a foolish dedication to my late wife, the publication of which would have annoyed me, and indeed is the only part of the business that could seriously have annoyed me, although it is my duty to protest against the whole. I have written to my attorney to do what he can to suppress it, although I fear that, after the precedent of Southey, there is little probability of an injunction being granted." The "fear" here expressed proved to be well based. The law gives no protection to a heretical book, and in fact refuses to acknowledge it, except as the object of a prosecution; and so the Court of Chancery connived at the sale of a work, the opinions of which it held to be pernicious.

The more exalted Platonical speculations of his later life naturally made Shelley discontented with the somewhat cold, though qualified, materialism of *Queen Mab*. But it is a mistake to describe that poem as utterly atheistical in its tendency. It is rather pantheistical, since, while it rejects the hypothesis of a creative God, it affirms the existence of "a pervading Spirit, coeternal with the universe." Passages might be quoted from it, full of deep yet modest piety, as regarded from the author's point of view — a point which must be conceded to the believers in *any* creed. The involuntary tendency of a poet to recognize spiritual existences constantly breaks forth, and peoples the world with Fairies and Genii. The immortality of the soul, and its essential difference from the body, are likewise acknowledged — nay, even passionately enforced. But, undoubtedly, the poem and the notes are anything but orthodox. Shelley regarded the conventional religion as gross, contradictory, and tending to oppression and cruelty; and history supplied him with many dismal facts in support of that view. He saw, moreover, that the Christianity of worldly-minded men is not sincere. — that their practice is at war with their profession; and, so seeing, he spoke out with all the vehemence of youth. For publishing these bold comments on the popular faith, Mr. Moxon, as late as 1840, was prosecuted and convicted. As a literary production, *Queen Mab* will always possess interest, because of the vigorous indications it contains of an expanding genius, already haunted with images of splendor and with utterances of sonorous melody; but it cannot be denied that it sometimes betrays an adherence to that conventional style of poetry which was then passing away from our literature, and from which Shelley himself afterwards widely diverged. The notes exhibit a large extent of reading; and, whatever may be thought of the doctrines enforced, no candid reader will refuse to admire the subtilty of reasoning and the mastery of style which are here evinced by a mere youth.

At Tanyralt, as at all other places, Shelley's benevolence was in constant activity. The reader has already seen how munificently it was exercised when the sea broke through the feeble barrier on which the safety of many of the poor cottagers depended; but this, though the most conspicuous, was not the only instance. Mr. Maddox, in subsequent years, told Captain Medwin, a relative of the poet, and one of his biographers, that Shelley was constantly relieving the humble and necessitous, and that he would visit them in their homes, and supply them, during the bleak winter months, with food, clothes, and fuel.

Yet this continual beneficence could not save Shelley from an attempt on his life, of a most atrocious and extraordinary kind; for the facts will not allow us to hope that the horrible scene was the creation of an over-excited and almost morbidly sensitive brain. It is true that there is something of a nightmare character in the incidents; but the testimony of Mrs. Shelley gives the stamp of reality to the affair. Miss Westbrook was also in the house at the time, and often, in after years, related the circumstance as a frightful fact. The details of this strange circumstance are given by Shelley and his wife in letters to Mr. Hookham:—

"My dear Sir,

"I have just escaped an atrocious assassination. Oh! send me 20*l*., if you have it!* You will perhaps hear of me no more. "—— friend,

"Percy Shelley."

* The incoherence of the few words here written by Shelley shows the agitated state of his mind at the time. It would appear that, after sending off the 20*l*. for the Hunt subscription, he was in want of money. Hence the request to Mr. Hookham for a little temporary accommodation, to enable him to make the necessary removal from Tanyralt

Postscript by Mrs. Shelley.

"Mr. Shelley is so dreadfully nervous to-day from having been up all night, that I am afraid what he has written will alarm you very much. We intend to leave this place as soon as possible, as our lives are not safe so long as we remain. It is no common robber we dread, but a person who is actuated by revenge, and who threatens my life, and my sister's as well. If you can send us the money, it will greatly add to our comfort.

"Sir, I remain your sincere friend,
"H. SHELLEY.
"T. Hookham, Esq."

Mr. Hookham answered this letter by sending a remittance, which was thus acknowledged:—

"*Bangor Ferry, March 6th*, 1813.
"MY DEAR FRIEND,

"In the first stage of our journey towards Dublin, we met with your letter. How shall I express to you what I felt of gratitude, surprise, and pleasure — not so much that the remittance rescued us from a situation of peculiar perplexity, but that one there was, who, by disinterested and unhesitating confidence, made amends to our feelings, wounded by the suspicion, coldness, and villany of the world. If the discovery of truth be a pleasure of singular purity, how far surpassing is the discovery of virtue!

"I am now recovered from an illness brought on by watching, fatigue, and alarm; and we are proceeding to Dublin, to dissipate the unpleasant impressions associated with the scene of our alarm.

"We expect to be there on the 8th. You shall then hear the details of our distresses. The ball of the assassin's pistols (he fired at me twice) penetrated my nightgown, and pierced the wainscot. He is yet undiscovered, though not unsuspected, as you will learn from my next.

"Unless you knew us all more intimately, you cannot conceive with what fervor and sincerity my wife and sister join with me to you in gratitude and esteem.

"Yours ever faithfully and affectionately,
"Percy B. Shelley.

"P. S. — Though overwhelmed by our own distresses, we are by no means indifferent to those of liberty and virtue. From the tenor of your letter, I augur that you have applied the 20*l*. I sent to the benefit of the Hunts. I am anxious to hear further of the success of this experiment. My direction is — 35 Great Cuffe Street, Dublin. By your kindness and generosity, we are perfectly relieved from all pecuniary difficulties. We only wanted a little breathing time, which the rapidity of our persecutions was unwilling to allow us. We shall readily repay the 20*l*. when I hear from my correspondent in London; but when can I repay the friendship, the disinterestedness, and the zeal of your confidence?

"*T. Hookham, Esq.*"

The most complete account of the attack is that contained in the following letter from Mrs. Shelley to Mr. Hookham: —

"35 *Cuffe Street, Stephen's Green, Dublin,*
March 11*th*, [1813].

"My dear Sir,

"We arrived here last Tuesday, after a most tedious passage of forty hours, during the whole of which time we were dreadfully ill. I am afraid no diet will prevent us from the common lot of suffering, when obliged to take a sea-voyage.

"Mr. S. promised you a recital of the horrible events that caused us to leave Wales. I have undertaken the task, as I wish to spare him, in the present nervous state of his health, everything that can recall to his mind the horrors of that night.

"On Friday night, the 26th of February, we retired to bed between ten and eleven o'clock. We had been in bed about half an hour, when Mr. S. heard a noise proceeding from one of the parlors. He immediately went down stairs with two pistols, which he had loaded that night, expecting to have occasion for them. He went into the billiard-room, where he heard footsteps retreating; he followed into another little room, which was called an office. He there saw a man in the act of quitting the room, through a glass door which opened into the shrubbery. The man then fired at Mr. S., which he avoided. Bysshe then fired, but it flashed in the pan. The man then knocked Bysshe down, and they struggled on the ground. Bysshe then fired his second pistol, which he thought wounded him in the shoulder, as he uttered a shriek and got up, when he said these words: — 'By God, I will be revenged! I will murder your wife; I will ravish your sister! By God, I will be revenged!' He then fled — as we hoped, for the night. Our servants were not gone to bed, but were just going, when this horrible affair happened. This was about eleven o'clock. We all assembled in the parlor, where we remained for two hours. Mr. S. then advised us to retire, thinking it impossible he would make a second attack. We left Bysshe and one man-servant, who had only arrived that day, and who knew nothing of the house, to sit up. I had been in bed three hours, when I heard a pistol go off. I immediately ran down stairs, when I perceived that Bysshe's flannel gown had been shot through, and the window-curtain. Bysshe had sent Daniel to see what hour it was, when he heard a noise at the window. He went there, and a man thrust his arm through the glass, and fired at him. Thank Heaven! the ball went through his gown, and he remained unhurt. Mr. S. happened to stand sideways; had he stood fronting, the ball must have killed him. Bysshe fired his pistol, but it would not go off; he then aimed a blow at him with an old sword, which we found in the house. The assassin attempted to get the sword from him, and just as he was getting it away, Dan rushed into the room, when he made his escape.

"'This was at four in the morning. It had been a most dreadful night; the wind was as loud as thunder, and the rain descended in torrents. Nothing has been heard of him; and we have every reason to believe it was no stranger, as there is a man of the name of Leeson, who, the next morning that it happened, went and told the shopkeepers of Tremadoc that it was a tale of Mr. Shelley's, to impose upon them, that he might leave the country without paying his bills. This they believed, and none of them attempted to do anything towards his discovery.

"We left Tanyralt on Saturday, and stayed, till everything was ready for our leaving the place, at the Solicitor-General of the county's house, who lived seven miles from us. This Mr. Leeson had been heard to say, that he was determined to drive us out of the country. He once happened to get hold of a little pamphlet which Mr. S. had printed in Dublin; this he sent up to Government. In fact, he was forever saying something against us, and that because we were determined not to admit him to our house, because we had heard his character, and, from many acts of his, we found that he was malignant to the greatest degree, and cruel.

"The pleasure we experienced on reading your letter you may conceive, at the time when every one seemed to be plotting against us.

"Pardon me, if I wound your feelings by dwelling on this subject. Your conduct has made a deep impression upon our minds, which no length of time can erase. Would that all mankind were like thee!"

After a short residence in Dublin, and a tour to the Lakes of Killarney, the Shelleys returned to London in May, 1813, and remained there until after the confinement of Mrs. Shelley, who, early in the summer, gave birth to a daughter, afterwards christened Ianthe Eliza.

Mr. Peacock, one of the poet's most intimate friends

at that time, has recently given in *Fraser's Magazine* an interesting account of Shelley's way of pleasing his infant.

"He was extremely fond of his child," says Mr. Peacock, "and would walk up and down a room with it in his arms for a long time together, singing to it a monotonous melody of his own making, which ran on the repetition of a word of his own coining. His song was — 'Yáhmani, yáhmani, yáhmani, yáhmani!' It did not please me, but, what was more important, it pleased the child, and lulled it when it was fretful. Shelley was extremely fond of his children. He was preëminently an affectionate father. But to this first-born there were accompaniments which did not please him. The child had a wet-nurse whom he did not like, and was much looked after by his wife's sister, whom he intensely disliked. I have often thought that, if Harriet had nursed her own child, and if this sister had not lived with them, the link of their married love would not have been so readily broken."

Shelley was now in severe pecuniary distress; for he received nothing from his father beyond the stipulated 200*l*. a year, and he had not found it possible to raise money on his future expectations. For the purpose of economy he retired to a small cottage in Berkshire, which bore the lofty title of High Elms, and where, in the society of a few friends, varied by frequent visits to London, some months glided by happily and quietly.

During this summer, Shelley paid a visit to Field Place, and his reception there is graphically told by a friend of the family (Captain Kennedy), who was then staying in the house: —

"At this time I had not seen Shelley; but the servants, especially the old butler, Laker, had spoken of him to me. He seemed to have won the hearts of the whole household. Mrs. Shelley often spoke to me of her son; her heart yearned after him with all the fondness of a mother's love. It was during the absence of his father and the three youngest children that the natural desire of a mother to see her son induced her to propose that he should pay her a short visit. At this time he resided somewhere in the country with his first wife and their only child, Ianthe. He walked from his house until within a few miles of Field Place, when a farmer gave him a seat in his travelling cart. As he passed along, the farmer, ignorant of the quality of his companion, amused Bysshe with descriptions of the country and its inhabitants. When Field Place came in sight, he told whose seat it was; and, as the most remarkable incident connected with the family, that young Master Shelley seldom went to church. He arrived at Field Place exceedingly fatigued. I came there the following morning to meet him. I found him with his mother and his two elder sisters in a small room off the drawing-room, which they had named Confusion Hall.

"He received me with frankness and kindliness, as if he had known me from childhood, and at once won my heart. I fancy I see him now, as he sat by the window, and hear his voice, the tones of which impressed me with his sincerity and simplicity. His resemblance to his sister Elizabeth was as striking as if they had been twins. His eyes were most expressive, his complexion beautifully fair, his features exquisitely fine; his hair was dark, and no peculiar attention to its arrangement was manifest. In person he was slender and gentlemanlike, but inclined to stoop; his gait was decidedly not military. The general appearance indicated great delicacy of constitution. One would at once pronounce of him that he was something different from other men. There was an earnestness in his manner, and such perfect gentleness of breeding, and freedom from everything artificial, as charmed every one. I never met a man who so immediately won upon me.

"The generosity of his disposition and utter unselfishness imposed upon him the necessity of strict self-denial in personal comforts. Consequently, he was obliged to be most economical in his dress. He one day asked us how we liked his coat, the only one he had brought with him. We said it was very nice; it looked as if new. 'Well,' said he, 'it is an old black coat which I have had done up, and smartened with metal buttons and a velvet collar.'

"As it was not desirable that Bysshe's presence in the country should be known, we arranged that, walking out, he should wear my scarlet uniform, and that I should assume his outer garments. So he donned the soldier's dress, and sallied forth. His head was so remarkably small that, though mine be not large, the cap came down over his eyes, the peak resting on his nose, and it had to be stuffed before it would fit him. His hat just stuck on the crown of my head. He certainly looked like anything but a soldier. The metamorphosis was very amusing; he enjoyed it much, and made himself perfectly at home in his unwonted garb. We gave him the name of Captain Jones, under which name we used to talk of him after his departure; but, with all our care, Bysshe's visit could not be kept a secret.

"I chanced to mention the name of Sir James Macintosh, of whom he expressed the highest admiration. He told me Sir James was intimate with Godwin, to whom, he said, he owed everything; from whose book, *Political Justice*, he had derived all that was valuable in knowledge and virtue. He discoursed with eloquence and enthusiasm; but his views seemed to me exquisitely metaphysical, and by no means clear, precise, or decided. He told me that he had already read the Bible four times. He was then only twenty years old.* He spoke of the Supreme Being as of infinite mercy and benevolence. He disclosed no fixed views of spiritual things; all seemed wild and fanciful. He said that he once thought the surrounding atmosphere was peopled with the spirits of the departed. He reasoned and spoke as a perfect gentleman, and treated my arguments, boy as I was (I had lately completed my sixteenth year), with as much consideration and respect as if I had been his equal in ability and attainments.

"Shelley was one of the most sensitive of human beings; he had a horror of taking life, and looked upon it

* As this was in the summer of 1813, Shelley must have been nearly, if not quite, twenty-one. — ED.

as a crime. He read poetry with great emphasis and solemnity; one evening he read aloud to us a translation of one of Goethe's poems, and at this day I think I hear him. In music he seemed to delight, as a medium of association; the tunes which had been favorites in boyhood charmed him. There was one, which he played several times on the piano with one hand, which seemed to absorb him; it was an exceedingly simple air, which, I understand, his earliest love (Harriet Grove) was wont to play for him. He soon left us, and I never saw him afterwards; but I can never forget him. It was his last visit to Field Place. He was an amiable, gentle being."

Towards the close of 1813, estrangements, which for some time had been slowly growing between Mr. and Mrs. Shelley came to a crisis. Separation ensued; and Mrs. Shelley returned to her father's house. Here she gave birth to her second child, — a son, who died in 1826.

The occurrences of this painful epoch in Shelley's life, and of the causes which led to them, I am spared from relating. In Mary Shelley's own words: — "This is not the time to relate the truth; and I should reject any coloring of the truth. No account of these events has ever been given at all approaching reality in their details, either as regards himself or others; nor shall I further allude to them than to remark that the errors of action committed by a man as noble and generous as Shelley, may, as far as he only is concerned, be fearlessly avowed by those who loved him, in the firm conviction that, were they judged impartially, his character would stand in fairer and brighter light than that of any contemporary."

Of those remaining who were intimate with Shelley at this time, each has given us a different version of this sad event, colored by his own views and personal feelings. Evidently Shelley confided to none of these friends. We, who bear his name, and are of his family, have in our possession papers written by his own hand, which in after years may make the story of his life complete, and which few now living, except Shelley's own children, have ever perused.

One mistake which has gone forth to the world, we feel ourselves called upon positively to contradict.

Harriet's death has sometimes been ascribed to Shelley. This is entirely false. There was no immediate connection whatever between her tragic end and any conduct on the part of her husband. It is true, however, that it was a permanent source of the deepest sorrow to him; for never during all his after life did the dark shade depart which had fallen on his gentle and sensitive nature from the self-sought grave of the companion of his early youth.

CHAPTER VII.

ENGLAND AND SWITZERLAND: JUDGMENT OF THE LORD CHANCELLOR: THE "REVOLT OF ISLAM."

To the family of Godwin, Shelley had, from the period of his self-introduction at Keswick, been an object of interest; and the acquaintanceship which had sprung up between them during the poet's occasional visits to London had grown into a cordial friendship. It was in the society and sympathy of the Godwins that Shelley sought and found some relief in his present sorrow. He was still extremely young. His anguish, his isolation, his difference from other men, his gifts of genius and eloquent enthusiasm, made a deep impression on Godwin's daughter Mary, now a girl of sixteen, who had been accustomed to hear Shelley spoken of as something rare and strange. To her, as they met one eventful day in St. Pancras Churchyard, by her mother's grave, Bysshe, in burning words, poured forth the tale of his wild past — how he had suffered, how he had been misled, and how, if supported by her love, he hoped in future years to enroll his name with the wise and good who had done battle for their fellow-men, and been true through all adverse storms to the cause of humanity.

Unhesitatingly, she placed her hand in his, and linked her fortune with his own; and most truthfully, as the remaining portions of these Memorials will prove, was the pledge of both redeemed.

The theories in which the daughter of the authors of *Political Justice* and of the *Rights of Woman* had been educated, spared her from any conflict between her duty and her affection. For she was the child of parents whose writings had had for their object to prove that marriage was one among the many institutions which a new era in the history of mankind was about to sweep away. By her father, whom she loved — by the writings of her mother, whom she had been taught to venerate — these doctrines had been rendered familiar to her mind. It was, therefore, natural that she should listen to the dictates of her own heart, and willingly unite her fate with one who was so worthy of her love.

The short peace of 1814 having opened the Continent, they went abroad, and, having visited some of the most magnificent scenes of Switzerland, returned to England from Lucerne by the Reuss and the Rhine. This river-navigation enchanted Shelley. He was never so happy as when he was in a boat, and, "in his favorite poem of *Thalaba*," as Mrs. Shelley records in her notes to her husband's works, "his imagination had been excited by a description of such a voyage." His pleasure must therefore have been keen.

On the death of Sir Bysshe, in January, 1815, Shelley's father inherited the title and the accumulated wealth. With respect to this event, Shelley records, in a journal which he kept: — "The will has been opened, and I am referred to Whitton" (Sir Timothy's legal adviser). "My father would not allow me to enter Field Place." Shelley Sidney — a half-brother of Sir Timothy — expressed his opinion that the will was a most extraordinary one. The death of the old baronet, however, placed the young poet in a better pecuniary position than he had ever yet occupied. Being now the direct heir to the estates, he could the more readily raise money for his immediate necessities; besides which, his father, yielding to the pressure of advice, allowed him 1,000*l.* a year. He was thus relieved from the painful stringency of his former condition.

In the winter months, at the commencement of this year, Shelley walked a hospital, for the purpose of acquiring some slight knowledge of surgery, which might enable him to alleviate the sufferings of the poor. Yet, at the very time he subjected himself to these painful and often harrowing experiences, he was himself in the most delicate state of health. In the spring he was said by an eminent physician to be in a rapid consumption; and so far had the malady progressed that abscesses were formed on his lungs. His fragile nature was shaken by frequent paroxysms of pain, during which he was often obliged to lie on the ground, or to have recourse to the perilous sedative of laudanum. He was at this time living in London. The symptoms of pulmonary disorder subsequently left him with a suddenness and completeness which seem to be unaccountable. A thorough change in his system supervened, and he was never again threatened with consumption; though he was at no time healthy, or free from the assaults of pain. This change, however, did not take place until some few years after the present date.

The summer of 1815 was partly occupied by a tour along the southern coast of Devonshire and a visit to Clifton. On the completion of these trips, Shelley rented a house on Bishopsgate Heath, on the borders of Windsor Forest, the air of which neighborhood did his health considerable service. The conclusion of the summer was very fine, and all things contributed to afford the worn spirits of Bysshe a brief interspace of happiness and calm. He visited the source of the Thames, together with a few friends, and on this occasion again indulged in the pleasure of boating — that pleasure which was in the end to lure him to his death. The party proceeded from Windsor to Cricklade in a wherry. "His beautiful stanzas in the churchyard of Lechlade," says Mrs. Shelley, in her collected edition of the poems, "were written on that occasion. *Alastor* was composed on his return. He spent his days under the oak shades of Windsor Great Park; and the magnificent woodland was a fitting study to inspire the various descriptions of forest scenery we find in the poem." This was the first production in verse which Shelley gave openly to the world.

In 1816, he again visited Switzerland, and made the acquaintance of Lord Byron, for the first time, at Sécheron's hotel at Geneva, where the former was staying when the latter arrived there. Both poets being ardent lovers of boating, they joined in the purchase of a small craft, in which, evening after evening, they made sailing excursions on the lake of Geneva, accompanied by Signor Polidori, a friend of Byron, though by no means of Shelley, who disliked him on account of the morbid vanity he was constantly exhibiting. Bysshe afterwards rented a house on the banks of the lake, and passed many days alone in the boat, reading or meditating, and resigning himself to the summer influences of winds and waters. On one occasion, when Shelley and Byron were sailing from Meillerie to St. Gingoux, a storm came on; the vessel was injured, and shipped a good deal of water; and, to make matters still worse, one of the boatmen stupidly mismanaged the sail. The loss of the boat seemed inevitable; and Shelley, being unable to swim, made up his mind that he should have to meet that death for which he was in fact only reserved until a later period. But the vessel righted, and got safely to the shore.

Mrs. Shelley has recorded that her husband's lines on *Mont Blanc*, and his *Hymn to Intellectual Beauty*, were written at this time. She thinks, however, that the genius of Shelley was in some measure checked by his association with Byron, "whose nature was utterly dissimilar to his own;" but that, at the same time, Shelley had a corresponding influence on Byron, as evinced in the abstractions of *Childe Harold*, then flowing from its author's pen.

The period was, indeed, rich in the production of works of genius. The famous "Monk" Lewis, as he is called, joined the society of the two English poets, and during some rainy weather he set them talking about ghost stories. Each was to write one of these fascinating toys of the imagination; and Mrs. Shelley's extraordinary romance of *Frankenstein* was the result, as far as herself was concerned, and indeed the only one of the proposed narratives which was completed. One evening, the recital by Lord Byron of the commencement of Coleridge's spectral poem, *Christabel*, conjured up in Shelley's mind, by an association of ideas, a vision of a beautiful woman with four eyes, two of which were glancing at him from out of her breast; and he rushed from the room in an agony of horror.

On the 30th of December, 1816 (after his return to England), Shelley's second marriage took place. She who was thenceforward the companion of his existence has left us some of the most interesting particulars which we possess of his brief remnant of life, and of his lamentable end. Her influence over him was of an important kind. His anxiety to aid the intelligence of the less instructed, and his efforts to promote the well-being of the poorer classes of his fellow-creatures, were as vivid and as strenuous as before; yet his mind, by gradually bending to milder influences, divested itself of much of that hostile bitterness of thought and expression with which he had hitherto attacked those political and social abuses which had seemed to him to be the principal obstacles to the progressive development of mankind.

His pecuniary struggles, his father's persevering anger,

and the calumnies of his unscrupulous enemies, had no longer the same power to embitter his existence, and to rouse his darker passions. From them he had now a sure refuge. Evil might be without; but by his hearth were sympathy, and encouragement, and love.

They had fixed upon the neighborhood of Marlow, in Buckinghamshire, for their winter quarters. While Shelley was looking out in this locality for a suitable residence, he received the following letter to aid him in his researches: —

"In the choice of a residence, dear Shelley, pray do not be too quick, or attach yourself too much to one spot. A house with a lawn, near a river or lake, noble trees or divine mountains — that should be our little mouse-hole to retire to; but never mind this. Give me a garden, and I will thank my love for many favors. If you go to London, you will perhaps try to procure me a good Livy; for I wish very much to read it. I must be more industrious, especially in learning Latin, which I neglected shamefully last summer at intervals; and those periods of not reading at all put me back very far. . . . . Adieu! Love me tenderly, and think of me with affection whenever anything pleases you greatly."

On the 22d of March, Shelley wrote as follows to Godwin: —

"MY DEAR GODWIN,

"IT was spring when I wrote to you, and winter when your answer arrived. But the frost is very transitory; every bud is ready to burst into leaf. It is a nice distinction you make between the development and the complete expansion of the leaves. The oak and the chestnut, the latest and the earliest parents of foliage, would afford you a still subtler subdivision, which would enable you to defer the visit, from which we expect so much delight, for six weeks. I hope we shall really see you before that time, and that you will allow the chestnut, or any other important tree, as he stands in the foreground, to be considered as a virtual representation of the rest.

"Will is quite well, and very beautiful. Mary unites with me in presenting her kind remembrances to Mrs. Godwin, and begs most affectionate love to you.

"Yours,
"P. B. SHELLEY.

"Have you read *Melincourt?* It would entertain you."

About this time, Shelley became acquainted, at Leigh Hunt's house, at Hampstead, with John Keats, and with the brothers James and Horace Smith. The genius of the former he at once recognized, and celebrated it, in a subsequent year, in the eloquent poem, *Adonais*. For Horace Smith Shelley had the most affectionate regard — a regard fully deserved by that excellent and warm-hearted wit.

But now came one of the greatest sorrows which Shelley ever had to encounter. Up to the time of his first wife's death, her children had resided with her and with her father; but, after that event, Shelley claimed them. Mr. Westbrook refused to give them up, and carried the case into Chancery, where he filed a bill, asseverating that the remaining parent of the children was unfit to have the charge of them, on account of the alleged depravity of his religious and moral opinions, in which he designed to bring them up. The case having been argued, judgment was pronounced by the Lord

Chancellor (Eldon), and it was decreed that Shelley should not be allowed to have the custody of his own offspring. He was forced, however, to set aside 200*l.* a year for their support; and this sum was deducted by Sir Timothy from his son's annuity. The children were committed to the care of a clergyman of the Church of England, and were of course educated in those principles which their father looked on with aversion. The son, as the reader has already seen, died when a youth; the daughter is still living.

As to the monstrous injustice of this decree, most men are now agreed; and no further remark need be made on so repellent a subject, except an expression of astonishment that the name of Dr. Parr should be found among Shelley's opponents. His testimony was given, and quoted very frequently, as to the respectability of the persons appointed, under Chancery, as guardians of the children.

The ensuing letter from the poet's legal adviser, written before the decision of the Lord Chancellor, contains some points of interest:—

"*Gray's Inn, 5th Aug.* 1817.
"My dear Sir,
"I enclose you the Master's report on the subject of the children, which I am sorry to say is against you. I am taking the necessary proceedings to bring the question before the Lord Chancellor, and it will come on for his decision some time next week, or, at any rate, before he rises, which is the 23d inst. One comfort is, that there could not be a weaker case against you than this is. The only support of Mr. Ken-

dall* is Dr. Parr, who is himself open to a great deal of observation, and who, except as a Greek scholar, does not stand high in any one's opinion.

"The Master, in the first place, omits to inquire what would be a proper plan for the education of the children, though ordered by the Chancellor to do so; and then he goes on to approve a proposal that Mr. Kendall should stand, in all respects, *loco parentis*, when the Lord Chancellor himself says that he has not yet made up his mind as to how far he would interfere against parental authority.

"I should think that the plaintiffs will find it a difficult matter to prevail on the Chancellor to confirm this unnatural proposal of abandoning these infants to the care of a stranger, of whom nobody interested in the welfare of the children knows anything,— who lives at a considerable distance from all the family,— who, from his ignorance of all the family, can have no object but to make the most of the children as a pecuniary transaction,— in short, who has nothing to recommend him but the affidavit of the venerable bridegroom, Dr. Parr.†

"As I objected to liberties being taken with your income, you will observe that the proposal is altered.

"Your faithful and obedient servant,
"P. W. LONGDILL."

Moved to fiery wrath by the cruel injustice which had been dealt out to him, Shelley wrote a terrible curse on the Lord Chancellor, which Mrs. Shelley published among her husband's poems. The outraged father speaks grandly and fearfully in these lines:—

"By thy most impious Hell, and all its terrors;
By all the grief, the madness, and the guilt

---

* One of the persons recommended as guardians for the children. —ED.

† Dr. Parr married, for the second time, in 1816, though then in his seventieth year.— ED.

Of thine impostures, which must be *their* errors,
    That sand on which thy crumbling power is built:

     *   *   *   *   *   *

" By all the hate which checks a father's love,
    By all the scorn which kills a father's care;
By those most impious hands that dared remove
    Nature's high bounds — by thee — and by despair,—

" Yes! the despair which bids a father groan,
    And cry, 'My children are no longer mine:
The blood within those veins may be mine own,
    But, Tyrant, their polluted souls are thine!'—

"I curse thee, though I hate thee not. O slave!
    If thou could'st quench the earth-consuming hell
Of which thou art a demon, on thy grave
    This curse should be a blessing. Fare thee well!"

In his *Masque of Anarchy* (written in 1819), Shelley has two stanzas, hot with scorn and sarcasm, on the man who had robbed him of his offspring:—

    " Next came Fraud, and he had on,
        Like Lord Eldon, an ermine gown:
        His big tears (for he wept well)
        Turn'd to mill-stones as they fell:

    " And *the little children*, who
        Round his feet play'd to and fro,
        Thinking every tear a gem,
        Had their brains knock'd out by them."

Towards the end of 1817, Shelley was obliged, owing to pecuniary difficulties, to stay for some time at the house of Leigh Hunt, who had by that time removed to Lisson Grove. He had been made answerable for certain liabilities incurred by his first wife, and the creditors pressed him severely; though until the demands were urged on him, he had no knowledge that any such claims existed; nor had he now an opportunity of verifying their exactness. He even ran some danger of arrest; but matters were at length settled. In the mean while, Mrs. Shelley resided at Marlow, in company with her children, and with a little daughter of Lord Byron, called Allegra, and sometimes Alba. Shelley returned to Marlow in the autumn.

On December 7th, he thus addressed Godwin: —

"*Marlow, December 7th,* 1817.
"MY DEAR GODWIN,

"To begin with the subject of most immediate interest: close with Richardson; and when I say this, what relief should I not feel from a thousand distressing emotions, if I could believe that he was in earnest in his offer! I have not heard from Longdill, though I wish earnestly for information.

"My health has been materially worse. My feelings at intervals are of a deadly and torpid kind, or awakened to a state of such unnatural and keen excitement, that, only to instance the organ of sight, I find the very blades of grass and the boughs of distant trees present themselves to me with microscopical distinctness. Towards evening I sink into a state of lethargy and inanimation, and often remain for hours on the sofa, between sleep and waking, a prey to the most painful irritability of thought. Such, with little intermission, is my condition. The hours devoted to study are selected with vigilant caution from among these periods of endurance. It is not for this that I think of travelling to Italy, even if I knew that Italy would relieve me. But I have experienced a decisive pulmonary attack; and, although at present it has passed away without any very considerable vestige of its existence, yet this symptom sufficiently shows the true nature of my disease to be consumption. It is to my advantage that this malady is in its nature slow, and, if one is sufficiently alive to its advances, is susceptible of cure from a warm climate. In the event of its assuming any decided shape, it would be my *duty* to go to Italy without delay; and it is only when that measure becomes an indispensable duty that, contrary to both Mary's feelings and to mine, as they regard you, I shall go to Italy. I need not remind you (besides the mere pain endured by the survivors) of the train of evil consequences which my death would cause to ensue. I am thus circumstantial and explicit, because you seem to have misunderstood me. It is not health, but life, that I should seek in Italy; and that, not for my own sake — I feel that I am capable of trampling on all such weakness — but for the sake of those to whom my life may be a source of happiness, utility, security, and honor, and to some of whom my death might be all that is the reverse.

"I ought to say, I cannot persevere in the meat diet. What you say of Malthus fills me, as far as my intellect is concerned, with life and strength. I believe that I have a most anxious desire that the time should quickly come that, even so far as you are personally concerned, you should be tranquil and independent. But when I consider the intellectual lustre with which you clothe this world, and how much the last generation of mankind may be benefited by that light, flowing forth without the intervention of one shadow, I am elevated above all thoughts which tend to you or myself as an individual, and become, by sympathy, part of those distant and innumerable minds to whom your writings must be present.

"I meant to have written to you about *Mandeville* * solely; but I was so irritable and weak that I could not write, although I thought I had much to say. I have read *Mandeville*, but I must read it again soon, for the interest is of that irresistible and overwhelming kind, that the mind, in its influence, is like a cloud borne on by an impetuous wind — like one breath-

---

* Godwin's novel, so called. — ED.

lessly carried forward, who has no time to pause, or observe the causes of his career. I think the power of *Mandeville* is inferior to nothing you have done; and, were it not for the character of Falkland,* no instance in which you have exerted that power of *creation*, which you possess beyond all contemporary writers, might compare with it. Falkland is still alone; power is, in Falkland, not, as in *Mandeville*, tumult hurried onward by the tempest, but tranquillity standing unshaken amid its fiercest rage. But *Caleb Williams* never shakes the deepest soul like *Mandeville*. It must be said of the latter, you rule with a rod of iron. The picture is never bright; and we wonder whence you drew the darkness with which its shades are deepened, until the epithet of tenfold might almost cease to be a metaphor. The *noun smorfia* touches some cord within us with such a cold and jarring power, that I started, and for some time could scarce believe but that I was Mandeville, and that this hideous grin was stamped upon my own face. In style and strength of expression, *Mandeville* is wonderfully great, and the energy and the sweetness of the sentiments scarcely to be equalled. Clifford's character, as mere beauty, is a divine and soothing contrast; and I do not think — if, perhaps, I except (and I know not if I ought to do so) the speech of Agathon in the *Symposium* of Plato — that there ever was produced a moral discourse more characteristic of all that is admirable and lovely in human nature, — more lovely and admirable in itself, — than that of Henrietta to Mandeville, as he is recovering from madness. Shall I say that, when I discovered that she was pleading all this time sweetly for her lover, and when at last she weakly abandoned poor Mandeville, I felt an involuntary, and, perhaps, an unreasonable pang? Adieu!

" Always most affectionately yours,

" P. S."

During the summer and autumn of 1817, Shelley had

* In the novel of *Caleb Williams*. — ED.

written the *Revolt of Islam* — a poem which was originally put forth under the title of *Laon and Cythna; or, the Revolution of the Golden City: a Vision of the Nineteenth Century.* Mr. Ollier (from whose house proceeded the first volume of Keats) was the chief publisher; and some copies of the poem, with the original name, were issued a little before Christmas. Some apprehension, on the score of the bold doctrines advocated in its pages, induced Mr. Ollier to arrest the progress of the work for a while, with a view to obtaining some modification of particular parts. Hereupon Shelley wrote to his publisher a letter, which is a remarkable specimen of the courage with which he defied conventional opinions: —

"*Marlow, December* 11*th*, 1817.
" DEAR SIR,

"IT is to be regretted that you did not consult your own safety and advantage (if you consider it connected with the non-publication of my book) before your declining the publication, after having accepted it, would have operated to so extensive and serious an injury to my views as now. The instances of abuse and menace, which you cite, were such as you expected, and were, as I conceived, prepared for. If not, it would have been just to me to have given them their due weight and consideration before. You foresaw, you foreknew, all that these people would say. You do your best to condemn my book before it is given forth, because you publish it, and then withdraw; so that no other bookseller will publish it, because one has already rejected it. You must be aware of the great injury which you prepare for me. If I had never consulted your advantage, my book would have had a fair hearing. But now it is first published, and then the publisher, as if the author had deceived him as to the contents of the work — and as if the inevitable consequence of its publication would be ignominy and punishment — and as if none should dare to touch it or look at it — retracts, at a period when nothing but the most extraordinary and unforeseen circumstances can justify his retraction.

"I beseech you to reconsider the matter, for your sake no less than for my own. Assume the high and the secure ground of courage. The people who visit your shop, and the wretched bigot who gave his worthless custom to some other bookseller, are not the public. The public respect talent; and a large portion of them are already undeceived, with regard to the prejudices which my book attacks. You would lose some customers, but you would gain others. Your trade would be diverted into a channel more consistent with your own principles. Not to say that a publisher is in no wise pledged to all the opinions of his publications, or to any; and that he may enter his protest with each copy sold, either against the truth or the discretion of the principles of the books he sells. But there is a much more important consideration in the case. You are, and have been to a certain extent, the publisher. I don't believe that, if the book was quietly and regularly published, the Government would touch anything of a character so refined, and so remote from the conceptions of the vulgar. They would hesitate before they invaded a member of the higher circles of the republic of letters. But, if they see us tremble, they will make no distinctions; they will feel their strength. You might bring the arm of the law down on us, by flinching now. Directly these scoundrels see that people are afraid of them, they seize upon them, and hold them up to mankind as criminals already convicted by their own fears. You lay yourself prostrate, and they trample on you. How glad they would be to seize on any connection of Hunt's, by this most powerful of all their arms — the terrors and self-condemnation of their victim. Read all the *ex officio* cases, and see what reward booksellers and printers have received for their submission.

"If, contrary to common sense and justice, you resolve to

give me up, you shall receive no detriment from a connection with me in small matters, though you determine to inflict so serious a one on me in great. You shall not be at a farthing's expense. I shall still, so far as my powers extend, do my best to promote your interest. On the contrary supposition, even admitting you derive no benefit from the book itself — and it should be my care that you shall do so — I hold myself ready to make ample indemnity for any loss you may sustain.

"There is one compromise you might make, though that would be still injurious to me. Sherwood and Neely wished to be the principal publishers. Call on them, and say that it was through a mistake that you undertook the principal direction of the book, as it was *my wish* that it should be theirs, and that I have written to you to that effect. This, if it would be advantageous to you, would be detrimental to, but not utterly destructive of my views. To withdraw your name entirely, would be to inflict on me a bitter and undeserved injury.

"Let me hear from you by return of post. I hope that you will be influenced to fulfil your engagement with me, and proceed with the publication, as justice to me, and, indeed, a well-understood estimate of your own interest and character, demand. I do hope that you will have too much regard to the well-chosen motto of your seal * to permit the murmurs of a few bigots to outweigh the serious and permanent considerations presented in this letter. To their remonstrances, you have only to reply, 'I did not write the book; I am not responsible; here is the author's address — state your objections to him. I do no more than sell it to those who inquire for it; and, if they are not pleased with their bargain, the author empowers me to receive the book and to return the money.' As to the interference of Government, nothing is more improbable that in any case it would be attempted; but, if it should,

---

* "In omnibus libertas."

it would be owing entirely to your perseverance in the groundless apprehensions which dictated your communication received this day, and conscious terror would be perverted into an argument of guilt.

"I have just received a most kind and encouraging letter from Mr. Moore on the subject of my poem. I have the fairest chance of the public approaching my work with unbiassed and unperverted feeling; the fruit of reputation (and you know for *what purposes* I value it) is within my reach. It is for you, now you have been once named as publisher, and have me in your power, to blast all this, and to hold up my literary character in the eye of mankind as that of a proscribed and rejected outcast. And for no evil that I have ever done you, but in return for a preference, which, although you falsely now esteem injurious to you, was solicited by Hunt, and conferred by me, as a source and a proof of nothing but kind intentions.

"Dear Sir,
"I remain your sincere well-wisher,
"Percy B. Shelley."

The poet, however, was afterwards convinced of the propriety of making certain alterations; and the work was issued in the following January under the title of the *Revolt of Islam*.

This eloquent and passionate poem was composed partly on the Thames, while the poet rocked idly in his boat "as it floated under the beech groves of Bisham;" partly during wanderings among the beautiful scenery of the neighborhood. The mingled luxuriance and wildness of the country surrounding his dwelling gave Shelley the greatest delight; but this pleasure was marred by the pain arising from the contemplation of the extreme poverty everywhere visible in Marlow. Many of the women of that town were (and are still) lacemakers — an occupation which, while it entails loss of health, is very ill-paid. The amount of distress existing in the winter of 1817–18 was very severe; the poor-laws were administered with rigor; the late war had frightfully augmented taxation, while the peace had thrown many persons, who had served as soldiers, back on the rural population; and a bad harvest had added to the other sources of human misery. "Shelley," says his widow, "afforded what alleviation he could. In the winter, while bringing out his poem, he had a severe attack of ophthalmia, caught while visiting the poor cottages." *

The poem at once inspired all lovers of literature with considerable interest in the author; but it found many severe critics. Even Godwin urged several objections to its general style; to which the poet replied in an interesting letter (dated December 11th, 1817), containing a very deeply-felt and accurate estimate of the peculiar tendencies of his own mind.

"I have read and considered," he writes, "all that you say about my general powers, and the particular instance of the poem in which I have attempted to develop them. Nothing can be more satisfactory to me than the interest which your admonitions express. But I think you are mistaken in some points with regard to the peculiar nature of my powers, whatever be their amount. I listened with deference and self-suspicion to your censures of *Laon and Cythna;* but the productions of mine which you commend hold a very low place in my own esteem, and

* Note to the *Revolt of Islam* in the collected edition of the Poems.

this reassured me, in some degree at least. The poem was produced by a series of thoughts which filled my mind with unbounded and sustained enthusiasm. I felt the precariousness of my life, and I resolved in this book to leave some records of myself. Much of what the volume contains was written with the same feeling, as real, though not so prophetic, as the communications of a dying man. I never presumed, indeed, to consider it anything approaching to faultless; but, when I considered contemporary productions of the same apparent pretensions, I will own that I was filled with confidence. I felt that it was in many respects a genuine picture of my own mind. I felt that the sentiments were true, not assumed; and in this have I long believed — that my power consists in sympathy, and that part of imagination which relates to sentiment and contemplation. I am formed, if for anything not in common with the herd of mankind, to apprehend minute and remote distinctions of feeling, whether relative to external nature or the living beings which surround us, and to communicate the conceptions which result from considering either the moral or the material universe as a whole. . . . . Yet, after all, I cannot but be conscious, in much of what I write, of an absence of that tranquillity which is the attribute and accompaniment of power. This feeling alone would make your most kind and wise admonitions, on the subject of the economy of intellectual force, valuable to me. And, if I live, or if I see any trust in coming years, doubt not but that I shall do something, whatever it may be, which a serious and earnest estimate of my powers will suggest to me, and which will be in every respect accommodated to their utmost limits."

It is not difficult to understand why Godwin failed to appreciate the new production of his son-in-law. He had formed his tastes in poetry by a life-long perusal of our old English masters — the men of the Shakspearean and Miltonic eras; and it was impossible that he could have gone to a better school. But the poetry of Shelley — excepting in as far as it was inspired, in its metaphysical part, by the genius of ancient Greece — was essentially modern in its character. It mingled the impalpable suggestions of mysticism with images of exotic splendor, tropical in the heat and glory of their hues, touched with a light that seemed to dawn from some remote and supernatural future, and often dim with the too great intensity of the writer's emotions and the excessive radiance in which he robed his subtle imaginings. The practical, acute, clear mind of Godwin could not live, with any comfort to itself, in this region of ethereal, though sublime magnificence; neither his temperament nor his intellectual habits fitted him for deriving any high degree of pleasure from a practice so opposed to his own. But Shelley has helped to make the times more poetical; and the flame-like energy and grandeur, the tumultuous passion, and the strange visionary beauty of the *Revolt of Islam* are now universally acknowledged.

In the same year, Shelley also wrote the highly mystical fragments of *Prince Athanase* — fragments, however, full of beauty and music; a large part of *Rosalind and Helen;* a few small poems; and a pamphlet advocating Parliamentary Reform, published under the signature of the "Hermit of Marlow." This political work is remarkable for the statesmanlike calmness of the writer's opinions, and the moderation of his demands. Shelley here proposed that committees should be formed with a view to polling the entire people on the subject which was then, as now, agitating the whole nation. He disavowed any wish to establish universal suffrage at once, or to do away with monarchy and aristocracy, while so large a proportion of the people remained disqualified by ignorance from sharing in the government of the country, though he looked forward to a time when the world would be enabled to "disregard the symbols of its childhood;" and he suggested that the qualification for the suffrage should be the registry of the voter's name as one who paid a certain small sum in *direct taxes*. Such were the views of a political thinker who was equally removed from being a Tory or a demagogue.

At the end of this year (1817), a relapse of the severe attack of ophthalmia, caught from his visits to the poor cottagers in his neighborhood, deprived Shelley of his usual resource of reading. In looking over the journal in which, from day to day, Mrs. Shelley was in the habit of noting their occupations, as well as passing events, one is struck with wonder at the number of books which they read in the course of the year. At home or travelling — before breakfast, or waiting for the mid-day meal — by the side of a stream, or on the ascent of a mountain — a book was never absent from

the hands of one or the other; and there were never
two books; one read while the other listened. The
catalogue of works perused, which I subjoin, would seem
to require the unremitting attention of unfettered leisure; yet at this time Shelley was greatly occupied with
affairs of business, and his mind was much harassed
by the Chancery suit with regard to his children.

"LIST OF BOOKS READ BY SHELLEY AND MARY IN 1817.

Symposium of Plato. ⎫
Plays of Æschylus.
Plays of Sophocles. ⎬ Greek.
Iliad of Homer.
Arriani Historia Indiæ.
Homer's Hymns. ⎭
Histoire de la Révolution Fran-
  çaise.
Apuleius.
Metamorphoses — Latin.
Coleridge's Biographia Litera-
  ria.
Political Justice.
Rights of Man.
Elphinstone's Embassy.
Several volumes of Gibbon.
Two volumes of Lord Chester-
  field's Letters.
Coleridge's Lay Sermons.

Memoirs of Count Grammont.
Somnium Scipionis.
Roderick Random.
Sir Philip Sydney's Arcadia.
Beaumont and Fletcher — three
  plays.
Waverley.
Epistolæ Plinii Secundi.
Vita Julii Cæsari. — Suetonius.
Davis's Travels in America.
Manuscrit venu de St. Hélène.
Buffon's Théorie de la Terre.
Lettres Persiennes.
Molière's George Dandin.
La Nouvelle Héloïse.
Godwin's Miscellanies.
Spenser's Faëry Queene.
First volume of Hume's Essays.
Besides many novels, poems, &c.

CHAPTER VIII.

ITALY: 1818.

The year 1818 was memorable in the life of Shelley, on account of his having at that date quitted England, to which he was destined never to return. The general state of his health, together with other motives, induced him to seek a more genial climate in the south of Europe. One of his most powerful reasons was a fear lest the Lord Chancellor might follow out some vague threat which he had uttered in delivering judgment, and deprive him of his infant son by his second wife. No attempt was made to act on this threat; but so much did Shelley fear that the outrage would be committed, that he addressed the child (who afterwards died at Rome) in some beautiful stanzas, signifying his readiness to abandon his country forever, rather than be parted from another of his offspring: —

> " The billows on the beach are leaping around it;
> The bark is weak and frail;
> The sea looks black, and the clouds that bound it
> Darkly strew the gale

Come with me, thou delightful child!
Come with me! Though the wave is wild
And the winds are loose, we must not stay,
Or the slaves of law may rend thee away.

* * * * *

"Rest, rest! shriek not, thou gentle child!—
  The rocking of the boat thou fearest,
And the cold spray, and the clamor wild?
  There, sit between us two, thou dearest, —
Me and thy mother. Well we know
The storm at which thou tremblest so,
With all its dark and hungry graves,
Less cruel than the savage slaves
Who hunt thee o'er these sheltering waves.

"This hour will in thy memory
  Be a dream of days forgotten:
We soon shall dwell by the azure sea
  Of serene and golden Italy,
  Or Greece, the Mother of the Free.
And I will teach thine infant tongue
  To call upon their heroes old
  In their own language, and will mould
Thy growing spirit in the flame
Of Grecian lore; that, by such name,
A patriot's birthright thou may'st claim."

In the early part of the year, Shelley was much occupied with matters of business in London; but in March they started for Italy. They went thither direct, avoiding even Paris, and did not pause till they arrived at Milan. From this city, the little Allegra was sent, under the care of a nurse, to her father at Venice.

The removal to Italy was advantageous to Shelley in

almost every respect. It is true that he left behind him friends to whom he was attached; but cares of various kinds, many of them springing from his lavish generosity, crowded round him in his native country, and the climate afflicted him with extreme suffering. His greatest pleasure — the free enjoyment of natural scenery — was marred by this sensitiveness to the influence of English weather.

The very first aspect of Italy (as Mrs. Shelley has recorded) enchanted him. The land appeared like "a garden of delight placed beneath a clearer and brighter heaven than any he had lived under before. He wrote long descriptive letters during the first year of his residence;" and in these we see, not merely the consummate handling of a master of prose composition, but a poet's appreciation of all forms of loveliness, whether of nature or of art.

A very romantic story touching this period of Shelley's life is told by Captain Medwin. He asserts that a married lady introduced herself to the poet in the year 1816, shortly before his departure for Switzerland, and, concealing her name, told him that his many virtues and the grandeur of his opinions in politics, morals, and religion, had inspired her with such an ardent passion for him that she had resolved on abandoning her husband, her family, and her friends, with a view to linking her fortunes to those of Shelley.

Of this strange narrative, it will be sufficient to say here that not the slightest allusion to it is to be found in any of the family documents.

The Shelleys stayed a month at Milan; and, after visiting the Lake of Como, proceeded to Leghorn, where they became acquainted with Mrs. Gisborne, a lady who had formerly been a most intimate friend of Mary Wollstonecraft (Mrs. Shelley's mother). The thoughtful character and amiable disposition of this lady seem to have bound the whole party in ties of friendship, which continued unbroken till the end.

At the Baths of Lucca, where the poet and his wife next went, *Rosalind and Helen*, begun at Marlow, was finished, at the request of Mrs. Shelley. Thence, in August, Shelley visited Venice; and, circumstances rendering it advisable that he should remain near at hand for a few weeks, he resided during that time at a villa which Lord Byron rented at Este, and which was kindly placed at his disposal. Here he was joined by his family, and here also more than one literary work was prosecuted. *I Capuccini* (such was the name of the residence) is described by Mrs. Shelley as "a villa built on the site of a Capuchin convent, demolished when the French suppressed religious houses. It was situated on the very overhanging brow of a low hill at the foot of a range of higher ones. The house was cheerful and pleasant; a vine-trellised walk — a Pergola, as it is called in Italian — led from the hall-door to a summer-house at the end of the garden, which Shelley made his study, and in which he began the *Prometheus;* and here also, as he mentions in a letter, he wrote *Julian and Maddalo*. A slight ravine, with a road in its depth, divided the garden from the hill, on which stood the ruins of the ancient castle of Este; whose dark, massive wall gave forth an echo, and from whose ruined crevices owls and bats flitted forth at night, as the crescent moon sank behind the black and heavy battlements. We looked from the garden over the wide plain of Lombardy, bounded to the west by the far Apennines, while, to the east, the horizon was lost in misty distance."

Julian and Maddalo is one of the most fervent, dramatic, and intense of its author's productions; and yet one of the most compact, highly wrought, and mature. The descriptions of Italian scenery are wonderfully minute and particular, when we consider that the poet had been only about half a year in the country. Of the magnificence of the word-pictures — especially in that gorgeous vision of a Venetian sunset, sphering in a transitory glory the sea, the ships, the palaces, the distant hills, and the ghastly madhouse — it would be difficult to say too much; while the soliloquy of the poor maniac is dusky and thick with human passion and pathos — the whole tragedy of a sorrowful life brought within the compass of a few pages. The poem, moreover, is interesting on account of the portraiture given by Shelley of Lord Byron, who is figured under the name of Maddalo — Julian being Shelley himself. The little Allegra is also described in lines of gentle pathos which have never been surpassed: —

> "The following morn was rainy, cold, and dim:
> Ere Maddalo arose, I call'd on him:
> And, whilst I waited, with his child I play'd;—
> A lovelier toy sweet Nature never made;

"A serious, subtle, wild, yet gentle being,
Graceful without design, and unforeseeing;
With eyes — oh! speak not of her eyes, which seem
Twin mirrors of Italian heaven, yet gleam
With such deep meaning as we never see
But in the human countenance. With me
She was a special favorite: I had nurs'd
Her fine and feeble limbs, when she came first
To this bleak world; and yet she seem'd to know,
On second sight, her ancient playfellow,
Less changed than she was, by six months or so.
For, after her first shyness was worn out,
We sat there, rolling billiard balls about,
When the Count enter'd."

While they were at Este, their little daughter, Clara, showed signs of suffering from the heat of the climate. Her indisposition being increased to an alarming extent by teething, the parents hastened to Venice for the best advice, but discovered at Fusina that, in their agitation, they had forgotten the passport. The soldiers on duty attempted to prevent their crossing the lagune; but Shelley, with his usual vehemence, augmented by the urgent nature of the case, broke through, and they reached Venice. Unhappily, it was too late; the little creature died just as they arrived.

At this period Shelley composed his exquisite descriptive poem, *Lines written among the Euganean Hills*. In November, he and Mrs. Shelley started southward, and on the 1st of December they arrived at Naples. In the mean while, they had hastily visited Ferrara, Bologna, and Rome, as well as other towns of less note. The winter was spent in the hot and indolent city of the south; and here the Shelleys lived very solitarily — too much so, according to the opinion of his widow, who thinks that a little intellectual society would have done great service to the spirits of her husband, now once more in a bad state of health, and often plunged into extreme gloom. He records this state of mind in his *Stanzas written in Dejection near Naples* (December, 1818), giving vent to his sorrow in lines which unite the utmost gentleness of pathos to the most lovely conceptions of poetry and the finest harmonies of verse:—

> "Yet now despair itself is mild,
>   Even as the winds and waters are:
> I could lie down like a tired child,
>   And weep away the life of care
>   Which I have borne, and yet must bear,
> Till death, like sleep, might steal on me,
>   And I might feel in the warm air
>   My cheek grow cold, and hear the sea
> Breathe o'er my dying brain its last monotony."

But this dejection — the result of many causes — gave place to a happier mood before the poet was snatched away from life.

The letters pertaining to this year may now follow in their regular sequence.

FROM GODWIN TO SHELLEY.

"*Skinner Street, June 8th*, 1818.

"MY DEAR SHELLEY,

"YOU are in a new country, and must be from day to day seeing objects and experiencing sensations, of which I should be delighted to hear. Write as to your equal, and, if that word is not discordant to your feelings, your friend. It would be strange indeed if we could not find topics of communication that may be gratifying to both. Let each of us dwell on those qualities in the other which may contribute most to the increase of mutual kindness. It is the judgment of the human species, and is fully accordant to my own experience, that the arrival and perusal of a letter from an absent friend is naturally one of the sources of the most delicious emotions of which man is susceptible.

"Since I began this letter, I have conceived the plan of a book which is, I think, a great desideratum in English history and biography, to be called *The Lives of the Commonwealth's Men*. I would confine myself to ten names: — Sir Henry Vane, Henry Martin, Henry Ireton, John Bradshaw, John Milton, John Hutchinson, Edmund Ludlow, Oliver St. John, Nathaniel Fiennes, Algernon Sidney. The whole might be comprised in two volumes, or perhaps in one. It has been the mode for more than a hundred and fifty years to load the Commonwealth's men (regicides, as they are often called) with all the abuse and scurrility that language can furnish. I would have them shown as they are — " Nothing extenuate, nor set down aught in malice;" — and perhaps they will be found equal to any ten men in the annals of the Roman republic. There were great and admirable personages among the Presbyterians — Hampden and Pym, for instance; these, fortunately for themselves, died early; but the Presbyterians have this slur upon them, that they contributed most actively, after the death of Cromwell, to bring back the King, and thus to occasion all the bloody, inhuman, and profligate scenes that followed. I would admit none into my list but such to whom I could apply Horace's rule, —

'Servetur ad imum,
Qualis ab incepto processerit, et sibi constet.'

"Now, this work I shall never write. All that I intended,

therefore, was to put down the plan of it in memorandum on a page of paper. But in my bed this morning I thought — Mary, perhaps, would like to write it; and I should think she is perfectly capable. The books to be consulted would be comparatively few: Noble's *Memoirs of the Protectorate House of Cromwell;* Whitlock's *Memorials of English Affairs under Charles the First;* Ludlow's *Memoirs;* Colonel Hutchinson's *Memoirs;* the trial of the twenty-nine Regicides; the trial of Sir Henry Vane; also, dying speeches of Corbet, Okey, and Barkstead. In a few instances, as I have observed in my letter of advice, the references of these authors might lead to further materials.

"By such a book at this, the English history, in one of its most memorable periods, would be made intelligible, which has never yet been the case. It has been slurred and confounded, and no grand and consistent picture of the men and their characters has ever been made out. There is a strong and inveterate prejudice in this country in favor of what these heroes styled 'the government of a single person.' I would at least have it shown that ten men, some of them never surpassed in ability, perhaps none of them in integrity, in this island, devoted themselves in heart and soul, with all their powers, to a purer creed.

"Very affectionately yours,

"W. GODWIN."

FROM MRS. SHELLEY TO MRS. GISBORNE.

"*Casa Bertini, Bagni di Lucca, June* 15, 1818.
"MY DEAR MADAM,

"IT is strange, after having been in the habit of visiting you daily now for so many days, to have no communication with you, and, after having been accustomed for a month to the tumult of Via Grande, to come to this quiet scene, where we hear no sound except the rushing of the river in the valley below. While at Levorno, I hardly heard the noise; but, when I came here, I felt the silence as a return to something very delightful from which I had been long absent. We live here in the midst of a beautiful scene, and I wish that I had the imagination and expressions of a poet to describe it as it deserves, and to fill you all with an ardent desire to visit it. We are surrounded by mountains covered with thick chestnut woods; they are peaked and picturesque, and sometimes you see peeping above them the bare summit of a distant Apennine. Vines are cultivated at the foot of the mountains. The walks in the woods are delightful; for I like nothing so much as to be surrounded by the foliage of trees, only peeping now and then through the leafy screen on the scene about me. You can either walk by the side of the river, or on commodious paths cut in the mountains; and, for rambles, the woods are intersected with narrow paths in every direction. Our house is small, but commodious, and exceedingly clean, for it has just been painted, and the furniture is quite new. We have a small garden, and at the end of it is an arbor of laurel trees, so thick that the sun does not penetrate it; nor has my prediction followed us, that we should everywhere find it cold. Although not hot, the weather has been very pleasant. We see the fire-flies in an evening, somewhat dimmed by the bright rays of the moon.

"And now I will say a few words of our domestic economy —albeit, I am afraid the subject has tired you out of your wits more than once. Signor Chiappa we found perfectly useless. He would talk of nothing but himself, and recommended a person to cook our dinner for us at three pauls a day. So, as it is, Paolo (whom we find exceedingly useful) cooks and manages for us, and a woman comes at one paul a day to do the dirty work. We live very comfortably, and, if Paolo did not cheat us, he would be a servant worth a treasure, for he does everything cleanlily and exactly, without teazing us in any way. So we lead here a very quiet, pleasant life, reading our canto of Ariosto, and walking in the evening among these delightful woods. We have but one wish. You know what that is, but you take no pity on us, and exile us from your presence so long that I quite long to see you again. Now we see no one. The Signor Chiappa is a stupid fellow, and the Casino is not open, that I know of — at least, it is not at all frequented. When it is, every kind of amusement goes on there, particularly dancing, which is divided into four parts — English and French country dances, quadrilles, waltzes, and Italian dances. These take place twice a week, on which evenings the ladies dress, but on others they go merely in a walking dress.

"We have found among our books a volume of poems of Lord Byron's, which you have not seen. Some of them I think you will like; but this will be a novelty to recommend us on our return I begin to be very much delighted with Ariosto; the beginning of the nineteenth canto is particularly beautiful. It is the wounding of Medoro, and his being relieved by Angelica, who, for a wonder, shows herself in the light of a sympathizing and amiable person.

"Affectionately yours,
"Mary Wollstonecraft Shelley."

FROM MRS. SHELLEY TO MRS. GISBORNE.

"*Bagni di Lucca, July* 2, 1818.

"My Dear Madam,

"An earthquake for the steam-engine, and thus to swallow up Mr. Reveley's* whole territory, is somewhat a harsh remedy; yet I could wish for one that could transport it (if you will not come without it) to these Bagni, where I am sure you would be enchanted with everything except the English that are crowded here to the almost entire exclusion of Italians, so that I think it would be easier to have a conversazione of Italians in England than here in their native

* Mr. Reveley was a son of Mrs. Gisborne by a former marriage. — Ed.

country. We see none but English; we hear nothing but English spoken. The walks are filled with English nursery maids — a kind of animal I by no means like — and dashing, staring Englishwomen, who surprise the Italians (who always are carried about in sedan chairs) by riding on horseback. For us, we generally walk, except last Tuesday, when Shelley and I took a long ride to *Il Prato Fiorito*, a flowery meadow on the top of one of the neighboring Apennines. We rode among chestnut woods, leaving the noisy cicala, and there was nothing disagreeable in it, except the steepness of the ascent. The woods about here are in every way delightful, especially when they are plain, with grassy walks through them. They are filled with sweet-singing birds, and not long ago we heard a cuckoo. Mr. Shelley wishes to go with me to Monte Pelerino — the highest of the Apennines — at the top of which there is a shrine. It is distant about twenty-two miles. Can it be there that the Italian palates were deceived by unwholesome food? (to talk of that hideous transaction in their own cool way); and would you think it advisable for us to make this pilgrimage? We must go on horseback and sleep in one of the houses on the mountain.

"I have had a letter from my father; he does not appear very well in health, but I hope the summer will restore him. He says in his letter: 'I was extremely gratified by your account of Mrs. Gisborne.'

"We are now in the 36th canto of *Ariosto*. How very entertaining it is, and how exceedingly beautiful are many of the stories! Yet I cannot think him so great a poet as Spenser, although, as I said before, a much better story-teller. I wonder if I shall like Tasso better?

"My dear Mrs. Gisborne,
"Yours affectionately and obliged,
"Mary W. Shelley."

FROM GODWIN TO MRS. SHELLEY.

"*Skinner Street, July 7th*, 1818.

"My dear Mary,

"You will, I dare say, be glad to hear that I am now over head and ears in my answer to Malthus. That painful complication of circumstances, which for four or five months suspended my labors, seems at present to have dispersed itself like a summer cloud. But I know that all these appearances are fallacious. I know that the tempest is brewing in the distance, and that at no very remote period it will pour all its fury upon my devoted head.* But this very consciousness gives new energy to my exertions. Providence, or by whatever other name we shall call that principle that presides over the affairs of men, has granted me an interval, however short, of cheerfulness and serenity; and (particularly at my time of life) such a favor is to be received as an inestimable present, which it becomes me most assiduously and vigilantly to improve.

"The Westminster election closes on Saturday, and the result of the whole in this division is, that the metropolis, which sends eight members — four for London, two for Westminster, and two for Southwark — has not sent, in its whole number, one old supporter of the present Administration. The members for Westminster are Romilly and Burdett; for Southwark, Calvert, a veteran Foxite, and Sir Robert Wilson; and for London, Alderman Wood, Alderman Morp, and Waithman (all stanch Oppositionists), and Mr. Wilson, a new man, who will, in all probability, vote for Government, but who is at least not an old supporter. Sir William Curtis for London — their right-hand man — is thrown out. The consequence of all this is, that everybody is of opinion that, if time had been given, and these examples had been sufficiently

---

* Godwin here alludes to pecuniary difficulties. — Ed.

early, the general defeat of the Ministry would have been memorable. As it is, it is computed that the Ministerial majority will immediately be diminished by forty or fifty votes; and sanguine people say, nobody can tell what that may end in.

"My occupations call me away, and I cannot add much to this letter. I am anxious to know what you are about, and could wish, as you kindly say on your part, that I could hear from you more frequently. I follow you in imagination under Italian skies, and amidst Italian scenery, and all the precious antiquities of that memorable region. I should be happy to hear of Shelley's health, of your occupations, and of the progress and improvement of your William.

"Farewell! Be useful, be respectable, be happy! Such is the prayer of your affectionate father,

"WILLIAM GODWIN.

"P. S.— Mr. Brougham has just lost his election for Westmoreland; but he appears to be sanguine of success at the next opportunity. He had 900 votes; his competitors, 1,100 and 1,200."

FROM MRS. SHELLEY TO MRS. GISBORNE.

"*Bagni di Lucca, August 17th*, 1818.

"MY DEAR MADAM,

"It gave me great pleasure to receive your letter after so long a silence, when I had begun to conjecture a thousand reasons for it, and, among others, illness, in which I was half right. Indeed, I am much concerned to hear of Mr. R.'s attacks, and sincerely hope that nothing will retard his speedy recovery. His illness gives me a slight hope that you might now be induced to come to the baths, if it were even to try the effect of the hot baths. You would find the weather cool; for we already feel in this part of the world that the year is declining, by the cold mornings and evenings. I have another selfish reason to wish that you would come, which I have a great mind not to mention; yet I will not omit it, as it might induce you. Shelley and C—— are gone; they went to-day to Venice on important business; and I am left to take care of the house. Now, if all of you, or any of you, would come and cheer my solitude, it would be exceedingly kind. I dare say you would find many of your friends here; among the rest there is the Signora Felicho, whom I believe you knew at Pisa.

"Shelley and I have ridden almost every evening. C—— did the same at first; but she has been unlucky, and once fell from her horse, and hurt her knee so as to knock her up for some time. It is the fashion here for all the English to ride; and it is very pleasant on these fine evenings, when we set out at sunset and are lighted home by Venus, Jupiter, and Diana, who kindly lend us their light after the sleepy Apollo is gone to bed. The road which we frequent is raised somewhat above, and overlooks, the river, affording some very fine points of view amongst these woody mountains.

"Still, we know no one; we speak to one or two people at the Casino, and that is all. We live in our studious way, going on with Tasso, whom I like, but who, now I have read more than half his poem, I do not know that I like so well as Ariosto. Shelley translated the *Symposium* in ten days. It is a most beautiful piece of writing. I think you will be delighted with it. It is true that in many particulars it shocks our present manners; but no one can be a reader of the works of antiquity unless they can transport themselves from these to other times, and judge not by our, but their, morality.

"Shelley is tolerably well in health; the hot weather has done him good. We have been in high debate — nor have we come to any conclusion — concerning the land or sea journey to Naples. We have been thinking that, when we want to go, although the equinox will be past, yet the equinoctial winds will hardly have spent themselves; and I cannot express to you how I fear a storm at sea, with two such young children as William and Clara. Do you know the periods when the Mediterranean is troubled, and when the wintry halcyon days come? However it may be, we shall see you before we proceed southward.

"We have been reading Eustace's *Tour through Italy*. I do not wonder the Italians reprinted it. Among other select specimens of his way of thinking, he says that the Romans did not derive their arts and learning from the Greeks; that Italian ladies are chaste, and the lazzaroni honest and industrious; and that, as to assassination and highway robbery in Italy, it is all a calumny — no such things were ever heard of. Italy was the garden of Eden, and all the Italians Adams and Eves, until the blasts of hell (*i. e.* the French — for by that polite name he designates them) came. By the by, an Italian servant stabbed an English one here, it was thought dangerously at first, but the man is doing better.

"I have scribbled a long letter, and I dare say you have long wished to be at the end of it. Well, now you are; so, my dear Mrs. Gisborne, with best remembrances,

"Yours obliged and affectionately,
"MARY W. SHELLEY."

In Mrs. Shelley's journal of this year are recorded two amusing ghost stories, which may find a place here, for the edification of believers in spectral appearances:—

"*Tuesday, October* 20*th*. — The Chevalier Mengaldo spends the evening at the Hoppners', and relates several ghost stories — two that occurred to himself.

"When the Chevalier was at the University, and very young, on returning home to pass the vacation he heard that the inhabitants of the town had been frightened by the mighty visitation of a ghost, who traversed the town from one end to the other; so much to their terror, that no one would venture out after dark. The Chevalier felt a great curiosity to see the ghost, and stationed himself at the window of a house of one of his friends, by which the shadow always passed. Twelve o'clock struck; no ghost appeared. One; half-past one. The Chevalier grew sleepy, and determined to return home. The town chiefly consisted, like most country towns, of one long street, and as the Chevalier, on his road home, was at one end of it, he saw at the other something white, like a rabbit or greyhound, that appeared to advance towards him. He perceived that as he advanced it grew larger and larger, and appeared to take a human form. The Chevalier could now no longer doubt but that it was the ghost, and felt his courage fail him, although he strove to master it as well as he could. The figure, as it approached, grew gigantic, and the Chevalier crouched behind a column as it passed, which it did with enormous footsteps. As it passed, it appeared all dressed in white; the face was long and white, and its hand appeared of itself capable of covering the whole body of Mengaldo.

" The Chevalier, when he was in the army, had a duel with a brother officer, and wounded him in the arm. He was very sorry at having wounded the young man, and attended him during its cure; so that when he got well they became firm and dear friends. Being quartered, I think, at Milan, the young officer fell desperately in love with the wife of a musician, who disdained his passion. The young man became miserable, and Mengaldo continually advised him to ask leave of absence — to hunt, to pay a visit, and in some way to divert his passion. One evening the young man came to Mengaldo, and said, 'Well, I have asked leave of absence, and am to have it early to-morrow morning; so lend me your fowling-piece and cartridges, for I shall go to hunt for a fortnight.' Mengaldo gave it him; and among his bird-shot were some bullets, put there for safety, in case, while hunting, he should be attacked by a wolf, &c.

" The young man said: 'Tell the lady I love that our conversation has been chiefly about her to-night, and that her name was the last I spoke.' 'Yes, yes,' said Mengaldo, 'I will say anything you please; but do not talk of her any more —

you must forget her.' On going away the young man embraced Mengaldo warmly; but the latter saw nothing more in it than his affection, combined with melancholy in separating himself from his mistress.

"When Mengaldo was on guard that night, he heard the report of a gun. He was first troubled and agitated by it, but afterwards thought no more of it, and when relieved from guard went to bed, although he passed a restless and sleepless night. In the morning early, some one knocked at the door. The man said he had got the young officer's leave of absence, and had taken it to his house. A servant had opened the door, and he had gone up stairs; but the officer's room-door was locked, and no one answered to his knocking; but something oozed through under the door that appeared like blood. Mengaldo was dreadfully terrified; he hurried to his friend's house, burst open the door, and found him stretched on the ground. He had blown out his brains, and his head and brains were scattered about the room, so that no part of the head remained on the shoulders. Mengaldo was grieved and shocked, and had a fever in consequence, which lasted some days. When he was well, he got leave of absence, and went into the country to try to divert his mind.

"One evening at moonlight, he was returning home from a walk, and passing through a lane with a hedge on both sides, so high that he could not see over it. As he walked along, he heard a rustling in the bushes beside him, and the figure of his friend issued from the hedge and stood before him, as he had seen him after his death, without his head. This figure he saw many times afterwards, always in the same place. It was impalpable to the touch, and never spoke, although Mengaldo often addressed it. Once he took another person with him. The same rustling was heard; the same shadow stepped forth; his companion was dreadfully terrified; he tried to cry, but his voice failed him, and he ran off as quickly as he could."

Under date " November 13th, 1818," Godwin thus

gossips with Shelley on the events of the day, and on his own projects: —

"I am at present deeply engaged upon Malthus. It goes on slowly, but so much the more surely (not the more surely as to its being ever finished, but the more surely) as to its being finally

> 'Fortis et in seipso totus teres atque rotundus,
> Externi ne quid valeat per læve morari,
> In quem maneat semper fortuna.'

I have just discovered a train of reasoning which, if I am not mistaken, will utterly and forever demolish his geometrical ratio.

* * * * * * *

"You have heard, of course, of the melancholy suicide of Sir Samuel Romilly. I do not remember any event that has produced so deep a public sensation. He was undoubtedly an admirable man; and I do not know any one whose parliamentary existence was so completely devoted to public good.

"You are also, I suppose, informed of the withdrawing the army of occupation from France. Lord Liverpool, we are told, has in consequence insisted upon a large reduction of our peace establishment, and made this measure the *sine quâ non* of his continuing in office. This is supposed to be owing to the turn matters took in the General Election. So far we have really made some advance in the scale of improvement.

"The last letters I received from Mary are of the date of August 3d and October 1st. In the October letter, she apparently labored under great depression of spirits, in consequence of the loss of her infant. I hope she has by this time recovered her accustomed tone, and is happy.

"Very affectionately yours,
"WILLIAM GODWIN."

FROM MRS. SHELLEY TO MRS. GISBORNE.

"*Naples, Dec.* 1818.

" MY DEAR MRS. GISBORNE,

" I HASTEN to answer your kind letter as soon as we are a little recovered from the fatigue of our long journey, although I still feel wearied and overcome by it,—so you must expect a very stupid letter. We set out from Este the day after I wrote to you. We remained one day at Ferrara and two at Bologna, looking at the memorials preserved of Tasso and Ariosto in the former town, and at the most exquisite pictures in the latter. Afterwards, we proceeded along the coast road by Rimini, Fano, Fossombrone, &c. We saw the divine waterfall, Terni, and arrived safely at Rome. We performed this journey with our own horses, with Paolo to drive us, which we found a very economical, but a very disagreeable way; so we shall not attempt it again. To you, who have seen Rome, I need not say how enchanted we were with the first view of Rome and its antiquities. One drawback they have at present, which I hope will be fully compensated for in the future. The ruins are filled with galley-slaves at work. They are propping the Coliseum, and making very deep excavations in the Forum. We remained a week at Rome, and our fears for the journey to Naples were entirely removed. They said here that there had not been a robbery on the road for eight months. This we found afterwards to be an exaggeration; but it tranquillized us so much that Shelley went on first, to secure us lodgings, and we followed a day or two after. We found the road guarded, and the only part of the road where there was any talk of fear was between Terracina and Fondi, when it was not thought desirable we should set out from the former place before daylight. Shelley travelled with a Lombard merchant and a Neapolitan priest. He remained only two nights on the road, and he went *veterino;* so you may guess he had to travel early and late. The priest, a great, strong, muscular fellow, was almost in convulsions with fear, to travel before daylight along the Pontine marshes. There was talk of two bishops murdered, and that touched him nearly. The robbers spare foreigners, but never Neapolitan men, if they are young and strong; so he was the worst off of the party. The merchant did not feel very comfortable, and they were both surprised at Shelley's quietness. That quiet was disturbed, however, between Capua and Naples, by an assassination committed in broad daylight before their eyes. A young man ran out of a shop on the road, followed by a woman armed with a great stick and a man with a great knife. The man overtook him, and stabbed him in the nape of the neck, so that he fell down instantly, stone dead. The fearful priest laughed heartily at Shelley's horror on the occasion.

"Well, we are now settled in comfortable lodgings, which Shelley took for three louis a week, opposite the Royal Gardens — you no doubt remember the situation. We have a full view of the bay from our windows; so I think we are well off. As yet, we have seen nothing; but we shall soon make some excursions in the environs.

"Ever yours affectionately,
"MARY W. SHELLEY."

CHAPTER IX.

"PROMETHEUS UNBOUND:" THE "CENCI."

The early part of the year 1819 was spent by the Shelleys at Naples, and was diversified by excursions to Pæstum, Pompeii, Herculaneum, Vesuvius, Baiæ, Lago d'Agnano, &c.; but in March they returned to Rome, where every day was occupied in explorations and visits, in wanderings among the sublime ruins of antiquity, and in meditations on the past. Their happiness, however, was soon interrupted by the death, in the early summer, of their son William — at that time their only surviving child. Shelley suffered the deepest anguish from this event; and the grief of Mrs. Shelley was no less. The child was buried in the English cemetery; in allusion to which place Shelley wrote: — "This spot is the repository of a sacred loss, of which the yearnings of a parent's heart are now prophetic; he is rendered immortal by love, as his memory is by death. My beloved child lies buried here. I envy death the body far less than the oppressors the minds of those whom they have torn from me. The one can only kill the body; the other crushes the affections."

Harping on the same mournful string, he thus addresses his dead child in verse:—

> "My lost William, thou in whom
> Some bright spirit lived, and did
> That decaying robe consume
> Which its lustre faintly hid,
> Here its ashes find a tomb;
> But beneath this pyramid
> Thou art not. If a thing divine,
> Like thee, can die, thy funeral shrine
> Is thy mother's grief and mine."

In the spring of 1819, Shelley wrote one of the greatest of his works, the *Prometheus Unbound*. The spot he selected for his study was that occupied by the ruined baths of Caracalla — a maze of gigantic chambers, open to the sky, and carpeted with verdure; of shattered towers, wreathed with a drapery of glorious weeds and trailing ivy, with which the stonework has become almost incorporated; of heaped masses of masonry, out of which spring groves of flowering shrubs; of broken arches, winding staircases, and hidden nooks for solitary thought. Here he worked with wonderful assiduity, and very soon completed the drama in three acts; the fourth was added several months after, when the poet was at Florence. All attentive readers of this wonderful work will agree with Mrs. Shelley in thinking that the lucid atmosphere of Rome, the exquisite vegetation of the surrounding wastes, and the sublime objects of art, whether of antiquity or of later times, which met his eyes in every direction, helped the sensitive imagination of Shelley to conceive those superhuman visions of loveliness and awful might which throng the scenes of *Prometheus Unbound*. But only his own subtle, and almost instinctive, apprehension of metaphysical analogies could have enabled him to endow his ideal characters with a language proper to the abstract ideas which they typify. This is the intuition of genius, which can not only create an imaginary world, but can govern it by laws in harmony with themselves and with that which they control. The personifications of Shelley's mythological drama are not the vague idealisms of a young poet seeking for effect; they have a deep psychological meaning. The poetry which they utter is like the language of beings wakening, in the fresh dawn of the world, to the mystery of their own emotions and the miraculous loveliness of the universe. We seem to behold the elemental splendor of things disarrayed of that indifference which springs from our superficial familiarity, and from the deadening effect of our conventional existence.

The drama, though written in 1819, was not published till 1820.

Several of Shelley's letters about this period have reference to a project, which he set on foot, of a steamboat to ply between Marseilles and Leghorn; the construction of this boat was to be managed by Mr. Reveley, the son of Mrs. Gisborne by a former marriage, to whom reference has already been made, and who was an engineer. The pecuniary profit was to belong solely to Mr. Reveley; but Shelley took a fervent interest in the undertaking, for its own sake. It was not puerile vanity, but the nobler feeling of honest pride, that made him enjoy the idea of being the first to introduce steam navigation into the Gulf of Lyons, and to glory in the consciousness of being in this manner useful to his fellow-creatures. Unfortunately, he was condemned to experience a failure. The prospects and views of his friends drew them to England, and the boat and engine were abandoned. Shelley was deeply disappointed yet it will be seen how generously he exculpates his friends to themselves, and relieves them from the regret they might naturally feel at having thus wasted his money and disappointed his desires.

FROM MRS. SHELLEY TO MRS. GISBORNE.

"*Rome, Monday, April* 26*th*, 1819.

"MY DEAR MRS. GISBORNE,

"WE already begin to feel, or think we feel, the effects of the Roman air, producing cold, depression, and even fever, to the feeblest of our party; so we emigrate a month earlier than we intended, and on the 7th of May leave this delightful city for the Bay of Naples, intending, if possible, to settle for some months at Castel del Mare. The physicians prognosticate good to Shelley from a Neapolitan summer. He has been very unwell lately, and is very far from well now; but I hope that he is getting up again.

"Yesterday evening, I met at a conversazione the true model of Biddy Fudge's lover — an Englishman with 'the dear Corsair expression, half savage, half soft,' with the beautiful mixture of ' Abelard and old Blucher,' and his forehead ' rather bald, but so warlike,' and his moustaches, on which the lamp shone with a fine effect. When I heard his name called Signor Colonello, I could not restrain a smile, which nearly degenerated into laughter when I thought we had Colonel Calicot in Rome. Presently he began, in very good

Italian, which, though Englishly pronounced, [was] yet better spoken than any other Englishman that I have heard, to give an account of his warlike feats, and how at Lisbon he had put to flight thirty well-armed and well-mounted robbers (he on foot), with two pistols that never missed their aim. There can be but one such man in the world, as you will be convinced when I tell you that, while I was admiring his extraordinary prowess, C—— whispered to me, "It is Colonel F——h."

"You asked me to tell you what I had heard of him at Venice. Only one or two shabby tricks too long for a letter; and that an officer who served in Spain, of the same regiment to which he pretends to belong, vows that there was no Colonel F——h there. Report says that he is a parson, and Lord B.'s nickname for his particular friend is the *Reverend Colonel F——h.*

"We have been very gay in Rome, as I dare say you have heard, with the visit of the Emperor of Austria, who, they whisper, wishes to take the Roman States into the keeping of the Holy Roman Empire; this would be a fall (to say the least of it) from nothingness to hell. There was a feast given at the Capitol. The three palaces were joined by a gallery, and the whole hung with silk, and illuminated in the most magnificent manner; and the dying Gladiator, surrounded by his Apollos and Venuses, shone forth very beautifully. There were very fine fireworks, and a supper not at all in the Italian taste, for there was an abundance which did honor to the old Cardinal who superintended the *fête*. Every one was pleased, and the Romans in ecstacies. I have not room to tell you how gracefully the old venerable Pope fulfilled the church ceremonies, or how surprised and delighted we were with the lighting up of St. Peter's; all that must serve for gossip when we meet. When will that be? We saw nobody at Naples; but we see a few people here. The Italian character does not improve upon us. By the by, we have given an introduction for you (which I do not think will be presented) to a Roman lady, a painter and authoress, very old, very miserly, and very mean — perhaps you know her. She says that she thinks she remembers your name.

"I am in better health and spirits than when I last wrote, and make no ceremony of writing without receiving answers. Shelley and C—— desire best remembrances.

"Affectionately yours,
"M. W. SHELLEY."

The ardor of intellectual creation must at this time have possessed Shelley to an extraordinary degree. No sooner had he finished the first three acts of *Prometheus Unbound*, than he began the *Cenci;* and, as the former work was written during the spring, and the date of the dedication of the latter is May 29th, the composition of the tragedy must have been pushed forward with great rapidity, though the work was not completed till a month or two after the date indicated. The dedication is to Leigh Hunt, and shows the high regard which Shelley entertained for the friend who, perhaps above all others, understood his nature and his genius. The origin of the tragedy is to be found in an old manuscript account of the story of the Cenci which a friend put into Shelley's hands while he was at Rome, and of which a translation is published by Mrs. Shelley in her edition of the poems. The poet's interest in the unhappy victim, Beatrice, was increased by seeing her portraits in the Colonna and Doria Palaces (the former by Guido); and he at first wished Mrs. Shelley to make the story the subject of a play by herself, as he conceived that she possessed a dramatic faculty, and that he had none whatever, — for the *Prometheus Unbound* is clearly not a drama in the ordinary sense of the word, but a poem, taking the form of action. He had already made one or two attempts of a more strictly dramatic kind, but had thrown them aside in disgust; nevertheless, he was persuaded by Mrs. Shelley to undertake the tragedy of the *Cenci*, and he frequently consulted her during its progress (the only time he submitted to her judgment any of his writings while they were being composed), and talked over the arrangement of the scenes from day to day.

While the work proceeded, the illness and death of the little boy, William, took place — an affliction which drove the broken-hearted parents to the neighborhood of Leghorn, where they took a small house (Villa Valsovano), about half-way between the city and Monte Nero. "Our villa," says Mrs. Shelley, "was situated in the midst of a *poderè;* the peasants sang as they worked beneath our window during the heats of a very hot summer, and in the evening the water-wheel creaked as the process of irrigation went on, and the fire-flies flashed from among the myrtle hedges. Nature was bright, sunshiny, and cheerful, or diversified by storms of a majestic terror, such as we had never before witnessed." A small terrace, roofed and glazed, at the top of the house, was converted by Shelley into a study; and here he could bask in the light and heat of an Italian summer (never too intense for him), or watch the processional march of the tempests over the near ocean. The greater part of the *Cenci* was written in this retreat.

Wishing to see his drama acted at Covent Garden,

with Miss O'Neil as the heroine, Shelley wrote to a friend in London (Mr. Peacock), requesting that he would open negotiations with the manager. In addressing Mr. Peacock, he says of the newly-completed work that his "principal doubt as to whether it would succeed as an acting play hangs entirely" on the frightful nature of the story; but he thinks that the delicacy with which he has treated the facts will remove any objection. It did not do so, however, for the manager declined to accept the work, on the ground anticipated by its author; yet, at the same time, he expressed his desire that the writer (whose name was not mentioned to him*) would compose a play on some other subject, adding that he would gladly produce it. In the same letter, Shelley observes:— "I am exceedingly interested in the question of whether this attempt of mine will succeed or not. I am strongly inclined to the affirmative, at present, founding my hopes on this, that, as a composition, it is certainly not inferior to any of the modern plays that have been acted, with the exception of *Remorse;* that the interest of the plot is incredibly greater and more real; and that there is nothing but what the multitude are contented to believe that they can understand, either in imagery, opinion, or sentiment." With respect to Miss O'Neil in the character of Beatrice, Shelley exclaims — "God forbid that I should see her play it! It would tear my nerves to pieces."

---

* The reason for this secrecy was a fear on the part of Shelley that, if the play were produced as his, his sister-in-law would hire people to hoot it off the stage.

In another letter, the poet writes: — "I have been cautious to avoid the introducing faults of youthful composition; diffuseness, a profusion of inapplicable imagery, vagueness, generality, and, as Hamlet says, 'words, words.'" The play is, in truth, a wonderful instance of mature judgment and self-control — the more extraordinary when we reflect that the author was barely seven-and-twenty when he wrote it, and that the peculiar tendency of his genius was towards an excessive affluence of imagination and fancy, and the embodiment of thoughts the most evanescent and impalpable in forms the most gorgeous and transcendent. The *Cenci* occupies entirely different ground. Everywhere we feel the earth under our feet. The characters are not personifications of abstract ideas, but are true human beings, speaking, indeed, a language exalted by passion, but, nevertheless, a language which has its roots in nature, and draws its sustenance from life. Awful are those revelations of the monstrous heart of the old man; tremendous in their hopeless agony and desolation those staggerings of the mind of Beatrice on the brink of madness; angelical, in its serene redemption from transitory error, that spirit of resignation and immortal love which rises, towards the close of the play, out of the hell of the earlier parts, and finds its most lovely expression in the final words. Never did poet more exquisitely show the triumph of Good over Evil than Shelley has done in that hushed and sacred ending. It is a voice out of the very depths of the suffering patience of humanity. But, indeed, the play throughout comes nearer to Shakspeare than any other writer has approached since Shakspeare's time.

Strange to say, however, Shelley, though frequently urged by his friends, would never again write in the same manner, asserting that his natural tastes lay in a totally different direction.

The first edition of the *Cenci* was printed in Italy, and sent to London for publication. It was received with a degree of enthusiasm to which no other work of Shelley attained during his life; and in 1821 a second edition was printed in England. In a letter to Mr. Ollier, his publisher, dated " Leghorn, September 6th, 1819," Shelley alludes both to *Prometheus Unbound* and to the *Cenci*.

FROM SHELLEY TO MR. OLLIER.

" Dear Sir,

"I received your packet with Hunt's picture about a fortnight ago; and your letter with Nos. 1, 2, and 3 yesterday, but not No. 4, which is probably lost or mislaid, through the extreme irregularity of the Italian post.

" The ill account you give of the success of my poetical attempts, sufficiently accounts for your silence; but I believe that the truth is, I write less for the public than for myself. Considering that perhaps the parcel will be another year on its voyage, I rather wish, if this letter arrives in time, that you would send the *Quarterly's* article by the post, and the rest of the *Review* in the parcel. Of course, it gives me a certain degree of pleasure to know that any one likes my writings; but it is objection and enmity alone that rouses my *curiosity*. My *Prometheus*, which has been long finished, is now being transcribed, and will soon be forwarded to you for publication. It is, in my judgment, of a higher character than anything I have yet attempted, and is perhaps less an imitation of anything that has gone before it. I shall also send you another work, calculated to produce a very popular effect, and totally in a different style from anything I have yet composed. This will be sent already printed. The *Prometheus* you will be so good as to print as usual. . . . .

"In the *Rosalind and Helen*, I see there are some few errors, which are so much the worse because they are errors in the sense. If there should be any danger of a second edition, I will correct them.

"I have read your *Altham*, and Keats's poem and Lamb's works. For the second in this list, much praise is due to me for having read it, the author's intention appearing to be that no person should possibly get to the end of it. Yet it is full of some of the highest and the finest gleams of poetry; indeed, everything seems to be viewed by the mind of a poet which is described in it. I think, if he had printed about fifty pages of fragments from it, I should have been led to admire Keats as a poet more than I ought, of which there is now no danger. In *Altham* you have surprised and delighted me. It is a natural story, most unaffectedly told; and, what is more, told in a strain of very pure and powerful English, which is a very rare merit. You seem to have studied our language to some purpose; but I suppose I ought to have waited for *Inesilla*.

"The same day that your letter came, came the news of the Manchester work, and the torrent of my indignation has not yet done boiling in my veins. I wait anxiously to hear how the country will express its sense of this bloody, murderous oppression of its destroyers. 'Something must be done. What, yet I know not.'*

"In your parcel (which I pray you to send in some safe manner, forwarding to me the bill of lading, &c., in a regular mercantile way, so that my parcel may come in six weeks, not twelve months) send me Jones's Greek Grammar and some sealing wax.

* A quotation from the *Cenci*. — ED.

"Whenever I publish, send copies of my books to the following people from me: —

"Mr. Hunt,   Mr. Keats,
"Mr. Godwin,   Mr. Thomas Moore,
"Mr. Hogg,   Mr. Horace Smith,
"Mr. Peacock,   Lord Byron (at Murray's).
"Yours, obliged and faithful,
"PERCY B. SHELLEY."

The reference to Keats in this letter is curious, considering the high admiration which Shelley afterwards felt for his writings. But the truth is that Keats's first volume (which is the book here alluded to) contained a great deal of what was raw, youthful, and weak, together with passages reflecting, as Shelley rightly says, "the highest and the finest gleams of poetry" — passages prophetic of the future achievements of the young genius.

Another letter to Mr. Ollier contains further allusion to the *Cenci,* and some scornful remarks on *Quarterly Review* slanders: —

"*Florence, Oct.* 15*th,* 1819.

"DEAR SIR,

"THE droll remarks of the *Quarterly,* and Hunt's kind defence, arrived as safe as such poison, and safer than such an antidote, usually do.

"I am on the point of sending to you 250 copies of a work which I have printed in Italy; which you will have to pay four or five pounds duty upon, on my account. Hunt will tell you the *kind of thing* it is, and in the course of the winter I shall send directions for its publication, *until the arrival of which directions, I request that you would have the kindness not* to open the box, *or, if by necessity, it is opened, to abstain from observing yourself, or permitting others to observe, what it con-*

tains.* I trust this confidently to you, it being of consequence. Meanwhile, assure yourself that this work has no reference, direct or indirect, to politics, or religion, or personal satire, and that this precaution is merely literary.

"The *Prometheus*, a poem in my best style, whatever that may amount to, will arrive with it, but in MS., which you can print and publish in the season. It is the most perfect of my productions.

"Southey wrote the article in question, I am well aware. Observe the impudence of the man in speaking of himself. The only remark worth notice in this piece is the assertion that I imitate Wordsworth. It may as well be said that Lord Byron imitates Wordsworth, or that Wordsworth imitates Lord Byron, both being great poets, and deriving from the new springs of thought and feeling, which the great events of our age have exposed to view, a similar tone of sentiment, imagery, and expression. A certain similarity all the best writers of any particular age inevitably are marked with, from the spirit of that age acting on all. This I had explained in my Preface, which the writer was too disingenuous to advert to. As to the other trash, and particularly that lame attack on my personal character, which was meant so ill, and which I am not the man to feel, 'tis all nothing. I am glad, with respect to that part of it which alludes to Hunt, that it should so have happened that I dedicate, as you will see, a work which has all the capacities for being popular to that excellent person. I was amused, too, with the finale; it is like the end of the first act of an opera, when that tremendous concordant discord sets up from the orchestra, and everybody talks and sings at once. It describes the result of my battle with their Omnipotent God; his pulling me under the sea by the hair of my head, like Pharaoh; my calling out like the devil who was *game* to the last; swearing and cursing in all comic and horrid oaths, like a French postilion on Mount Cenis; entreating everybody to drown themselves; pretend-

* The italics are Shelley's own. — ED.

ing not to be drowned myself when I *am* drowned; and, lastly, *being* drowned.*

"You would do me a particular kindness if you would call on Hunt, and ask him when my parcel went, the name of the ship, and the name of the captain, and whether he has any bill of lading, which, if he has, you would oblige me by sending, together with the rest of the information, by return of post, addressed to the Post-Office, Florence.

"Yours very sincerely,
"P. B. SHELLEY."

FROM SHELLEY TO MR. OLLIER.

"Florence, December 15th, 1819."

"DEAR SIR,

"PRAY give Mr. Procter my best thanks for his polite attention. I read the article you enclosed with the pleasure which every one feels, of course, when they are praised or defended; though the praise would have given me more pleasure if it had been less excessive. I am glad, however, to see the *Quarterly* cut up, and that by one of their own people. Poor Southey has enough to endure. Do you know, I think the article in *Blackwood* could not have been written by a favorer of Government, and a religionist. I don't believe any such one could sincerely like my writings. After all, is it not some friend in disguise, and don't you know who wrote it?

"There is one very droll thing in the *Quarterly*. They say that 'my chariot-wheels are broken.' Heaven forbid! My chariot, you may tell them, was built by one of the best makers in Bond Street, and it has gone several thousand miles in perfect security. What a comical thing it would be to make the following advertisement! — 'A report having prevailed, in consequence of some insinuations in the *Quarterly*

---

* Shelley's frequent allusions to his being drowned are very singular. — ED.

Review, that Mr. Shelley's chariot-wheels are broken, Mr. Charters, of Bond Street, begs to assure the public that they, after having carried him through Italy, France, and Switzerland, still continue in excellent repair.'

"When the box comes, you may write a note to Mr. Peacock; or it would be better to call on him, and ask if *my tragedy is accepted?* If not, publish what you find in the box. I think it will succeed as a publication. Let *Prometheus* be printed without delay. You will receive the additions, which Mrs. S. is now transcribing, in a few days. It has already been read to many persons. My *Prometheus* is the best thing I ever wrote.

"Pray what have you done with *Peter Bell?* Ask Mr. Hunt for it, and for some other poems of a similar character I sent him to give you to publish. I think *Peter* not bad in his way; but perhaps no one will believe in anything in the shape of a joke from me.

"Of course with my next box you will send me the *Dramatic Sketches*.* I have only seen the extracts in the *Examiner*. They have some passages painfully beautiful. When I consider the vivid energy to which the minds of men are awakened in this age of ours, ought I not to congratulate myself that I am a contemporary with names which are great, or will be great, or ought to be great?

"Have you seen my poem, *Julian and Maddalo?* Suppose you print that in the manner of Hunt's *Hero and Leander;* for I mean to write three other poems, the scenes of which will be laid at Rome, Florence, and Naples, but the subjects of which will be all drawn from dreadful or beautiful realities, as that of this was.

"If I have health —— but I will neither boast nor promise. I am preparing an octavo on reform — a commonplace kind of book — which, now that I see the passion of party will postpone the great struggle till another year, I shall not trouble myself to finish for this season. I intend it to be an

* By Mr. Procter. — Ed.

instructive and readable book, appealing from the passions to the reason of men.

"Yours very sincerely,
"P. B. S."

It will be seen from the date of the last two letters that the Shelleys had removed from Leghorn to Florence. They did so in the early part of October; but though Shelley was delighted with the latter city (one of the most glorious in Italy), he found that the air did not suit him, and early in the following year he moved again.

The "Manchester work," to which Shelley alludes in the letter of September 6th, was the slaughter, by a body of mounted yeomanry, of several wretched men and women who had attended a large reform meeting in the open air, at Peterloo, near the great cotton metropolis. This horrible affair suggested to Shelley his *Masque of Anarchy*, which he sent to Leigh Hunt to be published by him, if he thought fit, in the *Examiner*. Leigh Hunt, however, did not insert it, because he thought the public mind was hardly in a fit state to receive a poem which was of a nature rather to increase than to calm the excitement already existing with respect to the massacre; but he gave it to the world in a small volume which appeared in the year 1832. In this poem, as in the *Cenci*, Shelley has shown his capacity to speak directly to the heart; yet it is full of imagination, also, and of exquisite musical utterance. Several of his other minor poems written in this same year were likewise prompted by the political state of England, which at that time, under the profligate rule of the Prince Regent and the reactionary counsels of Lord Castlereagh, was fast becoming one with the worst Continental tyrannies. *Peter Bell the Third* was a satire on Wordsworth for deserting his youthful advocacy of liberty. It was not published till after Shelley's death.

The article in the *Quarterly Review* was a criticism on the *Revolt of Islam*. Shelley read it for the first time at a public room in Florence, and laughed loudly at its absurdity. Yet the calumnies it contained probably led to a dastardly attack on him at the Post-Office by an Englishman, who, addressing him as an Atheist, knocked him down, and ran off. Several efforts were made by Shelley to discover and punish the cowardly scoundrel; but they failed. The poor fanatic effectually shrouded himself in secrecy.

Writing to her friend, Mrs. Gisborne, from Florence, on the 5th of October, Mrs. Shelley reports a witty remark by her husband, which ought to be preserved. " Shelley," she records, " *Calderonized* on the late weather :· he called it an epic of rain, with an episode of frost, and a few similes concerning fine weather."

Shelley was at this time greatly troubled by the failure of his usual remittances from England, owing to some cause which he could not divine. In a letter to Mrs. Gisborne, dated October 14th, he says : —

" About Henry and the steam-engine, I am in torture until this money comes from London, though I am sure that it must and will come ; unless, indeed, my banker has broke, and then it will be my loss, not Henry's. A little delay will mend the matter. I would then write instantly to London an effectual letter, and by return of post all would be set right. It would then be a thing easily set straight; but, if it were not, you know me too well not to know that there is no personal suffering, or degradation, or toil, or anything that can be named, with which I do not feel myself bound to support this enterprise of Henry. But all this rodomontade only shows how correct Mr. Bielby's advice was, about the discipline necessary for my imagination. No doubt that all will go on with mercantile and commonplace exactness, and that you will be spared the suffering, and I the virtue, incident to some untoward event."

A week later, he wrote as follows to Mrs. Gisborne and her son:—

"*Florence, Oct. 21st,* 1819.

"MY DEAR FRIENDS,

"I SEND you a check for 111 sequins, 5 pauls, the produce of 50*l.*, to go on with. It must be presented and indorsed by Henry, to get the money. The 200*l.* will arrive in a few days.

"My sincerest congratulations to Mr. Gisborne on his arrival.

"I write these lines in a stationer's close to the Post-Office, and in great haste, not to miss the post.

"PERCY B. SHELLEY."

We next come to a letter of friendly reproof, addressed to Mr. Henry Reveley:—

"*October* 28*th,* 1819.

"MY DEAR HENRY,

"IN the first place, listen to a reproach: you ought to have sent me an acknowledgment of my last billet.

"Let you and I try if we cannot be as punctual and business like as the best of them. But no clipping and coining, if you please.

"Now take this that I say in a light just so serious as not to give you pain, In fact, my dear fellow, my motive for soliciting your correspondence, and that flowing from your own mind, and clothed in your own words, is, that you may begin to accustom to discipline yourself in the only practice of life in which you appear deficient. You know that you are writing to a person persuaded of all the confidence and respect due to your powers in those branches of science to which you have addicted yourself; and you will not permit a false shame with regard to the mere mechanical arrangement of words to overbalance the advantage arising from the free communication of ideas. Thus you will become day by day more skilful in the management of that instrument of their communication on which the attainment of a person's just rank in society depends. Do not think me arrogant. There are subjects of the highest importance, on which you are far better qualified to instruct me, than I am qualified to instruct you on this subject.

* * * * * *

"Your very faithful friend,
"P. B. S."

Addressing the Gisbornes on the same day, Shelley again refers to the unsatisfactory state of his finances:—

"*Florence, Oct.* 28*th*, 1819.

"MY DEAR FRIENDS,

"I RECEIVED this morning the strange and unexpected news that my bill of 200*l.* has been returned to Mr. Webb protested. Ultimately this can be nothing but delay, as I have only drawn from my banker's hands as much as to leave them still in possession of 80*l.* ; and this I positively know, and can prove by documents. By return of post (for I have not only written to my banker, but to private friends) no doubt Henry will be enabled to proceed. Let him, meanwhile, do all that can be done.

"Meanwhile, to save time, could not money be obtained temporarily, at Livorno, from Mr. W—— or Mr. G——, or any of your acquaintance, on my bills at three or six months, indorsed by Mr. Gisborne and Henry, so that he may go on with his work? If a month is of consequence, think of this.

"Be of good cheer, *Madonna mia;* all will go well. The enclosed is for Henry, and was written before this news, as he will see; but it does not, strange as it is, abate one atom of my cheer.

"Accept, dear Mrs. G., my best regards.

"Yours faithfully,
"P. B. S."

On November 13th, Shelley writes to Leigh Hunt:—
"Yesterday morning, Mary brought me a little boy. She suffered but two hours' pain, and is now so well that it seems a wonder that she stays in bed. The babe is also quite well, and has begun to suck. You may imagine that this is a great relief and a great comfort to me amongst all my misfortunes, past, present, and to come. . . . . Poor Mary begins (for the first time) to look a little consoled; for we have spent, as you may imagine, a miserable five months." The same domestic event is touched upon by Mrs. Shelley herself in a letter to Mrs. Gisborne:—

"*December* 1*st*, 1819.
"My dear Mrs. G.,

"The little boy is nearly three times as big as when he was born; he thrives well and cries little, and is now taking a right-down, earnest sleep, with all his heart in his shut eyes.

"There are some ladies come to this house who knew Shelley's family; the younger one was *enthousiasmée* to see him; the elder said that he was a very shocking man, but, finding that we became the mode, she melted, and paid us a visit. She is a little old Welshwoman, without the slightest education. She has got an Italian master, and has entered into the difficult part of the language, the singulars and plurals — the *il's* and the *lo's*, and is to turn masculines into feminines, and feminines into masculines; but she says she does not think she shall ever learn, for she cannot help mixing Welsh with her Italian — and, besides, it spoils her French. She speaks the sweetest French, as you may judge by her telling her master, '*Je ne peut lire aucune plus.*'

"The younger lady was a ward of one of Shelley's uncles. She is lively and unaffected. She sings well for an English *debûtante*, and, if she would learn the scales, would sing exceedingly well, for she has a sweet voice. So there is a great deal of good company for C——, who is as busy as a bee among them all, serving as an interpreter to their masters. She has a most excellent singing master, and he now teaches several other young ladies who are here. One who had had a very cross master in England, when told to sing *sol*, burst into tears. The poor man was aghast. '*Non capisco questo effetto.*'

"I do not know why I write all this gossip to you. Pray let us hear of you, and the steamboat, and the felucca.

"Affectionately yours,
"M. W. SHELLEY."

Writing to Mrs. Gisborne on December 15th, Mrs. Shelley says: —

"You see, my dear friend, by the receipt of your crowns, that we have recovered 100*l.* of our money. There is still 100*l.* in jeopardy; but we must hope, and perhaps, by dint of giving it up as lost, we may find it again. . . . . . . I have begun reading with Shelley the *Conquesta di Mexico*, by Solio. We have read very little yet. I send you something to amuse you — the bane and antidote. The bane from the *Quarterly*, the antidote from *Blackwood's Edinburgh Magazine*, a publication as furious as the *Quarterly*, but which takes up arms (singularly enough) in Shelley's defence. We half think that it must be Walter Scott, the only liberal man of that faction."

Some days later, Mrs. Shelley again wrote to her friend, Mrs. Gisborne:—

"*Florence, Dec. 28th*, 1819.
"MY DEAR MRS. GISBORNE,

"I AM glad you are pleased with the *Prometheus*. The last act, though very beautiful, is certainly the most mystic of the four. I am glad also that Spenser pleases you, for he is a favorite author of mine. In his days, I fancy, translations and plagiarisms were not considered so disgraceful as they are now. You have not all of him, and therefore perhaps you have not read the parts that I particularly admire * — the snowy Florimel, Belphœbe, and her Squire lover (who are half meant for Queen Elizabeth and Lord Essex). Britomart is only an imitation; she is cold and dull; but the others, and the lovely Una, are his own creations, and I own I like them better than Angelica, although, indeed, the thought of her night scene with Madora † came across me, and made me pause as I wrote the opinion. But, perhaps, it is not in pathos, but in simple description of beauty, that Spenser excels. His description of the Island of Bliss is an exact translation of Tasso's *Garden of Armida;* yet how is it that I find a greater simplicity and spirit in the translation than in the original? Yet, so it is.

"I think of beginning to read again — study I cannot, for I have no books, and I may not call simple reading study, for papa is continually saying and writing, that to read one book without others beside you, to which you may refer, is mere child's play; but still I hope now to get on with Latin and Spanish. Do you know that, if you could borrow for us

* In the *Faëry Queene*. — ED.
† See Ariosto's *Orlando Furioso*. — ED.

Rousseau's *Emile*, and Voltaire's *Essai sur l'Esprit des Nations* — either or both — you would oblige us very much.

"Shelley has given up the idea of visiting Leghorn before the finishing of the steamboat. He is rather better these last two or three days, but he has suffered dreadfully lately from his side. He seems a changed man. His numerous weaknesses and ailments have left him, and settled all in his side alone, for he never, any other winter, suffered such constant pain there.* It puts me in mind of the mountain of ills in the *Spectator*, where mankind exchange ills one with the other; then they all take up their old evils again as the most bearable. I do not know whether this is Shelley's case.

"Affectionately yours,
" M. W. Shelley."

---

* In another letter, Mrs. Shelley speaks of this pain having a rheumatic character. — Ed.

CHAPTER X.

THE POET'S LIFE AT PISA AND LEGHORN.

On the 26th of January, 1820, the Shelleys removed to Pisa. At that city they had friends, and could consult the celebrated physician Vaccà on the subject of the poet's ailments, though they received from him no other advice than to abstain from all medicine, and leave the constitution to right itself. Vaccà was as much puzzled as the other medical men to assign any cause for Shelley's painful symptoms; but, whatever might have been the nature of the complaint, the air of Pisa agreed better with the patient than that of any other place, and it was therefore determined on to remain there. Under the best of circumstances, however, Shelley was never entirely free from pain and ill-health.

In walking, riding, and studying, some months passed pleasantly away. When evening had set in, Shelley, according to his usual custom, would read aloud. A few weeks in the spring were spent at Leghorn, in a villa lent to them by their friends the Gisbornes, who were then absent in England. From this house Shelley addressed his letter in verse to Mrs. Gisborne — a composition of interwoven grace and humor, uttered in free and fluent heroic couplet, and containing a lovely picture of the scenery and influences by which the writer was surrounded : —

> "I see a chaos of green leaves and fruit
> Built round dark caverns, even to the root
> Of the living stems who feed them; in whose bowers
> There sleep in their dark dew the folded flowers.
> Beyond, the surface of the unsickled corn
> Trembles not in the slumbering air, and, borne
> In circles quaint and ever-changing dance,
> Like winged stars the fire-flies flash and glance,
> Pale in the open moonshine; but each one
> Under the dark trees seems a little sun, —
> A meteor tamed, — a fix'd star gone astray
> From the silver regions of the Milky Way.
> Afar, the Contadino's song is heard,
> Rude, but made sweet by distance; and a bird,
> Which cannot be a nightingale, and yet
> I know none else that sings so sweet as it
> At this late hour; — and then all is still."

The date of this poem is July 1st. While staying at the same house, Shelley wrote his divine *Ode to a Skylark*. The poem was suggested to him one evening by the bird itself, whose song attracted his attention as he was wandering with Mrs. Shelley among lanes shut in by myrtle hedges, and spangled with the erratic glory of the fire-flies.

Being alarmed for the safety of their only child, who was affected by the extreme heat of the summer, the parents left Leghorn in August for the baths of San Giuliano, which are situated four miles from Pisa. The water of the baths soothed the nervous irritability of Shelley, and the time appears to have been very agreeably spent, the country being beautiful and the climate brilliant. " During some of the hottest days of August," we read in the notes to the poems, " Shelley made a solitary journey on foot to the summit of Monte San Pelegrino — a mountain of some height, on the top of which there is a chapel, the object, during certain days in the year, of many pilgrimages." The undue exertion produced considerable lassitude and weakness in Shelley after his return; yet, in the three days immediately succeeding, he produced that gorgeous fantasy, the *Witch of Atlas*. He had conceived the idea during his walk.

In Mrs. Shelley's Journal, under date "August 25th," is recorded: — " Shelley writes *Ode to Naples;* begins *Swellfoot, the Tyrant* — suggested by the grunting of the pigs at the fair of San Giuliano, whilst he was reading aloud his *Ode to Liberty*." He compared this unmusical interruption to " the chorus of frogs in the satiric drama of Aristophanes." The object of Shelley's burlesque was to place in a ludicrous point of view the prosecution of Queen Caroline, which was then going forward; and the pigs were made to serve as chorus. On being finished, it was sent to England, where it was printed and published anonymously; but the Society for the Suppression of Vice, conceiving, in their ultra-sensitiveness, that its subject trenched too much on forbidden ground, threatened to prosecute, and the work was consequently withdrawn.

Several other poems (though none of great length) were written in the same year; among them, that delicate dream, that romance of metaphysical subtlety, finding its expression in the utmost affluence of fancy and imagination — the *Sensitive Plant*.

A singular circumstance brought to a termination the stay of the Shelleys at San Giuliano. "At the foot of our garden," writes Mrs. Shelley, "ran the canal that communicated between the Serchio and the Arno. The Serchio overflowed its banks, and, breaking its bounds, this canal also overflowed. All this part of the country is below the level of its rivers, and the consequence was that it was speedily flooded. The rising waters filled the square of the baths, in the lower part of which our house was situated. The canal overflowed in the garden behind; the rising waters on either side at last burst open the doors, and, meeting in the house, rose to the height of six feet. It was a picturesque sight at night, to see the peasants driving the cattle from the plains below to the hills above the baths. A fire was kept up to guide them across the ford; and the forms of the men and the animals showed in dark relief against the red glare of the flame, which was reflected again in the waters that filled the square."

Driven forth by this local deluge, Shelley and his wife took up their abode for the winter at Pisa, where the extreme mildness of the climate offered a great inducement to them to stay. The dreamy quiet of the half-depopulated old Republican city, moreover, delighted Shelley; and for the brief remainder of his life he lived for the most part there. Painful experience had taught him and Mrs. Shelley, when contemplating their infant son, to dread the heat in the south of the peninsula;

though, but for this fear, they would have continued to wander at will, being devoted lovers of travelling.

The appearance of the poet at this time showed a singular mixture of premature age and unusually prolonged youth. He walked with a stoop, and his hair was sprinkled with gray; but, when Mr. Trelawney was introduced to him some time afterwards, he found him looking like "a tall, thin stripling."

Some letters addressed to Mr. Ollier, during the year 1820, illustrate the progress of Shelley's intellectual labors:—

"*Pisa, Jan. 20th,* 1820.

"DEAR SIR,

"I SEND you the *Witch of Atlas*, a fanciful poem, which, if its merit be measured by the labor which it cost, is worth nothing; and the errata of *Prometheus*, which I ought to have sent long since — a formidable list, as you will see.

"I have lately, and but lately, received Mr. Gisborne's parcel, with reviews, &c. I request you to convey to Mr. Procter my thanks for the present of his works, as well as for the pleasure which I received from the perusal, especially of the *Dramatic Sketches*.

"The reviews of my *Cenci* (though some of them, and especially that marked 'John Scott,' are written with great malignity) on the whole give me as much encouragement as a person of my habits of thinking is capable of receiving from such a source, which is, inasmuch as they coincide with, and confirm, my own decisions. My next attempt (if I should write more) will be a drama, in the composition of which I shall attend to the advice of my critics, to a certain degree. But I doubt whether I *shall* write more. I could be content either with the Hell or the Paradise of poetry; but the torments of its Purgatory vex me, without exciting my powers sufficiently to put an end to the vexation.

"I have also to thank *you* for the present of one or two of your publications. I am enchanted with your *Literary Miscellany*, although the last article it contains has excited my polemical faculties so violently, that the moment I get rid of my ophthalmia I mean to set about an answer to it, which I will send to you, if you please. It is very clever, but, I think, very false.* Who is your commentator on the German Drama? He is a powerful thinker, though I differ from him *toto cœlo* about the Devils of Dante and Milton. If you know him personally, pray ask him, from me, what he means by receiving the *spirit into me;*† and (if really it is any good) how one is to get at it. I was immeasurably amused by the quotation from Schlegel, about the way in which the popular faith is destroyed — first the Devil, then the Holy Ghost, then God the Father. I had written a Lucianic essay to prove the same thing. There are two beautiful stories, too, in this *Miscellany*. It pleased me, altogether, infinitely. I was also much pleased with the *Retrospective Review* — that is, with all the quotations from old books in it; but it is very ill executed.

"When the spirit moves you, write and give me an account of the ill success of my verses.

"Who wrote the review, in your publication, of my *Cenci?* It was written in a friendly spirit, and, if you know the author, I wish you would tell him from me how much obliged I am to him for this spirit, more gratifying to me than any literary laud.   Dear Sir,

"Yours, very truly,
"P. B. S."

---

* The article (which was written by Mr. Peacock) was an Essay on Poetry, which the writer regarded as a worn-out delusion of barbarous times. — ED.

† The writer was the late Archdeacon Hare, who, despite his orthodoxy, was a great admirer of Shelley's genius. He contended that Milton erred in making the Devil a majestical being, and hoped that Shelley would in time humble his soul, and "receive the spirit into him." — ED.

"*Pisa, March 6th*, 1820.

"DEAR SIR,

"I DO not hear that you have received *Prometheus* and the *Cenci;* I therefore think it safest to tell you how and when to get them if you have not yet done so.

"Give the bill of lading Mr. Gisborne sent you to a broker in the city, whom you employ to get the package, and to pay the duty on the unbound books. The ship sailed in the middle of December, and will assuredly have arrived long before now.

"*Prometheus Unbound*, I must tell you, is my favorite poem; I charge you, therefore, specially to pet him and feed him with fine ink and good paper. *Cenci* is written for the multitude, and ought to sell well. I think, if I may judge by its merits, the *Prometheus* cannot sell beyond twenty copies. I hear nothing either from Hunt, or you, or any one. If you condescend to write to me, mention something about Keats.

"Allow me particularly to request you to send copies of whatever I publish to Horace Smith.

"May be you will see me in the summer; but in that case I shall certainly return to this 'Paradise of Exiles'* by the ensuing winter.

"If any of the Reviews abuse me, cut them out and send them. If they praise, you need not trouble yourself. I feel ashamed if I could believe that I should deserve the latter; the former, I flatter myself, is no more than a just tribute. If Hunt praises me, send it, because that is of another character of thing.

"Dear Sir,
"Yours very truly,
"PERCY B. SHELLEY."

"*Pisa, March 13th*, 1820.

"DEAR SIR,

"I AM anxious to hear that you have received the parcel

---

* This is a phrase which he himself applies to Italy in *Julian and Maddalo*. — ED.

from Leghorn, and to learn what you are doing with the *Prometheus*. If it can be done without great difficulty, I should be very glad that the *revised* sheets might be sent by the post to me at Leghorn. It might be divided into four partitions, sending me four or five sheets at once.

"My friends here have great hopes that the *Cenci* will succeed as a publication. It was refused at Drury Lane,* although expressly written for theatrical exhibition, on a plea of the story being too horrible. I believe it singularly fitted for the stage.

"Let me request you to give me frequent notice of my *literary interests* also.

"I am, dear Sir,
 "Your very obliged servant,
  "PERCY B. SHELLEY.

"I hope you are not implicated in the late plot.† Not having heard from Hunt, I am afraid that he, at least, has something to do with it. It is well known, since the time of Jaffier, that a conspirator has no time to think about his friends."

"*Pisa, May* 14*th*, 1820.
"DEAR SIR,
"I REPLY to your letter by return of post, to confirm what I said in a former letter respecting a new edition of the *Cenci*, which ought, by all means, to be instantly urged forward.

"I see by your account that I have been greatly mistaken in my calculations of the *profit* of my writings. As to the trifle due to me, it may as well remain in your hands.

"As to the printing of the *Prometheus*, be it as you will. But in this case, I shall repose or trust in your care respecting the correction of the press; especially in the lyrical parts,

---

* This is apparently a slip of the pen for Covent Garden. — ED.
† The Cato Street Conspiracy. — ED.

where a minute error would be of much consequence. Mr. Gisborne will revise it; he heard it recited, and will therefore more readily seize any error.

"If I had even intended to publish *Julian and Maddalo* with my name, yet I would not print it with *Prometheus*. It would not harmonize. It is an attempt in a different style, in which I am not yet sure of myself — a *sermo pedestris* way of treating human nature, quite opposed to the idealisms of that drama. If you print *Julian and Maddalo*, I wish it to be printed in some unostentatious form, accompanied with the fragment of *Athanase*, and exactly in the manner in which I sent it; and I particularly desire that my name be not annexed to the first edition of it, in any case.

"If *Peter Bell* be printed (you can best judge if it will sell or no, and there would be no other reason for printing such a trifle), attend, I pray you, particularly to completely concealing the author; and for Emma read Betty, as the name of Peter's sister. Emma, I recollect, is the real name of the sister of a great poet who might be mistaken for Peter. I ought to say that I send you poems in a few posts, to print at the end of *Prometheus*, better fitted for that purpose than any in your possession.

"Keats, I hope, is going to show himself a great poet; like the sun, to burst through the clouds, which though dyed in the finest colors of the air, obscured his rising. The Gisbornes will bring me from you copies of whatever may be published when they leave England.

"Dear Sir,
"Yours faithfully,
"P. B. Shelley."

"*Pisa, November* 10*th*, 1820.

"Dear Sir,
"Mr. Gisborne has sent me a copy of the *Prometheus*, which is certainly most beautifully printed. It is to be regretted that the errors of the press are so numerous, and in

many respects so destructive of the sense of a species of poetry which, I fear, even without this disadvantage, very few will understand or like. I shall send you the list of *errata* in a day or two.

"I send some poems to be added to the pamphlet of *Julian and Maddalo*. I think you have some other smaller poems belonging to that collection, and I believe you know that I do not wish my name to be printed on the title-page, though I have no objection to my being known as the author.

"I enclose also another poem, which I do not wish to be printed with *Julian and Maddalo*, but at the end of the second edition of the *Cenci*, or of any other of my writings to which my name is affixed, if any other should at present have arrived at a second edition, which I do not expect. I have a purpose in this arrangement, and have marked the poem I mean by a cross.

"I can sympathize too feelingly in your brother's misfortune.* It has been my hard fate also to watch the gradual death of a beloved child, and to survive him. Present my respects to your brother.

"My friend Captain Medwin is with me, and has shown me a poem on Indian hunting, which he has sent you to publish. It is certainly a very elegant and classical composition, and, even if it does not belong to the highest style of poetry, I should be surprised if it did not succeed. May I challenge your kindness to do what you can for it?

"You will hear from me again in a post or two. The *Julian and Maddalo*, and the accompanying poems, are all my saddest verses raked up into one heap. I mean to mingle more smiles with my tears in future.

"Your obedient servant,
"P. B. SHELLEY."

In addressing her friend, Mrs. Gisborne, on the 24th

---

* This letter was addressed to Mr. James Ollier, who was in partnership with his brother. The latter had just lost a daughter. — ED.

of March, 1820, Mrs. Shelley speaks of herself and her husband as being "very busy translating *Spinoza*. I write from his dictation," she adds; "and we get on. By the bye, I wish you would send me the volume of the *Encyclopædia* that gives a system of shorthand, for I want to learn one without delay."

Writing to the Gisbornes, on March 19th, Shelley says:— "Tell us of the steamboat. This steamboat is a sort of a symptote, which seems ever to approach and never to arrive. But courage! Horrible work this, in England!" (He is here again alluding to the Cato Street conspiracy, and to the disturbed state of things.) "Good and bad seem to have become inextricably entangled in our unhappy country."

On May 8th, the poet indulges (in again addressing Mrs. Gisborne) in a little playful raillery on the subject of Mrs. Shelley's handwriting:—

"I wonder what makes Mary think her letter worth the trouble of opening— except, indeed, she conceives it to be a delight to decipher a difficult scrawl. She might as well have put, as I will —'MY DEAR SIR,

"'? ? ? ! ! !

"'Yours, &c.'

"Take care of yourselves, and do *you* not forget your nightly journal. The silent dews renew the grass without effort in the night. I mean to write to you, but not to-day. All happiness attend you, my dear friend! As an excuse for mine and Mary's incurable stupidity, I send a little thing about poets, which is itself a kind of excuse for Wordsworth."

FROM MRS. SHELLEY TO MISS CURRAN.

"*Leghorn, June* 20*th*, 1820.

"My dear Miss Curran,

"It is a very long time since I heard from you, so that, if I did not know your dislike to writing, I should be afraid that something had happened — and that you were very ill. My heart, during all this time, was at Rome; but I cannot conjecture when I shall be really there. Still, a letter with the Roman postmark would be a pleasant thing; how much more welcome if from you!

"I am afraid you find great difficulties in executing our unhappy commission. Shelley and I therefore are induced to entreat you to have the kindness to order a plain stone to be erected, to mark the spot, with merely his name and dates (William Shelley, born Jan. 24th, 1816 — June 7th, 1819). You would oblige us more than I can express if you would take care that this should be done.

"Our little Percy is a thriving, forward child; but after what has happened I own it appears to me a failing cloud — all those hopes that we so earnestly dwell upon. How do you like the *Cenci?* It sells, you must know, of which I am very glad. If I could hear of any one going to Rome I would send you some other books to amuse you, for we had a parcel from England the other day; but we are entirely out of the world. It will give me great pleasure to hear from you, to know when you leave Rome, and how your pictures increase. Be sure I do not forget your nice study and your kind hospitality. Your study, how can I forget when we have so valuable a specimen of it, that is dearer to me than I can well say?

"Shelley desires his kindest remembrances. I would give a very great deal to look upon the divine city from the Trinita di Monti. Is not my heart there?

"From papa I have not heard a very long time. Affairs

seem going on there badly, but slower than a tortoise — I hope not so surely towards their apparent end.

"Farewell! I entreat you to write.

"Yours, with affection,
"Mary W. Shelley.

"P. S. — I have heard your brother's life of your father much praised."

FROM KEATS TO SHELLEY.

"*Hampstead, August* 10*th*, 1820.

"My dear Shelley,

"I am very much gratified that you, in a foreign country, and with a mind almost over-occupied, should write to me in the strain of the letter beside me. If I do not take advantage of your invitation,* it will be prevented by a circumstance I have very much at heart to prophesy. There is no doubt that an English winter would put an end to me, and do so in a lingering, hateful manner. Therefore, I must either voyage or journey to Italy, as a soldier marches up to a battery. My nerves at present are the worst part of me, yet they feel soothed that, come what extreme may, I shall not be destined to remain in one spot long enough to take a hatred of any four particular bedposts. I am glad you take any pleasure in my poor poem,† which I would willingly take the trouble to unwrite, if possible, did I care so much as I have done about reputation. I received a copy of the *Cenci*, as from yourself, from Hunt. There is only one part of it I am judge of — the poetry and dramatic effect, which by many spirits now-a-days is considered the Mammon. A modern work, it is said, must have a purpose, which may be the God. An artist must serve Mammon; he must have 'self-concentration' — selfishness, perhaps. You, I am sure, will forgive me for sincerely re-

---

* To go to Italy. — Ed.   † *Endymion.* — Ed.

marking that you might curb your magnanimity, and be more of an artist, and load every rift of your subject with ore. The thought of such discipline must fall like cold chains upon you, who perhaps never sat with your wings furled for six months together. And is not this extraordinary talk for the writer of *Endymion*, whose mind was like a pack of scattered cards? I am picked up and sorted to a pip. My imagination is a monastery, and I am its monk. I am in expectation of *Prometheus* every day. Could I have my own wish effected, you would have it still in manuscript, or be but now putting an end to the second act. I remember you advising me not to publish my first blights, on Hampstead Heath. I am returning advice upon your hands. Most of the poems in the volume I send you * have been written above two years, and would never have been published but for a hope of gain; so you see I am inclined enough to take your advice now. I must express once more my deep sense of your kindness, adding my sincere thanks and respects for Mrs. Shelley. In the hope of soon seeing you,

"I remain most sincerely yours,
"JOHN KEATS."

FROM MRS. SHELLEY TO MISS CURRAN.

"*Pisa, San Giuliano, August 17th*, [1820.]

"MY DEAR MISS CURRAN,

"I SHOULD have answered your letter before, but we have been in the confusion of moving. We are now settled in an agreeable house at the baths of San Giuliano, about four miles from Pisa, under the shadow of mountains, and with delightful scenery within a walk. We go on in our old manner, with no change. I have had many changes for the worse — one might be for the better — but that is nearly impossible.

* This was his last publication. — ED.

Our child is well and thriving, which is a great comfort; and the Italian stay gives Shelley health, which is to him a rare and substantial enjoyment.

"I did not receive the letter you mention to have written in March, and you also have missed one of our letters, in which Shelley acknowledged the receipt of the drawing you mention,* and requested that the largest pyramid might be erected, if they would encase it with white marble for 25*l*. However, the whole had better stand as I mentioned in my last; for, without the most vigorous inspection, great cheating would take place, and no female could detect them. When we visit Rome, we can do that which we wish. Many thanks for your kindness, which has been very great.

"How enraged all our mighty rulers are at the quiet revolutions which have taken place; it is said that some one said to the Grand Duke here, '*Ma si chiedono une constituzione qui!*' '*Ebene la dario subito*,' was the reply; but he is not his own master, and Austria would take care that that should not be the case. They say, Austrian troops are coming here, and the Tuscan ones will be sent to Germany. We take in *Galignani*, and would send them to you if you liked. I do not know what the expense would be, but I should think slight.

"If you recommence painting, do not forget Beatrice. I wish very much for a copy of that. You would oblige us greatly by making one. Pray let me hear of your health. We do not know when we shall be in Rome; circumstances must direct; and they dance about like will-o'-the-wisps, enticing and then deserting us. We must take care not to be left in a bog. Adieu! take care of yourself. Believe me, with sincere wishes for your health, and kind remembrances,

"Ever sincerely yours,
"MARY W. SHELLEY.

"P. S.—Who was he with the long memory who remem-

* Of the child William.—ED.

bered seeing me? Somehow, people always remember my features; even those have detected my identity who have not seen me since I was a month old; so I have hopes that, when I go to heaven, I shall easily be recognized by my old friends.

"Do you know, we lose many letters?—having spies (not Government ones) about us in plenty. They made a desperate push to do us a desperate mischief lately, but succeeded no further than to blacken us amongst the English; so, if you receive a fresh batch (or green bag) of scandal against us, I assure you it will be a lie. Poor souls! we live innocently, as you well know; if we did not, ten to one we should not be so unfortunate."

In a letter dated September 4th, 1820, Horace Smith communicates to Shelley his opinion of two of his recent works:—

"I got from Ollier last week a copy of the *Prometheus Unbound*, which is certainly a most original, grand, and occasionally sublime work, evincing, in my opinion, a higher order of talent than any of your previous productions; and yet, contrary to your own estimation, I must say I prefer the *Cenci*, because it contains a deep and sustained human interest, of which we feel a want in the other. Prometheus himself certainly touches us nearly; but we see very little of him after his liberation; and, though I have no doubt it will be more admired than anything you have written, I question whether it will be so much read as the *Cenci*.

"Your letter, stating your sudden intention of going to Paris, turned up the other day, with all the postmarks of the world upon it, except, I believe, Jerusalem and Seringapatam. Did you intrust it to the Wandering Jew?"

FROM SHELLEY TO MR. JOHN GISBORNE.

"*Pisa, Oct.* 29*th*, 1820.

" DEAR FRIEND,

" CAN you tell me anything about Arabic grammars, dictionaries, and manuscripts, and whether they are vendible at Leghorn, and whether there are any native Arabs capable of teaching the language? Do not give yourself any trouble about the subject; but if you could answer or discover an answer to these questions without any pains, I should be very much obliged to you. My kind regards to Mrs. G. and Henry.

" Yours very truly,

" P. B. SHELLEY."

CHAPTER XI.

SHELLEY AND BYRON AT PISA.

EARLY in the year 1821, the Shelleys made the acquaintance of Mr. and Mrs. Williams, the former of whom was drowned with the poet. Mrs. Shelley says of him that no man " ever existed more gentle, generous, and fearless." Like his illustrious friend, he was a great lover of boating, and the two were frequently on the water together, before the day which proved fatal to both. Shelley, indeed, enjoyed a good deal of his favorite recreation during this year. The shallow waters of the Arno, on which no ordinary vessel can float, did not prove any obstacle to him; he contrived a boat "such as the huntsmen carry about with them in the Maremma, to cross the sluggish but deep streams that intersect the forest — a boat of laths and pitched canvas."* In this he frequently took little trips on the Arno, though his Italian friends, seeing the peril which he ran, used to remonstrate with him, and to prophesy — with too much truth — that

* Mrs. Shelley.

the amusement would lead to his death. On one occasion, when he had been with a friend down the Arno and round the coast to Leghorn, he returned by the canal, when the skiff got entangled amongst some weeds, and was upset. The intense cold made Shelley faint; but no further harm was done. "Once," writes Mrs. Shelley, "I went down with him to the mouth of the Arno, where the stream, then high and swift, met the tideless sea, and disturbed its sluggish waters. It was a waste and dreary scene; the desert sand stretched into a point surrounded by waves that broke idly, though perpetually, around."

But the water was far from engrossing Shelley's thoughts at this time. The south of Europe had awakened from its lethargy into a state of high political excitement, and it seemed as if the age of liberty were dawning in several places. Spain and Naples had been revolutionized in the previous year; and the northern and central parts of Italy now endeavored to follow the example. Several insurrectionary movements were attended by temporary success; Tuscany alone, owing to the benevolent rule of its prince, remained tranquil; but, in the end, the patriots were crushed beneath the weight of Austrian armies. At the same period, however, a revolution began in a country farther east, which was destined to result, to a certain extent, in success, though Shelley did not live long enough to behold the issue. Greece declared itself independent of Ottoman domination; and these combined attacks on the general foe filled Shelley with the utmost enthusiasm. Some Greeks were at that time at Pisa; and amongst them was Prince Mavrocordato, to whom *Hellas* is dedicated. On the 1st of April, this gentleman called on the Shelleys, and told them that his cousin, Prince Ipsilanti, had issued a proclamation (a copy of which he brought with him), and that Greece thenceforward would be free. The emotions of joy and hope kindled by this intelligence in the mind of the poet produced the lyrical drama of *Hellas,* of which Shelley records, in his preface, that it was " written at the suggestion of the events of the moment, is a mere improvise, and derives its interest (should it be found to possess any) solely from the intense sympathy which the author feels with the cause he would celebrate." Nevertheless, it contains passages of great power, and lyrics of the utmost sweetness.

In the same year, Shelley wrote that piece of radiant mysticism and rapturous melody, *Epipsychidion.* The subject of this poem — " the noble and unfortunate Lady Emilia V——," was the daughter of an Italian count, and was shut up in a convent by her father until such time as he could find for her a husband of whom he approved. In this dreary prison, Shelley saw her, and was struck by her amazing beauty, by the highly cultivated grace of her mind, and by the misery which she suffered in being debarred from all sympathy. She was subsequently married to a gentleman chosen for her by her father; and, after pining in his society, and in the marshy solitudes of the Maremma, for six years, she left him, with the consent of her parent, and died of consumption in a dilapidated old mansion at Florence. This occurred long after the death of Shelley, who used frequently to visit her while she was living in the convent, and to do his utmost to ameliorate her wretched condition. In return, she was in the habit of sending him bouquets of flowers; and one of these presents he thus acknowledged:—

> "Madonna, wherefore hast thou sent to me
>   Sweet basil and mignonette?
> Embleming love and health, which never yet
> In the same wreath might be.
>   Alas! and they are wet!
> Is it with thy kisses or thy tears?
>   For never rain or dew
>   Such fragrance drew
> From plant or flower. The very doubt endears
>   My sadness ever new,
> The sighs I breathe, the tears I shed, for thee."

Another of Shelley's compositions belonging to the year 1821 is his *Adonais*. This is a monody on the death of Keats, who expired at Rome on the 27th of December, 1820, of consumption. He was attended in his last illness by his friend, Mr. Severn, who devoted himself to the dying man. They were alone, and were overtaken by poverty; and Mr. Severn (who was an artist) not only watched by the bedside of the young poet, day and night, soothing him in the midst of his frightful paroxysms of mental and bodily anguish, but painted small pictures during his leisure moments, and, sallying forth unobserved, sold them to procure the necessary funds. Yet even this beautiful devotion could not save Keats from death; and he now lies in the Protestant burial-ground, whither the ashes of him who has celebrated his genius in verse lasting as his own were destined shortly to follow him.

Adonais abounds in passion and poetry; in bursts of eloquent grief; in profound glimpses into the divine mystery of the universe and of the soul of man; and of keen, arrowy flashes of scorn, directed against those hirelings of party who endeavored to crush the genius of Keats, simply because he was known to be the friend of men who dared to speak on behalf of freedom when to do so was considered an eighth deadly sin. But Shelley was mistaken in supposing that the death of Keats was accelerated by the contemptible treatment he had met with. He regarded such things with indifference, and died from causes of a much deeper kind.

Of the funeral of Keats, Shelley records in the preface to *Adonais*, that he " was burried in the romantic and lonely cemetery of the Protestants, under the pyramid which is the tomb of Cestius, and the massy walls and towers, now mouldering and desolate, which formed the circuit of ancient Rome. The cemetery is an open space among the ruins, covered in winter with violets and daisies. It might make one in love with death, to think that one should be buried in so sweet a place."

On the 29th of November, 1821, Shelley wrote to Mr. Severn, from Pisa, on the subject of the death of Keats:—

" DEAR SIR,

"I SEND you the elegy on poor Keats, and I wish it were better worth your acceptance. You will see, by the preface, that it was written before I could obtain any particular account of his last moments; all that I still know was communicated to me by a friend, who had derived his information from Colonel Finch. I have ventured to express, as I felt, the respect and admiration which your conduct towards him demands.

"In spite of his transcendent genius, Keats never was, nor ever will be, a popular poet; and the total neglect and obscurity in which the astonishing remnants of his mind still lie, was hardly to be dissipated by a writer who, however he may differ from Keats in more important qualities, at least resembles him in that accidental one, a want of popularity.

"I have little hope, therefore, that the poem I send you will excite any attention, nor do I feel assured that a critical notice of his writings would find a single reader. But for these considerations, it had been my intention to have collected the remnants of his compositions, and to have published them with a life and criticism. Has he left any poems, or writings of whatsoever kind, and in whose possession are they? Perhaps you would oblige me by information on this point.

"PERCY B. SHELLEY."

With respect to his *Epipsychidion*, and to one or two other poems, Shelley thus writes to Mr. Ollier:—

"*Pisa, Feb.* 16*th*, 1821.

"DEAR SIR,

"I SEND you three poems — *Ode to Naples*, a sonnet, and a longer piece, entitled *Epipsychidion*. The two former are my own; and you will be so obliging as to take the first opportunity of publishing according to your own discretion.

"The longer poem, I desire, should not be considered as my own; indeed, in a certain sense, it is a production of a portion of me already dead; and in this sense the advertisement is no fiction.* It is to be published simply for the esoteric few; and I make its author a secret, to avoid the malignity of those who turn sweet food into poison; transforming all they touch into the corruption of their own natures. My wish with respect to it is, that it should be printed immediately in the simplest form, and merely one hundred copies; those who are capable of judging and feeling rightly with respect to a composition of so abtruse a nature, certainly do not arrive at that number — among those, at least, who would ever be excited to read an obscure and anonymous production; and it would give me no pleasure that the vulgar should read it. If you have any bookselling reason against publishing so small a number as a hundred, merely, distribute copies among those to whom you think the poetry would afford any pleasure, and send me, as soon as you can, a copy by the post. I have written it so as to give very little trouble, I hope, to the printer, or to the person who revises. I would be much obliged to you if you would take this office on yourself.

"Is there any expectation of a second edition of the *Revolt of Islam?* I have many corrections to make in it, and one part will be wholly remodelled. I am employed in high and new designs in verse; but they are the labors of years, perhaps.

"We expect here every day the news of a battle between the armies of Austria and Naples. The latter have advanced upon Rome; and the first affair will probably take place in the Ecclesiastical States. You may imagine the expectation of all here.

"Pray send me news of my intellectual children. For

---

* In his preface he speaks of the poem as having been written by a person who " died at Florence, as he was preparing for a voyage to one of the wildest of the Sporades, which he had bought, and where it was his hope to have realized a scheme of life suited, perhaps, to that happier and better world of which he is now an inhabitant, but hardly practicable in this." The preface is signed " S." — ED.

Prometheus, I expect and desire no great sale. The *Cenci* ought to have been popular.

"I remain, dear Sir,
"Your very obedient servant,
"Percy B. Shelley."

Some idea of the reception given to the *Epipsychidion* may be derived from a letter written by Shelley, in the course of October, to Mr. Gisborne. He here says:—

"The *Epipsychidion* is a mystery; as to real flesh and blood, you know that I do not deal in those articles; you might as well go to a gin-shop for a leg of mutton, as expect anything human or earthly from me. I desired Ollier not to circulate this piece, except to the συνετὀι, and even they, it seems, are inclined to approximate me to the circle of a servant-girl and her sweetheart. But I intend to write a Symposium of my own, to set all this right."

FROM SHELLEY TO MR. OLLIER.

"*Pisa, Feb.* 22*d*, 1821.

"Dear Sir,

"Peacock's essay is at Florence at present. I have sent for it, and will transmit to you my paper [on Poetry] as soon as it is written, which will be in a very few days. Nevertheless, I should be sorry that you delayed your Magazine through any dependence on me. I will not accept anything for this paper, as I had determined to write it, and promised it you, before I heard of your liberal arrangements; but perhaps in future, if I think I have any thoughts worth publishing, I shall be glad to contribute to your Magazine on those terms. Meanwhile, you are perfectly at liberty to publish the *Ode to Naples*, the sonnet, or any short piece you may have of mine.

"I suppose *Julian and Maddalo* is published. If not, do not add the *Witch of Atlas* to that peculiar piece of writing; you may put my name to the *Witch of Atlas*, as usual. The piece I last sent you, I wish, as I think I told you, to be printed immediately, and that anonymously. I should be very glad to receive a few copies of it by the box, but I am unwilling that it should be any longer delayed.

"I doubt about *Charles the First*; but, if I do write it, it shall be the birth of severe and high feelings. You are very welcome to it on the terms you mention, and, when once I see and feel that I can write it, it is already written.* My thoughts aspire to a production of a far higher character; but the execution of it will require some years. I write what I write chiefly to inquire, by the reception which my writings meet with, how far I am fit for so great a task, or not. And I am afraid that your account will not present me with a very flattering result in this particular.

"You may expect to hear from me within a week, with the answer to Peacock. I shall endeavor to treat the subject in its elements, and unveil the inmost idol of the error.

"If any Review of note abuses me excessively, or the contrary, be so kind as to send it me by post.

"If not too late, pray send me by the box the following books: The most copious and correct history of the discoveries of Geology. If one publication does not appear to contain what I require, send me two or three. A history of the late war in Spain; I think one has been written by Southey. Major *Somebody's* account of the siege of Zaragoza; it is a little pamphlet. Burnet's *History of his Own Times*; and the *Old English Drama*, 3 vols.

"Excuse my horrible pens, ink, and paper. I can get no pen that will mark; or, if you will not excuse them, send me out some English ones.

---

* The play was never finished. — ED.

"I am delighted to hear of Procter's success, and hope that he will proceed gathering laurels. Pray tell me how the *Prometheus Unbound* was received.
   "Dear Sir,
    "Your very obliged servant,
     "PERCY B. SHELLEY."

FROM THE SAME TO THE SAME.

      "*Pisa, June 8th*, 1821.
"DEAR SIR,
 "You may announce for publication a poem entitled *Adonais*. It is a lament on the death of poor Keats, with some interposed stabs on the assassins of his peace and of his fame; and will be preceded by a criticism on *Hyperion*, asserting the due claims which that fragment gives him to the rank which I have assigned him. My poem is finished, and consists of about forty Spenser stanzas. I shall send it you, either printed at Pisa, or transcribed in such a manner as it shall be difficult for the reviser to leave such errors as *assist* the obscurity of the *Prometheus*. But, in case I send it printed, it will be merely that mistakes may be avoided; [so] that I shall only have a few copies struck off in the cheapest manner.

"If you have interest enough in the subject, I could wish that you inquired of some of the friends and relations of Keats respecting the circumstances of his death, and could transmit me any information you may be able to collect, and especially as to the degree in which, as I am assured, the brutal attack in the *Quarterly Review* excited the disease by which he perished.

"I have received no answer to my last letter to you. Have you received my contribution to your Magazine?
   "Dear Sir,
    "Yours very sincerely,
     "P. B. SHELLEY."

FROM SHELLEY TO MR. OLLIER.

"*Pisa, March* 20*th*, 1821.

" DEAR SIR,

"I SEND you the *Defence of Poetry*, Part I. It is transcribed, I hope, legibly.

" I have written nothing which I do not think necessary to the subject. Of course, if any expressions should strike you as too unpopular, I give you the power of omitting them; but I trust you will, if possible, refrain from exercising it. In fact, I hope that I have treated the question with that temper and spirit as to silence cavil. I propose to add two other parts in two succeeding Miscellanies. It is to be understood that although you may omit, you do not alter or add.

" Pray let me hear from you soon.
" Dear Sir,
" Yours very sincerely,
" P. B. S."

FROM THE SAME TO THE SAME.

"*Pisa, September* 25*th*, 1821.

" DEAR SIR,

" IT will give me great pleasure if I can arrange the affair of Mrs. Shelley's novel with you to her and your satisfaction. She has a specific purpose in the sum which she instructed me to require; and, although this purpose could not be answered without ready money, yet I should find means to answer her wishes in that point, if you could make it convenient to pay one third at Christmas, and give bills for the other two thirds at twelve and eighteen months. It would give me peculiar satisfaction that you, rather than any other person, should be the publisher of this work; it is the product of no slight labor, and, I flatter myself, of no common talent. I doubt not it will give no less credit than it will receive from your names. I trust you know me too well to believe that my judgment deliberately given in testimony of the value of any production is influenced by motives of interest or partiality.

"The romance is called *Castruccio, Prince of Lucca*, and is founded (not upon the novel of Macchiavelli under that name, which substitutes a childish fiction for the far more romantic truth of history, but) upon the actual story of his life. He was a person who, from an exile and an adventurer, after having served in the wars of England and Flanders in the reign of our Edward the Second, returned to his native city, and, liberating it from its tyrants, became himself its tyrant, and died in the full splendor of his dominion, which he had extended over the half of Tuscany. He was a little Napoleon, and, with a dukedom instead of an empire for his theatre, brought upon the same all the passions and the errors of his antitype. The chief interest of the romance rests upon Euthanasia, his betrothed bride, whose love for him is only equalled by her enthusiasm for the liberty of the republic of Florence, which is in some sort her country, and for that of Italy, to which Castruccio is a devoted enemy, being an ally of the party of the Emperor. This character is a masterpiece : and the keystone of the drama, which is built up with admirable art, is the conflict between these passions and these principles. Euthanasia, the last survivor of a noble house, is a feudal countess, and her castle is the scene of the exhibition of the knightly manners of the time. The character of Beatrice, the prophetess, can only be done justice to in the very language of the author. I know nothing in Walter Scott's novels which at all approaches to the beauty and the sublimity of this — creation, I may almost say, for it is perfectly original; and, although founded upon the ideas and manners of the age which is represented, is wholly without a similitude in any fiction I ever read. Beatrice is in love with Castruccio, and dies; for the romance, although interspersed with much lighter matter, is deeply tragic, and the shades darken and gather as the catastrophe approaches. All the manners, customs, opinions of the age are introduced; the superstitions, the heresies, and the religious persecutions, are displayed; the minutest circumstance of Italian manners in that age is not omitted; and the whole seems to me to constitute a living and a moving picture of an age almost forgotten. The author visited the scenery which she describes in person; and one or two of the inferior characters are drawn from her own observation of the Italians, for the national character shows itself still in certain instances under the same forms as it wore in the time of Dante.* The novel consists, as I told you before, of three volumes, each at least equal to one of the *Tales of my Landlord*, and they will be very soon ready to be sent. In case you should accept the present offer, I will make one observation which I consider of essential importance. It ought to be printed in half volumes at a time, and sent to the author for her last corrections by the post. It may be printed on thin paper like that of this letter, and the expense shall fall upon me. Lord Byron has his works sent in this manner; and no person, who has either fame to lose or money to win, ought to publish in any other manner.

"By the bye, how do I stand with regard to these two great objects of human pursuit? I *once* sought something nobler and better than either; but I might as well have reached at the moon, and now, finding that I have grasped the air, I should not be sorry to know what substantial sum, especially of the former, is in your hands on my account. The gods

---

* The book here alluded to was ultimately published under the title of *Valperga*. Mrs. Shelley received 400*l.* for the copyright; and this sum was generously devoted to the relief of Godwin's pecuniary difficulties. In a letter to Mrs. Gisborne, dated June 30th, 1821, Mrs. Shelley says that she first formed the conception at Marlow; that this took a more definite shape at Naples; that the work was delayed several times; and that it was "a child of mighty slow growth." It was also, she says, a work of labor, as she had read and consulted a great many books.— ED.

have made the reviewers the almoners of this worldly dross, and I think I must write an ode to flatter them to give me some; if I would not that they put me off with a bill on posterity, which when my ghost shall present, the answer will be —'no effects.'

"*Charles the First* is conceived, but not born. Unless I am sure of making something good, the play will not be written. Pride, that ruined Satan, will kill *Charles the First*, for his midwife would be only *less than him whom thunder has made greater*. I am full of great plans; and, if I should tell you them, I should add to the list of these riddles.

"I have not seen Mr. Procter's *Mirandola*. Send it me in the box, and pray send me the box immediately. It is of the utmost consequence; and, as you are so obliging as to say you will not neglect my commissions, pray send this without delay. I hope it *is* sent, indeed, and that you have recollected to send me several copies of *Prometheus*, the *Revolt of Islam*, and the *Cenci*, &c., as I requested you. Is there any chance of a second edition of the *Revolt of Islam?* I could materially improve that poem on revision. The *Adonais*, in spite of its mysticism, is the least imperfect of my compositions, and, as the image of my regret and honor for poor Keats, I wish it to be so. I shall write to you, probably, by next post, on the subject of that poem, and should have sent the promised criticism for the second edition, had I not mislaid, and in vain sought for, the volume that contains *Hyperion*. Pray give me notice against what time you want the second part of my *Defence of Poetry*. I give you this Defence, and you may do what you will with it.

"Pray give me an immediate answer about the novel.

"I am, my dear Sir,

"Your very obliged servant,

"PERCY B. SHELLEY.

"I ought to tell you that the novel has not the smallest tincture of any peculiar theories in politics or religion."

FROM SHELLEY TO MR. OLLIER.

"*Pisa, Nov.* 11*th*, 1821.

"Dear Sir,

"I send you the drama of *Hellas*, relying on your assurance that you will be good enough to pay immediate attention to my literary requests. What little interest this poem may ever excite, depends upon its immediate publication; I entreat you, therefore, to have the goodness to send the MS. instantly to a printer, and the moment you get a proof despatch it to me by the post. The whole might be sent at once. Lord Byron has his poem sent to him in this manner, and I cannot see that the inferiority in the composition of a poem can affect the powers of a printer in the matter of despatch, &c. If any passages should alarm you in the notes, you are at liberty to suppress them; the poem contains nothing of a tendency to danger.

"Do not forget my other questions. I am especially curious to hear the fate of *Adonais*. I confess I should be surprised if *that* poem were born to an immortality of oblivion.

"Within a few days I may have to write to you on a subject of greater interest. Meanwhile, I rely on your kindness for carrying my present request into immediate effect.

"Dear Sir,
"Your very faithful servant,
"Percy B. Shelley.

"I need not impress on you the propriety of giving a speedy answer to Mrs. S.'s proposal. Her volumes are now ready for the press. The *Ode to Napoleon* to print at the end."

The calumnies heaped upon Shelley by his unscrupulous detractors often gave him great pain. In writing to Mr. Ollier, on the 11th of June, 1821, he says:—"I hear that the abuse against me exceeds all bounds. Pray, if you see any one article particularly outrageous, send it me. As yet, I have laughed; but woe to these scoundrels if they should once make me lose my temper! I have discovered that my calumniator in the *Quarterly Review* was the Rev. Mr. Milman. Priests have their privilege."

Malicious reports seemed to track him wherever he went; and one of these is the subject of some letters which will be found below. Mrs. Shelley writes in her journal, under date August 4th:—"Shelley is gone to see Lord Byron at Ravenna. This is his [Shelley's] birthday; seven years are now gone—what changes! We now appear tranquil; yet who knows what wind— But I will not prognosticate evil; we have had enough of it. When we arrived in Italy, I said, all is well if it were permanent. It was more passing than an Italian twilight. I now say the same: may it be a Polar day! —yet that, too, has an end." They had passed a very pleasant summer, having both derived great enjoyment from frequently going to see some friends living at the village of Pugnano. They reached that place by the canal, "which, fed by the Serchio, was, though an artificial, a full and picturesque stream, making its way under verdant banks sheltered by trees that dipped their boughs into the murmuring waters. By day, multitudes of ephemera darted to and fro on the surface; at night, the fire-flies came out among the shrubs on the banks; the cicale at noonday kept up their hum; the aziola cooed in the quiet evening."* Yet, as Mrs. Shelley

* Notes to the Poems.

prognosticated in her diary, their happiness was soon to be dashed. Shelley writes from Ravenna on August 7th: —

"My dearest Mary,

"I arrived last night at ten o'clock, and sat up talking with Lord Byron until five o'clock this morning. I then went to sleep, and now awake at eleven, and, having despatched my breakfast as quick as possible, mean to devote the interval until twelve, when the post departs, to you. . . . .

"Lord Byron has told me of a circumstance that shocks me exceedingly, because it exhibits a degree of desperate and wicked malice for which I am at a loss to account. When I hear such things, my patience and my philosophy are put to a severe proof, whilst I refrain from seeking out some obscure hiding-place, where the countenance of man may never meet me more.

* * * * *

"Imagine my despair of good; imagine how it is possible that one of so weak and sensitive a nature as mine can run further the gauntlet through this hellish society of men. *You* should write to the Hoppners a letter refuting the charge, in case you believe and know, and can prove that it is false; stating the grounds and proofs of your belief. I need not dictate what you should say; nor, I hope, inspire you with warmth to rebut a charge which you only effectually *can* rebut."

To this letter, Mrs. Shelley thus replied: —

"My dear Shelley,

"Shocked beyond all measure as I was, I instantly wrote the enclosed. If the task be not too dreadful, pray copy it for me. I cannot.

"Read that part of your letter which contains the accusation. I tried, but I could not write it. I think I could as soon have died. I send also Elise's last letter; enclose it or not, as you think best.

"I wrote to you with far different feelings last night, beloved friend. Our bark is indeed 'tempest-tost;' but love me, as you have ever done, and God preserve my child to me, and our enemies shall not be too much for us. Consider well if Florence be a fit residence for us. I love, I own, to face danger; but I would not be imprudent.

"Pray get my letter to Mrs. H. copied, for a thousand reasons. Adieu, dearest! Take care of yourself — all yet is well. The shock for me is over, and I now despise the slander; but it must not pass uncontradicted. I sincerely thank Lord Byron for his kind unbelief.

"Affectionately yours,
"M. W. S."

"*Friday.*

"Do not think me imprudent in mentioning C.'s illness at Naples. It is well to meet facts. They are as cunning as wicked. I have read over my letter; it is written in haste; but it were as well that the first burst of feeling should be expressed. No letters."

FROM SHELLEY TO MRS. SHELLEY.

"*Thursday, Ravenna.*

"I HAVE received your letter with that to Mrs. Hoppner. I do not wonder, my dearest friend, that you should have been moved. I was at first, but speedily regained the indifference which the opinion of anything or anybody, except our own consciousness, amply merits, and day by day shall more receive from me. I have not recopied your letter — such a measure would destroy its authenticity — but have given it to Lord Byron, who has engaged to send it, with his own comments, to the Hoppners.

"People do not hesitate, it seems, to make themselves panders and accomplices to slander; for the Hoppners had exacted from Lord Byron that these accusations should be concealed from *me*. Lord Byron is not a man to keep a secret, good or bad; but, in openly confessing that he has not done so, he must observe a certain delicacy, and therefore wished to send the letter himself; and indeed this adds weight to your representations.

"Have you seen the article in the *Literary Gazette* on me? They evidently allude to some story of this kind. However cautious the Hoppners have been in preventing the calumniated person from asserting his justification, you know too much of the world not to be certain that this was the utmost limit of their caution. So much for nothing.

* * * * *

"My greatest comfort would be utterly to desert all human society. I would retire with you and our children to a solitary island in the sea; would build a boat, and shut upon my retreat the floodgates of the world. I would read no reviews, and talk with no authors. If I dared trust my imagination, it would tell me that there are one or two chosen companions, besides yourself, whom I should desire. But to this I would not listen. Where two or three are gathered together, the devil is among them; and good, far more than evil, impulses — love, far more than hatred — has been to me, except as you have been its object, the source of all sorts of mischief. So, on this plan, I would be *alone*, and would devote, either to oblivion or to future generations, the overflowings of a mind which, timely withdrawn from the contagion, should be kept fit for no baser object. But this it does not appear that we shall do.

"The other side of the alternative (for a medium ought not to be adopted) is to form for ourselves a society of our own class, as much as possible, in intellect or in feelings; and to connect ourselves with the interests of that society. Our roots never struck so deeply as at Pisa, and the transplanted tree flourishes not. People who lead the lives which we led until last winter, are like a family of Wahabee Arabs pitching their tent in the middle of London. We must do one thing or the other; for yourself — for our child — for our existence. The calumnies, the sources of which are probably deeper than we perceive, have ultimately for object the depriving us of the means of security and subsistence. You will easily perceive the gradations by which calumny proceeds to pretext, pretext to persecution, and persecution to the ban of fire and water. It is for this — and not because this or that fool, or the whole court of fools curse and rail — that calumny is worth refuting or chastising."

But from these painful details let us pass to other subjects.

At one time during the year 1821, Shelley thought of taking a farm situated amongst chestnut and pine-woods on one of the hills near the Serchio — a position commanding a magnificent prospect. Another fancy was to settle still further in the maritime Apennines at Massa. His greatest desire, however, was to spend his summers on the shores of the sea; and, having one day made an excursion to Spezzia, he was so delighted with the beauty of the bay, that he ultimately took a house there. This was not until the following year; for it was long before a suitable residence could be found. The Villa Magni was the name of the house, and it was the last which Shelley occupied.

He looked forward, with great pleasure, to seeing Leigh Hunt in the autumn of 1821; but the gratification was delayed till the following summer. The journalist was to join Lord Byron in the production of a quarterly magazine, to be called the *Liberal*, and Byron wished Shelley to unite with them. This the latter declined to do, because, according to Mrs. Shelley, he did not like to appear desirous of acquiring readers by associating his poetry with the writings of more popular authors; and also because that association might have had the effect of shackling him in the expression of his opinions. But he subsequently modified his determination, to the extent of contributing a few of his productions, though he always refused to be in any way connected with the undertaking in a pecuniary point of view. The first number did not appear till shortly after his death.

On the 1st of November, Byron arrived at Pisa, where he established himself. Leigh Hunt did not reach Italy till several months later. Shelley was now a good deal in the society of Byron; between whom and himself, however, a perfect cordiality seemed never to exist. The author of *Childe Harold* has confessed in one of his letters, that, much as he admired and esteemed Shelley, the feeling did not amount to entire friendship — an emotion which he could realize only with regard to one of the companions of his childhood. And Shelley, in the presence of Byron, felt somewhat oppressed by the weight of what he conceived to be his Lordship's superior poetical powers; though on this point the world is rapidly reversing contemporary judgment. In writing to a friend, Shelley speaks of Byron's genius reducing him to despair; an excess of modesty to which, perhaps, may be attributed the comparatively small number of his compositions at this time.

On the 28th of March, Horace Smith, who had kindly undertaken the management of Shelley's money matters in London, addressed a letter to his friend, touching the sudden stoppage of his income: —

"My dear Shelley,

"I called to-day at Brookes and Co.'s for your money, as usual, and was not a little surprised to be told that they had received notice *not to advance anything more on your account, as the payments to them would in future be discontinued;* but they could give me no information why this alteration had occurred, or whether you were apprised of it. Perhaps you have been, though you could hardly have failed to mention it to me. But I will call again, and endeavor to get some solution of the apparent mystery. Meantime, if you are in any straits, you had better draw on me, at the Stock Exchange, for what you want. I would remit you, but that, knowing you are not over-regular in matters of business, you may, perhaps, have made new arrangements for your money, and, through inadvertency, omitted to apprise me.

"Now that Italy has become the scene of war, a letter from you now and then, when you have any recent political news, would not only be gratifying, but, perhaps, useful in the way of business. The papers of to-day affirm that the Spanish Constitution has been proclaimed at Florence; and, for my own part, I have little doubt that, if the Austrians be defeated in the first instance, (which God grant!) the whole of Italy will be convulsed and revolutionized. In this anxious suspense, I must await the course of events, and hope to receive some communications from you.

"You ask in what periodical works I write. Principally in Baldwin's *London Magazine*, under various signatures, but generally H.; and also in the *New Monthly*, edited by Campbell, the poet. Poor Scott! what a melancholy termination! and how perfectly unnecessary!* Christie and the two seconds will surrender and take their trial at the Old Bailey

---

* Scott was the editor of the *London Magazine*, and was killed in a duel with a Mr. Christie, arising out of some strong remarks which he (Scott) had made on the writers in *Blackwood's Magazine*. The seconds were blamed for allowing another interchange of shots; but they were acquitted on their trial. — Ed.

Sessions next month. We are raising a subscription for Scott's family.

"You never said anything of Keats, who I see died at Rome under lamentable circumstances, and whom all lovers of poetry may regret, as a young genius destined to do great things. I have a sympathetic feeling for your ophthalmia, having myself lately suffered from a complaint in the eyes, but am now nearly recovered.

"Nothing strikingly new in literature, or in our domestic policy, although the battle between the suffering agriculturists and the fund-holders is obviously approximating. They (the former) already hope to abolish the malt-tax, on which our nominal sinking fund mainly relies. Another bad year, and they *must* reduce the interest, or replace the alarming defalcation of revenue by new loans. It is all working together for good; for it is by this explosion only that we can have the smallest chance of Reform.

"If I learn anything further about the money, I shall write you again shortly. Meantime, I am always,
"Dear Shelley,
"Yours most faithfully,
"HORATIO SMITH."

In his zeal for his friend's cause, Horace Smith thus addressed Sir Timothy Shelley on the subject of the money:—

"*Fulham, April* 13*th*, 1821.

"SIR,

"THOUGH I have not the honor of your acquaintance, I venture to hope that the circumstances which I am about to state will plead my excuse for intruding myself upon your attention. I feel pride in declaring myself the particular friend of Mr. Percy Bysshe Shelley, for whom I have been in the habit of receiving his quarterly income, and remitting it myself to Italy, for the purpose of saving brokerage and agency charges. Knowing my intimacy with your son, Dr.

Hume* applied to me last year, stating that he was in arrear; at which I expressed my surprise, as I assured him that Mr. Shelley never drew more than 220*l*., leaving the 30*l*. regularly for his use. I mentioned his application in more than one letter to Italy, and on the 14th of November wrote to Dr. Hume the following letter: —

["In this letter † I gave an extract of P. B. S.'s letter to me, saying he had scrupulously and regularly left the 30*l*. in the banker's hands, and they had orders to pay it regularly; expressing my own conviction that Dr. H. would get it on application.]

"To this letter I never received any reply; from which I very naturally concluded that the money was paid, and expressed this belief and conviction in my next communication to Mr. Shelley. Thus the affair rested till I called, on the 28th March last, with my usual order on Messrs. Brookes and Co. for 220*l*.; by whom I was informed that the payment of Mr. Shelley's income was stopped — whether permanently or temporarily, they could not tell me; nor could they afford me any explanation whatever, none having been given to them. This inexplicable occurrence was made known by me to Mr. Shelley on the following day.

"It was not until after a good deal of personal trouble and inquiry that I learned the real state of the case, and the institution of legal proceedings; and, having a thorough conviction that Mr. Shelley had left the money at the bankers, I believed it to be paid. I called on Messrs. Wright and Co., and found, as I suspected, that the money had all along been *lying in their hands* to the amount of Dr. Hume's claim within a trifle (which I presume are postages or some petty charges, with which Mr. Shelley was unacquainted), and that they had

---

* The custodian of Shelley's children by his first wife. — E<small>D</small>.

† The part here enclosed in brackets was inserted in a copy of the letter to Sir Timothy, afterwards sent by Horace Smith to his friend. A copy, in full, of the letter to Dr. Hume was of course sent to the baronet. — É<small>D</small>.

only been prevented paying it at once by the want of a regular, formal check or order. You will observe he says, in his letter to me: — 'I have regularly and scrupulously left 30*l.* from my income for Dr. Hume's draft;' but it is probable that, although he told the bankers he left it for Dr. Hume, he omitted to lodge a regular credit for his drafts — an oversight for which his inexperience of business supplies a sufficient explanation and excuse. Why this inquiry was not made at the bankers before the institution of law proceedings; why no application was made to me to get the irregularity rectified, which I would have pledged myself to have done; why nothing was said to him; why 250*l.* was finally impounded to pay 120*l.* — are points of which I will not offer any solution.

"I cannot find that Mr. Shelley has received from any quarter the smallest intimation of these proceedings. He has been left in a foreign country without the means of present subsistence, and must have been exposed to the most distressing suspense and anxiety from the sudden announcement of the cessation of his income without a syllable of explanation.

"To conduct so harsh and unmerited, and evincing such a total disregard to his feelings, you, sir, I am sure, would never have become a party, but from some great misapprehension of the real circumstances of the case. It is to remove this erroneous impression, and to prove to you, as I trust I have done effectually, that Mr. Shelley has been guilty of nothing but a little ignorance of the precise forms of bankers' business, that I have ventured to trouble you with this long explanation. My sincere respect and attachment to that gentleman would not allow me to be silent when I thought him aggrieved; and, in the hope that this feeling will plead my excuse for intruding upon your time, I beg to subscribe myself respectfully, &c., &c.,

"H. SMITH."

FROM HORACE SMITH TO SHELLEY.

"*Fulham, April* 17*th*, 1821.

"My dear Shelley,

"I wrote you on the 3d of this month, and I have been engaged in warlike operations for you ever since. I have a long story to tell. Determined to ferret out the mystery of this Chancery suit, I went from one place to another making inquiries; and, as Dr. Hume made no reply to my first letter, I wrote him a second, which, after an interval of several days, extorted the reply of which I send you a copy. On the same day when this came to hand, I called on Mr. Longdill, whom I understood to be your friend, when he at once confessed that he was a party to the proceedings against you, in order, as he said, to get Dr. Hume paid, whom he had himself recommended as custodian to the children.* He did not seem to believe that the 30*l*. had been left at Brookes's, and I found had never written to you, as he asked where you were. I went to the bankers'—back to him—was told by him that the law charges were now all incurred, and that it was too late to stay proceedings. From him I came home, chewing the cud of indignation, and, on my arrival, Hume's letter was put into my hand, whence I found that Sir Timothy was also made a party, and observed the alacrity with which Mr. Whitton had recommended Chancery applications, and the impounding of 250*l*. to pay 120*l*. On a review of the whole affair, it did appear such a cowardly cabal against an absent man—it evinced such an insulting indifference to your feelings—it appeared so cruel that, amid so many parties (some calling themselves your friends), not one could be found to give a hint to you or me—that, in a towering passion, I sat down and wrote to Dr. Hume, finding the utmost difficulty to

* It will be recollected that, at the time of Lord Eldon's decree Mr. Longdill was Shelley's legal adviser; which renders his subsequent conduct very extraordinary. — Ed.

restrain my indignation within civil bounds. Read this letter, and tell me whether I do not deserve credit for subduing my feelings to such temperate language.

"Yesterday, I wrote to Sir Timothy, of which also you have a copy, and in which no want of respect can be imputed to me. This night, I have received the enclosed from Mr. Longdill, whose conscience, I suppose, has directed some of my innuendoes to his own bosom, and, with the usual self-betrayal of a man who feels he has done wrong, he has recourse to vulgarity and abuse.

"From Sir Timothy I do not expect any reply, and here, therefore, so far as I am concerned, the matter will probably end. My bitter and uncontrollable scorn of all paltry underhand proceedings may have led me to interfere unnecessarily or intemperately; but, as I thought it very likely that your conduct had been blazoned to Sir Timothy in the blackest colors, I determined on letting him know how the matter really stood. Perhaps it might not be amiss if you were to write him a respectful, explanatory letter.

"You will observe that Mr. Westbrooke is a party to the suit, and probably, as there can be no defence, it will be decided against you; but I suppose they will make some arrangement for cancelling the order in the event of the death of one or both of the children. I suppose, also, you will have the pleasure of paying the law charges of this application; but, as I have cut myself off from the honor of any communication with the gentlemen who have treated you with so much respect, I must receive my next intelligence from you, which pray give me, soon as you can.

"As affairs seem all settling in Italy, I resume my intention of taking you by the hand. My wife has a daughter, and is doing perfectly well. I expect we shall be ready to start in July or August. Will that be too hot, and would you preferably recommend October? Let me hear from you fully, and believe me always, My dear Shelley,

"Yours very sincerely,
"HORATIO SMITH."

FROM HORACE SMITH TO SHELLEY.

"*London, April* 19*th*, 1821.

"Dear Shelley,

"I wrote you on the 17th inst., with a budget of letters relative to this lawsuit; and annexed I hand you a copy of Sir Timothy's reply, received yesterday. I am most glad that I wrote to him, for it turns out that my conjecture that he was unacquainted with the affair is correct, and that the law proceedings were literally *cooked up* by the lawyers. It appears a most scandalous liberty in Mr. Whitton, not only to make your father a party without his privity, but actually to stop your money on his own authority. I have this day written a few lines to Sir Timothy, stating that I had seen a letter at Wright's from Whitton, certainly *implying* that he *had* communicated with Sir T.; and I leave the lawyer to get out of this dilemma as well as he can. Of Whitton I know nothing; but I seem to dislike him by instinct. Having written you so many letters lately, I have nothing further to say than to repeat the pleasant assurance that I shall this summer or autumn take you by the hand, when we can talk over all these matters

"I am, my dear Shelley,
"Ever yours,
"Horatio Smith."

FROM SIR TIMOTHY SHELLEY TO HORACE SMITH.

"*Bath*, 17*th April*, 1821.

"Sir,

"Your letter of the 13th inst. I received this day. 'Tis the first intimation I have had of the business you allude to, either in law proceedings or otherwise, more than last year I did hear the payment had been countermanded; but, hearing nothing further, I concluded it had been rectified.

"I shall lay your letter before my solicitor, to be informed of any circumstances that may have necessarily arisen that concern my name as a party.

"I have the honor to be, Sir,
"Your obedient servant,
"T. SHELLEY."

FROM HORACE SMITH TO SHELLEY.

"*Paris, August* 30*th,* 1821.

"MY DEAR SHELLEY,

"I WROTE you on the 10th, and have since had the pleasure of receiving yours, by Mr. and Mrs. Gisborne, who made a very short stay here, and left us a few days ago for England.

"He handed me also your poem on Keats's death, which I like, with the exception of the *Cenci,* better than anything you have written, finding in it a great deal of fancy, feeling, and beautiful language, with none of the metaphysical abstraction which is so apt to puzzle the uninitiated in your productions. It reminded me of *Lycidas,* more from the similarity of the subject than anything in the mode of treatment.

"You must expect a fresh stab from Southey whenever he has an opportunity. Mrs. G. also left me a copy for Moore, who is residing in the neighborhood of Paris, though I have not seen him.

"About a fortnight ago, my wife became worse, and the weather setting in about the same time with an unusual intensity of heat, so completely overcame her that I was obliged to have medical advice, and the physician (an Englishman settled here) dissuades me from taking her to a more southern latitude. Terrified at the intensity of the heat here, where unfortunately it has been of a very uncommon fierceness, she now dreads encountering the sun of Italy; and, in the face of these insuperable dissuasives, I cannot of course proceed. The disappointment and vexation of this sudden overthrow of all my long cherished plans is not less painful to me than the cause of it is distressing. I have also to regret the trouble I have unnecessarily given you, and the disappointment (for I have vanity enough to believe you will think it such) to which I have exposed you. In the midst of these more serious annoyances, I have hardly time to attend to the petty inconveniences to which we must be subjected by wintering here without any of our clothes, books, or comforts, all of which have been shipped to Leghorn. I think of taking a house at Versailles, but at present I am quite unsettled in everything. When I have arranged my plans, I shall write to you again; till when, and always,

"I am, my dear Shelley,

"Your very sincere and disappointed friend,

"HORATIO SMITH.

Towards the close of December, Mrs. Shelley wrote a letter to Mrs. Gisborne, in which she says: —

"Since writing my last letter, we have heard of the departure of Hunt,* and now anxiously await his arrival. He will be more comfortable than he dreams of now; for Lord Byron has furnished the *pian terreno* of his own house for him, so that (more lucky than the rest of the economical English, who come here) he will find clean and spacious apartments, with every comfort about him, and a climate — such a climate! We dine in a room without a fire, with all the windows open; a tramontano reigns, which renders the sky clear, and the warm sun pours into our apartments. It is cold at night, but as yet not uncomfortably so; and it now verges towards Christmas-day. I am busy in arranging Hunt's rooms, since that task devolves upon me.

"Lord Byron is now living very sociably, giving dinners to his male acquaintance, and writing divinely. Perhaps by

---

* Leigh Hunt and his family had indeed departed, but were driven back by stress of weather; so that their voyage was postponed for some months. — ED.

this time you have seen *Cain*, and will agree with us in thinking it his finest production. Of some works one says — one has thought of such things, though one could not have expressed them so well. It is not thus with *Cain*. One has, perhaps, stood on the extreme verge of such ideas, and from the midst of the darkness which had surrounded us the voice of the poet now is heard, telling a wondrous tale.

"Our friends in Greece are getting on famously. All the Morea is subdued, and much treasure was acquired with the capture of Tripoliza. Some cruelties have ensued; but the oppressor must in the end buy tyranny with blood; such is the law of necessity. The young Greek Prince you saw at our house is made the head of the Provisional Government in Greece. He has sacrificed his whole fortune to his country; and, heart and soul, is bent upon her cause.

"You will be glad to hear that Shelley's health is much improved this winter. He is not quite well, but he is much better. The air of Pisa is so mild and delightful, and the exercise on horseback agrees with him particularly. Williams, also, is quite recovered. We think that we may probably spend next summer at La Spezzia — at least, I hope that we shall be near the sea.

"The clock strikes twelve. I have taken to sit up rather late this last month, and, when all the world is in bed or asleep, find a little of that solitude one cannot get in a town through the day. Yet daylight brings with it all the delights of a town residence, and all the delights of friendly and social intercourse — few of the pains; for my horizon is so contracted that it shuts most of those out.

"Most sincerely yours,
"Mary W. S."

CHAPTER XII.

THE BAY OF SPEZZIA.

The end now rapidly approaches. We have arrived at the year which saw the close of Shelley's short life; but a few minor incidents remain to be recorded before we stand in the presence of death.

The winter of 1822 was spent at Pisa. Shelley, during part of the time, was engaged on the dramatic fragment, *Charles the First* — a subject which he had at one time proposed to Mrs. Shelley; but, being dissatisfied with the progress he was making, he threw aside the conception, and devoted his thoughts to a mystical poem in the *terza rima*, called the *Triumph of Life* — also left incomplete, and the last of his long productions. He likewise, about the same time, made several translations from Goethe, Calderon, Homer, &c., with a view to their publication in the *Liberal*.

In the January of this year, or towards the end of the previous December, Shelley became acquainted with Mr. Trelawny, who called on him at Pisa, and who, in his recently published *Recollections of the last Days of Shelley and Byron*, has given an interesting account of his introduction. It was dusk when he arrived at the poet's residence, and through the open door of the room he observed a pair of glittering eyes. Mrs. Williams, who lived in the same house, exclaimed, " Come in, Shelley; it's only our friend Tre, just arrived." Thus encouraged, the poet glided in, in some confusion, but holding out both his hands cordially. He was habited in a jacket, which he seemed to have outgrown, and which added to his juvenile appearance. A book was in his hand, which proved to be Calderon's *Magico Prodigioso;* and, being asked to read some passages, he made an extempore rendering of several parts with marvellous ease and rapidity, accompanying his translation by a masterly analysis of the genius of the author, and a lucid interpretation of the story. Suddenly he disappeared; and Mrs. Williams, in answer to the astonishment of Mr. Trelawny, said, " Oh, he comes and goes like a spirit; no one knows when or where." Shelley, however, had simply gone to fetch his wife. From this time until the poet's death, Mr. Trelawny was on intimate terms with him.

Mrs. Shelley's opinion of their new friend may be gathered from an entry in her journal, under date January 19th, 1822 : —

" Trelawny is extravagant — partly natural, and partly, perhaps, put on; but it suits him well; and, if his abrupt, but not unpolished, manners be assumed, they are nevertheless in unison with his Moörish face (for he looks Oriental, though not Asiatic), his dark hair, his Herculean form. And then there is an air of extreme good-nature, which pervades his whole countenance, especially when he smiles,— which assures me that his heart is good. He tells strange stories of himself — horrific ones — so that they harrow one up; while with his emphatic, but unmodulated, voice, his simple, yet strong language, he portrays the most frightful situations. Then, all these adventures took place between the ages of thirteen and twenty. I believe them now I see the man; and, tired with the every-day sleepiness of human intercourse, I am glad to meet with one who, among other valuable qualities, has the rare merit of interesting my imagination."

And, in a letter addressed to Mrs. Gisborne on the 9th of February, Mrs. Shelley says:— "Trelawny [is] a kind of half-Arab Englishman, whose life has been as changeful as that of Anastasius, and who recounts the adventures of his youth as eloquently and well as the imagined Greek. He is clever; for his moral qualities, I am yet in the dark. He is a strange web, which I am endeavoring to unravel. I would fain learn if generosity is united to impetuousness, nobility of spirit to his assumption of singularity and independence. He is six feet high; raven black hair which curls thickly and shortly like a Moor's; dark gray, expressive eyes; overhanging brows; upturned lips, and a smile which expresses good-nature and kind-heartedness. His voice is monotonous, yet emphatic; and his language, as he relates the events of his life, energetic and simple. Whether the tale be one of blood and horror, or of irresistible comedy, his company is delightful, for he excites me to think, and, if any evil share the intercourse, that time will unveil."

It was not many months before the writer had a terrible means of judging the sterling worth and kindness of her new friend's character.

The fatal project of the boat was suggested by Mr. Trelawny very early in the year; and, on the 15th of January, as recorded in Williams's journal, the former gentleman brought with him the model of an American schooner, after which design it was proposed that a craft thirty feet long should be built. It appears, however, that ultimately a design to which Williams had taken a fancy was adopted. Mr. Trelawny at once wrote to Captain Roberts, a nautical friend, at Genoa, to commence the work directly. Shelley and Williams were to be the joint proprietors of this boat, which, when completed, was called the "Don Juan." On the passage in Williams's diary recording the discussion of the details of the project, Mrs. Shelley has written this note:—

"Thus, on that night — one of gayety and thoughtlessness — Jane's * and my miserable destiny was decided. We then said, laughing, to each other: 'Our husbands decide without asking our consent, or having our concurrence; for, to tell you the truth, I hate this boat, though I say nothing.' Said Jane, 'So do I; but speaking would be useless, and only spoil their pleasure.' How well I remember that night! How short-sighted we are! And now that its anniversary is come and gone, methinks I cannot be the wretch I too truly am."

A mysterious intimation of the great calamity that was

---

* Mrs. Williams.

fast approaching seems to have hung like a cloud over the spirits of Mrs. Shelley at this time. She records in her diary that, on the evening of February 7th, she went to a ball; and this gives rise to some singular reflections. "During a long, long evening in mixed society," she writes, "how often do one's sensations change; and, swift as the west wind drives the shadows of clouds across the sunny hills or the waving corn, so swift do sentiments pass, painting, yet not disfiguring the serenity of the mind. It is then that life seems to weigh itself, and hosts of memories and imaginations, thrown into one scale, make the other kick the beam. You remember what you have felt, what you have dreamt; yet you dwell on the shadowy side, and lost hopes and death (such as you have seen it) seem to cover all things with a funeral pall. The time that was, is, and will be, presses upon you, and, standing the centre of a moving circle, you 'slide giddily as the world reels.'* You look to Heaven, and would demand of the everlasting stars, that the thoughts and passions which are your life may be as ever-living as they. You would demand of the blue Empyrean that your mind might be as clear as it, and that the tears which gather in your eyes might be the shower that would drain from its profoundest depths the springs of weakness and sorrow. But — a thousand swift, consuming lights supply the place of the eternal ones of Heaven. The enthusiast suppresses her tears, crushes her opening thoughts, and — all is changed. Some word, some look,

---

* These words are from the *Cenci*. — ED.

excites the lagging blood — laughter dances in the eyes — and the spirits rise proportionably high.

> 'The Queen is all for revels; her light heart,
> Unladen from the heaviness of state,
> Bestows itself upon delightfulness.'

"Sometimes I awaken from my visionary monotony, and my thoughts flow, until, as it is exquisite pain to stop the flowing of the blood, so is it painful to check expression, and make the overflowing mind return to its usual channel. I feel a kind of tenderness to those whoever they may be (even though strangers), who awaken this strain, and touch a chord so full of harmony and thrilling music."

When this was written, Shelley was away, in company with Williams, on a visit to Spezzia, where they were seeking for a house. They were absent about four days, returning on the 11th of February. Under that date, Mrs. Shelley writes in her journal: —

"What a mart this world is! Feelings, sentiments, more invaluable than gold or precious stones, are the coin; and what is bought? Contempt, discontent, and disappointment, if, indeed, the mind be not loaded with drearier memories.

"And what say the worldly to this? Use Spartan coin; pay away iron and lead alone; and store up your precious metal. But, alas! from nothing, nothing comes; or, as all things seem to degenerate, give lead, and you will receive clay. The most contemptible of all lives is when you live in the world, and none of your passions or affections are called into action. I am convinced I could not live thus; and as Sterne says that in solitude he would worship a tree, — so, in the world, I should attach myself to those who bore the semblance of those qualities which I admire. But it is not this that I want. Let me love the trees, the skies and the ocean, and that all-encompassing Spirit of which I may soon become a part. Let me, in my fellow-creature, love that which is, and not fix my affection on a fair form endued with imaginary attributes. Where goodness, kindness, and talent are, let me love and admire them at their just rate, neither adding nor diminishing; and, above all, let me fearlessly descend into the remotest caverns of my own mind, carry the torch of self-knowledge into its dimmest recesses — but too happy if I dislodge any evil spirit, or enshrine a new deity in some hitherto uninhabited nook."

An amusing anecdote is related by Mrs. Shelley in a letter to Mrs. Gisborne, dated March 7th. "So," she exclaims, " H. is shocked that, for good neighborhood's sake, I visited the *piano di sotto*. Let him reassure himself; instead of a weekly, it was only a monthly, visit. In fact, after going three times, I stayed away. He preached against Atheism, and, they said, against Shelley. As he invited me himself to come, this appeared to me very impertinent; so I wrote to him, to ask him whether he intended any personal allusion. He denied the charge most entirely. This affair, as you may guess, among the English at Pisa made a great noise. Gossip here is of course out of all bounds. Some people have given them something to talk about. I have seen little of it all; but that which I have seen makes me long most eagerly for some sea-girt isle where, with Shelley, my babe, my books and horses, we might give the rest to the winds. This we shall not have. For the present, Shelley is entangled with Lord Byron, who is in a terrible fright lest he should desert him. We shall have boats, and go somewhere on the sea-coast, where, I dare say, we shall spend our time agreeably enough."

An exciting, and even perilous, event occurred to Shelley about this time. Together with Lord Byron, Trelawny, Count Gamba the younger, a Captain Hay, and a Mr. Taaffe, he was riding home outside the gates of Pisa, on horseback, with the ladies following in a carriage. Suddenly "a mounted dragoon" — to quote the account given by Williams in his diary — " dashed through their party, and touched Taaffe's horse as they passed in an insolent and defying manner. Lord Byron put spurs to his horse, saying that he should give some account of such insolence. Shelley's horse, however, was the fleetest, and, coming up to the dragoon, he crossed and stopped him, till the party arrived; but they had now reached the gate where a guard was stationed, and, finding himself so well supported, he drew his sword, and, after abusing them all as '*maladetti Inglesi*,' began to cut and slash to the right and left, (and what signified it to him whether he had the blood of all the English here?) saying that he arrested them all. ' Do that if you can,' said Lord Byron, and dashed through the guard with young Count Gamba, and reached home to bring arms for what he expected would turn out a serious scuffle. The dragoon, finding the rest of the party intended to force their way, made a desperate cut at Shelley, who took off his cap, and, warding the blow from the sharp part of the sabre, the hilt struck his head and knocked him off his horse. The fellow was repeating his cut at Shelley while down, when Captain Hay parried it with a cane he had in his hand; but the sword cut it in two, and struck Captain Hay's face across the nose. A violent scene now took place, and the dragoon tried to get into the town and escape, when Lord B. arrived, and, half drawing a sword-stick to show that he was armed, the fellow put up his sword, and begged Lord Byron to do the same. It was now dark, and, after walking a few paces with Lord Byron, he put his horse into a gallop, and endeavored to get off; but, on passing Lord Byron's house, a servant had armed himself with a pitchfork, and speared him as he passed. He fell from his horse, and was carried to the hospital.

"Trelawny had finished his story * when Lord Byron came in — the Countess fainting on his arm, Shelley sick from the blow, Lord Byron and the young Count foaming with rage, Mrs. Shelley looking philosophically upon this interesting scene, and Jane and I wondering what the devil was to come next. Taaffe, after having given his deposition at the police-office, returned to us with a long face, saying that the dragoon could not live out the night. All now again sallied forth to be the

* The foregoing facts were related to Williams by Trelawny, who was the first to arrive at Shelley's house. — ED.

first to accuse, and, according to Italian policy, not wait to be accused.

"9 *o'clock*. — The report already in circulation about Pisa is 'that a party of peasants, having risen in insurrection, made an attack upon the guard, headed by some Englishmen; and that the guard maintained their ground manfully against an awful number of armed insurgents. One Englishman, whose name was Trelawny, left dead at the gate, and Lord Byron mortally wounded,' who is now telling me the tale, and Trelawny drinking brandy and water by his side.

"10 *o'clock*. — How the attack ought to have been conducted is now agitating; all appear to me to be wrong.

"11 *o'clock*. — Disperse to our separate homes.

"*March 25th*. — At seven this morning, an officer from the police called here, demanding my name, country, profession, and requesting to have an account of my actions between the hours of six and eight yesterday evening. My servants told him I was asleep, but that they could inform him that I was engaged in a very bloody scene * between those hours. 'Then he must come to the police-office.' 'Ask him,' said I, 'if I am to bring the scene with me, or the whole play as far as I have written.'

"12 *o'clock*. — Shelley comes. The wounded dragoon much worse. Hear that the soldiers are confined to their barracks, but they swear to be revenged on some

* Williams here jocosely alludes to a play which he was writing at the time. — ED.

of us. A report is abroad that Taaffe is the assassin, and is now confined in Lord B.'s house, guarded by bull-dogs, &c., to avoid the police. This he himself overheard while walking down the Lung Arno. Shelley and Trelawny think it necessary to go around. A skaite-strap is therefore substituted for a pistol-belt, and my pistols so slung to Trelawny's waist.

"2 *o'clock.* — Sallied forth. Very much stared and pointed at. Called on Lord B. Heard that extreme unction had been administered to the dragoon, whose wound is considered mortal. A deposition is drawn up, and sent, with all the signatures concerned, to the police. The Grand Duke is expected to-night."

Notwithstanding the severity of his wound, the dragoon recovered, and there is no account of the servant being banished, as some writers have stated. But Lord Byron shortly afterwards left Pisa, which he probably found it necessary to do, in consequence of the fray.

Shelley exhibited great activity in this affair; and on another occasion, when a man at Lucca had been condemned to be burnt alive for sacrilege, he proposed to Lord Byron and Captain Medwin that they should at once arm, mount, and, setting off for the spot, endeavor to rescue the man when brought out for execution, and to carry him beyond the frontiers. Pending this last resource, however, they got up, together with other English residents, a petition to the Grand Duke; and the sentence on the prisoner was commuted to hard labor at the galleys.

In writing to Mr. Gisborne on the 10th of April, Shelley makes some allusion to his study of Goethe's *Faust*. He observes: — "I have been reading over and over again *Faust*, and always with sensations which no other composition excites. It deepens the gloom, and augments the rapidity, of ideas, and would therefore seem to me an unfit study for any person who is a prey to the reproaches of memory and the delusions of an imagination not to be restrained. And yet the pleasure of sympathizing with emotions known only to few, although they derive their sole charm from despair and the scorn of the narrow good we can attain in our present state, seems more than to ease the pain which belongs to them. Perhaps all discontent with the less (to use a Platonic sophism) supposes the sense of a just claim to the greater, and that we admirers of *Faust* are on the right road to Paradise."

The Shelleys and Williamses left Pisa on the 26th of April for their new house, the Villa Magni, situated in a wild spot in the Bay of Spezzia, on the very border of the sea, and under the shadow of a steep hill which rose behind it. The proprietor of the estate was insane, and had at one time rooted up the olives on the hill side, and planted forest trees in their places. This, as Mrs. Shelley records in her notes to the poems, gave the plantation an unusually English appearance. Dark, heavy-foliaged walnut and ilex trees, however, overhung the white stone house behind; while in front stretched the tideless bay, shut in by strange visions of jagged cliffs and multiform rocks, with the near castle of Lerici to the east, and Porto Venere far off to the west. The situation was so solitary that there was only one footpath over the beach, which trailed its uncertain course along very rough ground towards Lerici. In the other direction, there was no path at all.

The weather in this rocky nook was often characterized by a savage grandeur. The sirocco would come raging along, bringing a wide dimness with it. Squalls were of frequent occurrence, churning up the foam from the blue waters of the bay; the wind appeared seldom to lull in that exposed situation; and the sea roared so incessantly, that Mrs. Shelley says it almost seemed as if they were on shipboard. But the sunshine often broke out over the precipitous shores, the dark foliage, and the wavering ocean, kindling all objects with the lustre and glory of the Italian atmosphere; and the sea would become quiet for a time.

Wild as were the elements and the spot, the natives were wilder still. Their manners were almost savage, with a mixture of the fierce revelry of Bacchanals. They frequently passed the night on the beach, singing rough, half frantic songs, and dancing fantastically among the waves that broke and tumbled on the shore. All the circumstances were of the most picturesque kind; but some of the pains of isolation must also have been felt by the English strangers. "We could get," writes Mrs. Shelley, "no provisions nearer than Sarzana, at a distance of three miles and a half off, with the torrent of the Magra between; and even there the supply was very deficient. Had we been wrecked on an island of the South Seas, we could scarcely have felt ourselves further from civilization and comfort; but where the sun shines the latter becomes an unnecessary luxury, and we had enough society among ourselves. Yet I confess housekeeping became rather a toilsome task, especially as I was suffering in my health, and could not exert myself actively."

Mr. Trelawny says that the villa looked more like a boat-house or a bathing-house than a place to live in. The terrace, or ground-floor, was unpaved, and had been used for the storing of boat gear, &c.; and the single story over it was divided into a saloon and four small rooms, with one chimney for cooking.

The fatal boat arrived on the 12th of May. She was brought round from Genoa by some English seamen, who, according to the entry in Williams's Journal, spoke highly of her performances. The writer adds: — "She does indeed excite my surprise and admiration. Shelley and I walked to Lerici, and made a stretch off the land to try her; and I find she fetches whatever she looks at. In short, we have now a perfect plaything for the summer." This last sentence now sounds like a ghastly dalliance with death. Mr. Trelawny did not think so highly of the boat as Williams; and Captain Roberts, the builder, had always protested against the model, but to no effect, for the self-love of Williams blinded him to the faults of his design. The sailors who navigated her from Genoa to Spezzia reported to Mr. Trelawny, according to that gentleman's account, "that they had been out in a rough night, that she was a ticklish boat to manage, but had sailed and worked well." They cautioned Shelley and Williams on the necessity for careful management, but seemed to think that, with two good seamen, all would be right. Shelley, however, only retained an English lad, about eighteen years of age.

Shelley's delight was now perfect. He was surrounded by friends whom he esteemed; he was expecting the arrival of another friend, for whom he entertained an affectionate regard; and he was enabled to spend a large part of his time in his favorite element. The weather became fine, and the whole party often passed their evenings on the water. Shelley and Williams sailed frequently to Massa; or, when the weather was unfavorable, amused themselves by altering the rigging, or by building a light boat of canvas and reeds, in which they might be enabled to float in waters too shallow for the "Don Juan." Thus aided, they explored a good deal of the coast of Italy. Shelley always had writing materials on board the larger vessel; and much of the *Triumph of Life* was composed as the poet glided down the purple seas of southern Europe, within sight of noble objects of natural scenery, made trebly glorious by the crowding memories of a splendid history and the golden halo of poetical associations. Sometimes, at night, when the sea was calm and the moon free from clouds, Shelley would go alone in his little shallop to some of the caves that opened from the rocky precipices on to the bay, and would sit weaving his wild verses to the measured beating of the waves as they crept up towards the shore. The stanza in which he was writing (the *terza rima*) has a strange affinity, in its endless and interlinked progression, with the trooping of the sea waves towards the land; and a fanciful ear may please itself by hearing in the lines of the *Triumph of Life*, as in an ocean shell, the distant murmuring of the Bay of Spezzia.

The wildness of the objects by which he was constantly surrounded — the solemnity of the solitude in which he had voluntarily placed himself, broken occasionally by the uproar of the half civilized men and women from the adjacent districts — the abrupt transitions of his life from sea to land, and from land to sea — the frequent recurrence of appalling storms, and the lofty, but weird, abstractions of the poem he was composing, — contributed to plunge the mind of Shelley into a state of morbid excitement, the result of which was a tendency to see visions. One night, loud cries, were heard issuing from the saloon. The Williamses rushed out of their room in alarm; Mrs. Shelley also endeavored to reach the spot, but fainted at the door. Entering the saloon, the Williamses found Shelley staring horribly into the air, and evidently in a trance. They waked him, and he related that a figure wrapped in a mantle came to his bedside, and beckoned him. He must then have risen in his sleep, for he followed the imaginary figure into the saloon, when it lifted the hood of its mantle, ejaculated, "*Siete sodis fatto?*" * and vanished. The dream is said to have been suggested by an incident occurring in a drama attributed to Calderon.

Another vision appeared to Shelley on the evening of

" * Are you satisfied?"

May 6th, when he and Williams were walking together on the terrace. The story is thus recorded by the latter in his diary:—

"Fine. Some heavy drops of rain fell without a cloud being visible. After tea, while walking with S. on the terrace, and observing the effect of moonshine on the waters, he complained of being unusually nervous, and, stopping short, he grasped me violently by the arm, and stared steadfastly on the white surf that broke upon the beach under our feet. Observing him sensibly affected, I demanded of him if he was in pain; but he only answered by saying, 'There it is again! there!' He recovered after some time, and declared that he saw, as plainly as he then saw me, a naked child [Allegra, who had recently died] rise from the sea and clasp its hands as if in joy, smiling at him. This was a trance that it required some reasoning and philosophy entirely to wake him from, so forcibly had the visions operated on his mind. Our conversation, which had been at first rather melancholy, led to this, and my confirming his sensations by confessing that I had felt the same, gave greater activity to his ever-wandering and lively imagination."

Thus passed the first half of the year 1822. It was one of the happiest periods of Shelley's life; but it did not produce much literary fruit. One of the poet's most perfect small productions, however, must be referred to this date:— the address *To a Lady with a Guitar*. In that exquisite trifle, Shelley pictures himself as Ariel; and, addressing the lady, he says:—

> "Now, alas! the poor sprite is
> Imprison'd, for some fault of his,
> In a body like a grave:
> From you he only dares to crave,
> For his service and his sorrow,
> A smile to-day, a song to-morrow."

He little knew how soon the spirit was to be emancipated from its "grave" by the liberator, Death!

The very last verses written by Shelley took the form of a little poem welcoming Leigh Hunt to Italy. This has, unfortunately, been lost.

CHAPTER XIII.

SHELLEY'S DEATH AND OBSEQUIES.

LEIGH HUNT arrived at Genoa on the 14th of June, and was heartily welcomed by Shelley, in a letter which he wrote to him. But so desirous was the latter of seeing his friend personally, that he determined to go in his boat with Williams to Leghorn, where Hunt had speedily proceeded, to arrange with Lord Byron the final preliminaries of the *Liberal.* Shelley at this time was in high spirits; Mrs. Shelley, on the contrary, was exceedingly depressed (owing, no doubt, to ill-health), and was haunted by a profound presentiment of coming evil, which had saddened her during the whole time she had lived in the Bay of Spezzia. The weather was now intensely hot, though the breeze which sprang up from the sea at noon cooled the air for a while, and set the waters sparkling. A great drought had prevailed for some time; prayers for rain were put up in the churches, relics were paraded through the towns; and the unusual character of the weather seemed to betoken that any change would be ushered in by a violent storm. Shelley, however, was not the man to be deterred by such portents from his contemplated journey; nor was his friend and companion, Williams. They accordingly disregarded the warning which Mr. Trelawny had given them some months before, with respect to the difference between the waters of the land-locked bay and those of the open sea beyond.

On the 1st of July, they left the Villa Magni, never to return. Mrs. Shelley was to have accompanied them, but her ill-health prevented her. They reached Leghorn in safety, and Shelley proceeded with Leigh Hunt to Pisa, where the two friends were accommodated with a floor in Lord Byron's palace, the furnishing of which, however, was done by Shelley. Byron had by this time been persuaded by Moore and some of his other friends in London that the projected magazine, about which he had been very anxious at first, would be injurious to his fame and interests; and Shelley now found him so desirous of making any possible retreat from his engagements, that, had he not feared he might damage his friend's interests, he would have quarrelled outright with the noble poet.* He was very much out of spirits when he left him; and that was the last interview they ever had.

Shelley appeared to Leigh Hunt to be far less hopeful than in former days, though otherwise unchanged. The two spent a delightful afternoon together during the brief stay of Shelley at Pisa, visiting the objects of note, and more especially the cathedral. Here the noble music of the organ deeply affected Shelley, who warmly

* See Trelawny's *Recollections of the Last Days of Shelley and Byron*, p. 109.

assented to a remark of Leigh Hunt, that a divine religion might be found out, if charity were really made the principle of it, instead of faith.

He left for Leghorn on the night of the same day. His departure from that place seems to have been hastened by a gloomy letter which he received from Mrs. Shelley, who was probably still trembling under that "shadow of coming misery" which she describes as moving her to agony, and as making her scarcely able to let her husband go from her side on the expedition which ultimately caused his death. For himself, he disregarded these ghostly presentiments, and had recently remarked that the only warning he had found infallible was that, whenever he felt peculiarly joyous, he was certain that some disaster was about to ensue.

On Monday, July 8th, Shelley and Williams set sail in the "Don Juan" for Serici. Trelawny was to have gone with them in Byron's vessel, the "Bolivar," but was detained for want of some necessary legal permit. They left about three P. M., when the Genoese mate of the "Bolivar" observed to Mr. Trelawny that they would soon have too much breeze. Black, ragged clouds were by this time coming up from the southwest; and the mate, pointing to what he called "the smoke on the water," observed that "the devil was brewing mischief." The waves were speedily covered with a sea-fog, in which Shelley's boat was hidden from the view of Mr. Trelawny. It was intensely hot; the atmosphere was heavy and moveless to an oppressive degree, and a profound silence spread far over the ocean. By half-past six o'clock it was almost dark; the sea looked solid and lead-colored; an oily scum was on the surface; the wind was beginning to wake, in short, panting gusts; and big drops of rain struck the water, rebounding as they fell. "There was a commotion in the air," says Mr. Trelawny, who records these particulars, "made up of many threatening sounds, coming upon us from the sea." The vessels in the harbor were all in hurried movement, and the tempest soon came crashing and glaring, in the fury of thunder, wind, rain, and lightning, over the port and the open waters. The storm only lasted about twenty minutes, and during its progress Captain Roberts watched Shelley's vessel with his glass from the top of the Leghorn lighthouse. The yacht had made Via Reggio when the storm began. "When the cloud passed onward," writes Mrs. Shelley, "Roberts looked again, and saw every other vessel sailing on the ocean, except the little schooner, which had vanished." Mr. Trelawny thought for some time that his friends would return to port; but he waited for them in vain.

The night was somewhat tempestuous. At daybreak Mr. Trelawny inquired of the crews of the various boats which had returned to harbor if they had seen anything of the missing vessel. They said they had not; though the Genoese mate of the "Bolivar" pointed out, on board a fishing-boat, an English-made oar, which he thought he recognized as belonging to the "Don Juan." The crew protested it was not so; but it seems that in Italy the fact of rendering assistance to a drowning stranger entails a long and rigorous quarantine at the next port, if the circumstance should be known there. On the morning of the third day, Mr. Trelawny rode over to Pisa, and told his fears to Lord Byron and Leigh Hunt. The latter was literally tongue-tied with horror; and the former was also greatly alarmed. Mr. Trelawny then despatched the "Bolivar" to cruise along the coast, sent a courier as far as Nice, and made the most minute investigations himself.

In the meanwhile, Mrs. Shelley and Mrs. Williams remained in miserable suspense in their wild home on the shores of the Bay of Spezzia. "The sea, by its restless moaning," writes the former,* "seemed to desire to inform us of what we would not learn." "If ever Fate whispered of coming disaster," she remarks in her notes to the poems of 1822, "such inaudible, but not unfelt, prognostics hovered around us. The beauty of the place seemed unearthly in its excess; the distance we were at from all signs of civilization — the sea at our feet, its murmurs or its roaring forever in our ears — all these things led the mind to brood over strange thoughts, and, lifting it from every-day life, caused it to be familiar with the unreal. A sort of spell surrounded us; and each day, as the voyagers did not return, we grew restless and disquieted; and yet, strange to say, we were not fearful of the most apparent danger."

At length, however, came the dreadful inference that the voyagers had perished in the storm. It was nothing more than an inference at first, though a strong one.

* Preface to the *Posthumous Poems*.

Mr. Trelawny was informed at Via Reggio that a punt, a water-keg, and some bottles, had been picked up on the beach. He recognized them as having belonged to Shelley's boat; but for some time the two miserable women at the Villa Magni clung to the desperate hope that the "Don Juan" might have been driven towards Elba or Corsica, and that the three lives on board might thus have been saved. Many days more passed in horrible uncertainty; and, on one of these, Mrs. Shelley, animated by the strength of her terrors, proceeded to Pisa, (though she had not yet recovered from her illness,) and rushing into Lord Byron's room with a face of marble, passionately demanded where her husband was. Of course his Lordship was unable to give her any information, and she refused to be calmed or comforted. Byron afterwards informed Lady Blessington that he never saw anything in dramatic tragedy to equal the terror of Mrs. Shelley's appearance on that day.

The worst ultimately revealed itself with a certainty which left no further room for even the faintest hope. Two bodies were found on the shore: one near Via Reggio; the other close to the tower of Migliarino, at the Bocca Lericcio. They lay about four miles apart. Mr. Trelawny went to see both, and recognized the first as the corpse of Shelley, and the second as that of Williams. Williams was nearly undressed, having evidently made an attempt to swim. He had on one of his boots, which Mr. Trelawny recognized by comparing it with another belonging to the same owner. Shelley had probably gone down at once, for he was unable to swim, and had always declared (according to Mr. Trelawny) that, in case of wreck, he would vanish instantly, and not imperil others in the endeavor to save him. His right hand was clasped in his breast, and he appears to have been reading Keats's last volume of poems at the time of the catastrophe; as the book, doubled back, was found thrust away, seemingly in haste, into a side pocket. In another pocket was a volume of Sophocles. The copy of Keats was lent by Leigh Hunt, who told Shelley to keep it till he could give it to him again with his own hands. As the lender would receive it from no one else, it was burnt with the body.

When the two corpses were discovered, fourteen days had elapsed since the loss of the yacht. A third week passed before the body of the young sailor, Charles Vivian, was found on the shore, four miles from the other two. It was a mere skeleton, and its identity could only be guessed at from the locality in which the waves had thrown it.

Subsequently, the boat was discovered off Via Reggio. She had gone down in fifteen fathoms water, but does not appear to have capsized; for various things were found in her exactly as they had been placed on starting. Captain Roberts took possession of the vessel, but failed in endeavoring to make her seaworthy. "Her shattered planks now lie rotting," says Mrs. Shelley, writing in 1839, "on the shore of one of the Ionian islands on which she was wrecked."

On a close examination, Captain Roberts found many

of the timbers on the starboard quarter broken; the two masts had been carried away, the bowsprit broken off, and the gunwale stove in; and the hull was half full of blue clay. The probability seems to be that the yacht was run down by a felucca during the squall.

Having identified the bodies of Williams and Shelley, Mr. Trelawny proceeded to the Villa Magni, in order that he might communicate to the two widows the sad intelligence that they must no longer cling to hope. It will be seen in one of the ensuing letters, contained in the next chapter, with what depth of feeling he discharged this terrible office.

According to Italian laws, everything cast by the sea on to the shore must be burned, to prevent the possible introduction of the plague. Through the instrumentality of Mr. Dawkins, our consul at Florence, Mr. Trelawny was allowed to superintend the cremation, and to convey the ashes, when all was over, to the widows. He exerted himself with indefatigable zeal, and at length got matters ready for the final ceremony. A body of soldiers had been despatched to the Bocca Lericcio (where the corpse of Williams had been temporarily buried in the sand), to see that the quarantine regulations were not contravened. The remains lay near the gnarled root of a pine tree; and, while the soldiers collected fuel from a stunted pine wood hard by, and from the wrecks scattered along the coast, the functionaries of the Health Office shovelled out the sand, and laid bare the corpse — now "a shapeless mass of bones and flesh," as Mr. Trelawny states in his account. On seeing the black silk handkerchief which the dead man had worn round his neck, Lord Byron (who was present, together with Leigh Hunt) observed — "The entrails of a worm hold together longer than the potter's clay of which man is made." The relics were then cast into the furnace, which had been constructed, under the direction of Mr. Trelawny, of iron bars and strong sheet-iron. "Don't repeat this with me," said Byron; "let my carcass rot where it falls." Frankincense, salt, wine, and oil, were thrown on the pyre; a light was set to the materials; and, after a few hours' fierce burning, the remains were found to be reduced to dark-colored ashes and some fragments of the larger bones. The relics were then screwed down in a box and placed in Byron's carriage.

This took place on the 15th of August. On the following day, the same ceremony was performed with regard to the corpse of Shelley, which lay near Via Reggio, and which, like that of Williams, had been temporarily buried in the sand. Mr. Trelawny, Lord Byron, and Leigh Hunt, were again present, and a guard of soldiers, as on the former occasion, stood by. The spot was wild, lonely, and inexpressibly grand. In front, lay the broad, bright waters of the Mediterranean, with the islands of Elba, Capraji, and Gorgona, in view; the white marble peaks of the Apennines closed the prospect behind, cooling the intense glare of the mid-day sun with the semblance of snow; and all between stretched the sands (yellow against the blue of the sea), and a wild, bare, uninhabited country, parched by the saline air, and exhibiting no other vegetation than a few stunted and bent tufts of underwood. A row of high, square watch-towers, stood along the coast; and above, in the hot stillness, soared a solitary curlew, which occasionally circled close to the pile, uttering its shrill scream, and defying all attempts to drive it away.

The body was placed entire in the furnace, and wine, frankincense, &c., as in the case of Williams, were cast on to the pyre. The flames, which were of a rich golden hue, broad and towering, glistened and quivered, and threw out, together with the sunlight, so intense a heat, that the atmosphere became tremulous and wavy. Leigh Hunt witnessed the ceremony from Lord Byron's carriage, occasionally drawing back when he was too much overcome to allow his emotions to be seen; while Byron himself, finding his fortitude unequal to the occasion, left before the conclusion of the rites.

The ashes of Shelley were deposited in the Protestant burial-ground at Rome, by the side of his son William, and of his brother-poet Keats. An inscription in Latin, simply setting forth the facts, was written by Leigh Hunt, and Mr. Trelawny added a few lines from Shakspeare's *Tempest* (one of Shelley's favorite plays):—

> "Nothing of him that doth fade,
> But doth suffer a sea-change
> Into something rich and strange."

The same gentleman also planted eight cypresses round

the spot, of which seven were flourishing in 1844, and probably are still.*

And so the sea and the earth closed over one who was great as a poet, and still greater as a philanthropist; and of whom it may be said, that his wild, spiritual character, seems to have fitted him for being thus snatched from life under circumstances of mingled terror and beauty, while his powers were yet in their spring freshness, and age had not come to render the ethereal body decrepit, or to wither the heart which could not be consumed by fire.

* The facts, on which the foregoing description of the burning of the bodies is based, are derived from Captain Medwin's *Conversations of Lord Byron*; Mr. Trelawny's *Recollections of the Last Days of Shelley and Byron*; and Leigh Hunt's *Autobiography*.

CHAPTER XIV.

MARY SHELLEY.

A WIDOW at four-and-twenty years of age; left in a foreign land, with no certain income, and with a child to support; coldly regarded by her husband's family, and possessed of no influential friends in England; — Mrs. Shelley now entered on a struggle, which she has described as "lonely" and "unsolaced," but which she encountered in the true spirit of heroism, and lived to see crowned with success, and rewarded by happier days.

The first emotions of horror at the death of her husband gave place to grief of a calmer, but intenser, kind. It will be seen in the ensuing letters, and in the journal which follows them, how deep was the agony which the young widowed heart endured; how abiding the sense of loss; how omnipresent the recollection of him, whose genius now became associated with all sights and sounds of earth, sky, and ocean. Italy had been the chosen land of Shelley; and his widow, though meeting everywhere with some ghost of old companionship, some memory of that which had vanished forever in this life, clung for a long while to the country which had witnessed her greatest joy and her wildest sorrow. She very speedily, however, left the Bay of Spezzia, and took up her residence at Pisa.

But she was not without comforters in her grief. Foremost among the letters she received from England must be placed one from her father, who, on the 9th of August, 1822, writes: —

"My poor girl! What do you mean to do with yourself? You surely do not mean to stay in Italy? How glad I should be to be near you, and to endeavor by new expedients each day to make up for your loss! But you are the best judge. If Italy is a country to which in these few years you are naturalized, and if England is become dull and odious to you, then stay.

"I should think, however, that now you have lost your closest friend, your mind would naturally turn homewards, and [to] your earliest friend. Is it not so? Surely we might be a great support to each other, under the trials to which we are reserved. What signify a few outward adversities, if we find a friend at home?

"Above all, let me entreat you to keep up your courage. You have many duties to perform; you must now be the father, as well as the mother; and I trust you have energy of character enough to enable you to perform your duties honorably and well.

"Ever and ever most affectionately yours,
"W. GODWIN."

FROM MRS. SHELLEY TO MISS CURRAN.

"*Pisa, July 26th*, 1822.

"MY DEAR MISS CURRAN,

"You will have received my letter concerning the pictures, and now I have another request to make. Your kindness to us when we were both so unhappy* — your great kindness — makes me do this without that feeling of unwillingness which I have in asking favors of any other person. Besides, you are unhappy, and therefore can better sympathize with and console the miserable. You would greatly oblige me, if you would get me from one of those shops in the Piazza di Spagna two mosaic stones, about as large as a half-crown piece. On one I wish an heart's-ease to be depicted; they call these flowers in Italian *Socera huora,* or *Viola far falla, Viola regolina, Viola renagola;* on the other (I think I have seen such a one), a view of the tomb of Cestius. I remember, also, that in one of your rooms there was a view of this place, and the people of the house might part with it, or a modern artist at Rome might make one for me, which would give me great pleasure. The difficulty is to pay you for these things; but as soon (if you have the extreme kindness to fulfil my requests) as I know what money you spend for me, I will take care it shall be remitted to you without delay.

"Will you indeed, my dear Miss Curran, do as I ask you? Alas! these trifles (not the picture — that is no trifle) serve as a kind of vent for those sentiments of personal affection and attentions which are so cruelly crushed forever. In a little poem of his are these words: 'Pansies let my flowers be.' Pansies are heart's-ease; and in another he says, that pansies mean memory. So I would make myself a locket to wear in eternal memory, with the representation of his flower, and with his hair; such things must now do instead of words of love, and the dear habit of seeing him daily. Pity me, then, and indulge me.

"In my last letter I was so selfish, that I did not ask after your welfare. Pray write to me. I must ever be grateful to you for your kindness to us in misfortune; and how much more when, through your talents and your goodness, I shall possess the only likeness that is of my husband's earthly form.

---

* From the loss of their son William, at Rome. — ED.

"My little Percy is well — not so beautiful as William, though there is some resemblance.

"Yours ever truly,
"MARY W. SHELLEY."

FROM THE SAME TO THE SAME.

"*Pisa, August* 14*th,* 1822.

"MY DEAR MISS CURRAN,

"I HAVE written two letters to you, requesting that favor now nearer my heart than any other earthly thing — the picture of my Shelley. Perhaps you have been at Gensano, and that delays your reply; perhaps you have altered your residence, and have not received my letters.

"I am well; so is my boy. We leave Italy soon; so I am particularly anxious to obtain this treasure, which I am sure you will give me as soon as possible. I have no other likeness of him; and, in so utter desolation, how invaluable to me is your picture!* Will you not send it? Will you not answer me without delay? Your former kindness bids me hope everything.

"Very sincerely yours,
"M. W. SHELLEY."

FROM MRS. SHELLEY TO MRS. GISBORNE.

"*Pisa, September* 10*th,* 1822.

"AND so here I am! I continue to exist; to see one day succeed the other; to dread night, but more to dread morning, and hail another cheerless day. My boy, too, is, alas! no consolation. When I think how he loved him — the plans he had for his education — his sweet and childish voice strikes me to the heart. Why should he live in this world of pain and anguish? And if he went I should go too, and we should all sleep in peace.

* Of Shelley. — ED.

"At times I feel an energy within me to combat with my destiny — but again I sink. I have but one hope, for which I live — to render myself worthy to join him; and such a feeling sustains me during moments of enthusiasm; but darkness and misery soon overwhelm the mind, when all near objects bring agony alone with them. People used to call me lucky in my star; you see now how true such a prophecy is!

"I was fortunate in having fearlessly placed my destiny in the hands of one who — a superior being among men, a bright planetary spirit enshrined in an earthly temple — raised me to the height of happiness. So far am I now happy, that I would not change my situation as *his* widow with that of the most prosperous woman in the world; and surely the time will at length come when I shall be at peace, and my brain and heart be no longer alive with unutterable anguish. I can conceive but of one circumstance that could afford me the semblance of content — that is, the being permitted to live where I am now, in the same house, in the same state, occupied alone with my child, in collecting his manuscripts, writing his life, and thus to go easily to my grave.

"But this must not be! Even if circumstances did not compel me to return to England, I would not stay another summer in Italy with my child. I will at least do my best to render him well and happy; and the idea that my circumstances may at all injure him is the fiercest pang my mind endures.

"I wrote you a long letter, containing a slight sketch of my sufferings. I sent it, directed to Peacock, at the India House, because accident led me to believe that you were no longer in London. I said in that, that on that day (Aug. 15) they had gone to perform the last offices for him; however I erred in this, for on that day those of Edward* were alone fulfilled, and they returned on the 16th to celebrate Shelley's. I will say nothing of the ceremony, since Trelawny has written an account of it, to be printed in the forthcoming journal.† I

---

* Captain Williams. — ED.   † The *Liberal*. — ED.

will only say, that all except his heart (which was inconsumable) was burnt, and that two days ago I went to Leghorn and beheld the small box that contained his earthly dress. Those smiles — that form. Great God! no — he is not there; he is with me, about me — life of my life, and soul of my soul! If his divine spirit did not penetrate mine, I could not survive to weep thus.

"I will mention the friends I have here, that you may form an idea of our situation. Mrs. Williams and I live together. We have one purse, and, joined in misery, we are for the present joined in life.

"The poor girl withers like a lily. She lives for her children, but it is a living death. Lord Byron has been very kind. But the friend to whom we are eternally indebted is Trelawny. I have, of course, mentioned him to you as one who wishes to be considered eccentric, but who was noble and generous at bottom. I always thought so, even when no fact proved it; and Shelley agreed with me, as he always did, or rather, I with him. We heard people speak against him on account of his vagaries; we said to one another, 'Still we like him; we believe him to be good.' Once, even, when a whim of his led him to treat me with something like impertinence, I forgave him, and I have now been well rewarded. In my outline of events, you will see how unasked he returned with Jane and me from Leghorn to Lerici; how he stayed with us miserable creatures twelve days there, endeavoring to keep up our spirits; how he left us on Thursday, and, finding our misfortune confirmed, then without rest returned on Friday to us, and, again without rest, returned with us to Pisa on Saturday. These were no common services. Since that, he has gone through, by himself, all the annoyances of dancing attendance on consuls and governors, for permission to fulfil the last duties to those gone, and attending the ceremony himself. All the disagreeable part, and all the fatigue, fell on him. As Hunt said, 'He worked with the meanest, and felt with the best.' He is generous to a distressing degree; but after all these benefits to us, what I most thank him for is this:— when on that night of agony — that Friday night — he returned to announce that hope was dead for us; when he had told me that, his earthly frame being found, his spirit was no longer to be my guide, protector and companion in this dark world,— he did not attempt to console me; that would have been too cruelly useless; but he launches forth into, as it were, an overflowing and eloquent praise of my divine Shelley, till I was almost happy that I was thus unhappy, to be fed by the praise of him, and to dwell on the eulogy that his loss thus drew from his friend.

"God knows what will become of me! My life is now very monotonous as to outward events; yet how diversified by internal feeling! How often, in the intensity of grief, does one instant seem to fill and embrace the universe! As to the rest — the mechanical spending of my time — of course I have a great deal to do, preparing for my journey. I make no visits, except one, once in about ten days, to Mrs. Mason. Trelawny resides chiefly at Leghorn, since he is captain of Lord Byron's vessel, the 'Bolivar.' He comes to see us about once a week, and Lord Byron visits us about twice a week, accompanied by the Guiccioli; but seeing people is an annoyance which I am happy to be spared. Solitude is my only help and resource. Accustomed, even when he was with me, to spend much of my time alone, I can at those moments forget myself, until some idea, which I think I would communicate to him, occurs, and then the yawning and dark gulf again displays itself, unshaded by the rainbows which the imagination had formed. Despair, energy, love, desponding and excessive affliction, are like clouds driven across my mind, one by one, until trees blot the scene, and weariness of spirit consigns me to temporary repose.

"I shudder with horror when I look back upon what I have suffered; and when I think of the wild and miserable thoughts that have possessed me, I say to myself: 'Is it true that I ever felt thus?' And then I weep in pity for myself; yet each day adds to the stock of sorrow, and death is the only end. I would study, and I hope I shall. I would write, and, when I am settled, I may. But were it not for the steady hope I entertain of joining him, what a mockery would be this world! Without that hope, I could not study or write; for fame and usefulness (except as far as regards my child) are nullities to me. Yet I shall be happy if anything I ever produce may exalt and soften sorrow, as the writings of the divinities of our race have mine. But how can I aspire to that?

"The world will surely one day feel what it has lost, when this bright child of song deserted her. Is not *Adonais* his own elegy? And there does he truly depict the universal woe which should overspread all good minds, since he has ceased to be their fellow-laborer in this worldly scene. How lovely does he paint death to be, and with what heartfelt sorrow does one repeat that line —

'But I am chain'd to time, and cannot thence depart!'

How long do you think I shall live? As long as my mother? Then eleven long years must intervene. I am now on the eve of completing my five-and-twentieth year. How drearily young for one so lost as I! How young in years for one who lives ages each day in sorrow! Think you that those moments are counted in my life as in other people's? Ah, no! The day before the sea closed over mine own Shelley, he said to Marianne,* 'If I die to-morrow, I have lived to be older than my father. I am ninety years of age.' Thus also may I say. The eight years I passed with him were spun out beyond the usual length of a man's life; and what I have suffered since will write years on my brow, and entrench them in my heart. Surely I am not long for this world. Most sure should I be were it not for my boy; but God grant that I may live to make his early years happy!

"Well, adieu! I have no events to write about, and can therefore only scrawl about my feelings. This letter, indeed, is

* Mrs. Leigh Hunt. — ED.

only the sequel of my last. In that I closed the history of all that can interest me. That letter I wish you to send my father; the present one, it is best not.

"I suppose I shall see you in England some of these days; but I shall write to you again before I quit this place. Be as happy as you can, and hope for better things in the next world. By firm hope you may attain your wishes. Again adieu!

"Affectionately yours,
"M. W. SHELLEY."

FROM MRS. SHELLEY TO MRS. GISBORNE.

"*Genoa, September* 17*th*, 1822.

"I AM here alone in Genoa; quite, quite alone! Jane has left me to proceed to England, and, except my sleeping child, I am alone. Since you do not communicate with my father, you will perhaps be surprised, after my last letter, that I do not come to England. I have written to him a long account of the arguments of all my friends to dissuade me from that miserable journey; Jane will detail them to you; and therefore I merely say now that, having no business there, I am determined not to spend that money, which will support me nearly a year here, in a journey, the sole end of which appears to me the necessity I should be under, when arrived in London, of being a burden to my father. When my crowns are gone, if Sir T. refuses, I hope to be able to support myself by my writings and mine own Shelley's MSS. At least, during many long months, I shall have peace as to money affairs; and one evil the less is much to one whose existence is suffering alone. Lord Byron has a house here, and will arrive soon; I have taken a house for the Hunts and myself, outside one of the gates. It is large and neat, with a *podère* attached. We shall pay about eighty crowns between us; so I hope that I shall find tranquillity from care this winter — though that may be the last of my life so free. Yet I do not hope it, though I say so; — hope is a word that belongs not to my situation.

"He — my own beloved — the exalted and divine Shelley, has left me alone in this miserable world — this earth canopied by the eternal starry heaven, where he is — where — Oh, my God! Yes — where I shall one day be!

" Jane quitted me this morning at four. After she left me, I again went to rest, and thought of Herghano, its halls, its cypresses, the perfume of its mountains, and the gayety of our life beneath their shadow. Then I dozed awhile, and in my dream saw dear Edward most visibly. He came, he said, to pass a few hours with us, but could not stay long. Then I woke, and the day began. I went out — took Hunt's house — but, as I walked, I felt that which is with me the sign of unutterable grief. I am not given to tears; and, though my most miserable fate has often turned my eyes to fountains, yet oftener I suffer agonies unassuaged by tears. But, during these last sufferings, I have felt an oppression at my heart I never felt before. It is not a palpitation, but a *stringemento* which is quite convulsive, and, did I not struggle greatly, would cause violent hysterics. Looking on the sea, or hearing its roar — his dirge — it comes upon me; but these are corporeal sufferings I can get over. That which is insurmountable is the constant feeling of despair that shadows me; I seem to walk on a narrow path with fathomless precipices all around me; yet where can I fall? I have already fallen, and all that comes of bad or good is a mere mockery.

" Those about me have no idea of what I suffer; none are sufficiently interested in me to observe that, though my lips smile, my eyes are blank, or to notice the desolate look that I cast upwards towards the sky. Pardon, dear friend, this selfishness in writing thus. There are moments when the heart must *sfogare*, or be suffocated; and such a moment is this. When quite alone, my babe sleeping, and dear Jane having just left me, it is with difficulty I prevent myself from flying from mental misery by bodily exertion, when to run into that vast grave (the sea), until I sink to rest, would be a pleasure to me; and, instead of this, I write, and as I write I say, ' Oh

God! have pity on me!' At least, I will have pity on you. Good night! I will finish this when people are about me, and I am in a more cheerful mood. Good night! I will go look at the stars; they are eternal; so is he — so am I.

"You have not written to me since my misfortune. I understand this; you first waited for a letter from me, and that letter told you not to write. But answer this as soon as you receive it. Talk to me of yourself, and also of my English affairs. I am afraid that they will not go on very well in my absence; but it would cost more to set them right than they are worth. I will, however, let you know what I think my friends ought to do, that when you talk to Peacock, he may learn what I wish. A claim should be made on the part of Shelley's executors for a maintenance for my child and myself from Sir Timothy. Lord Byron is ready to do this or any other service for me that his office of executor demands from him. But I do not wish it to be done separately by him, and I wait to hear from England before I ask him to write to Whitton on the subject. Secondly, Ollier must be asked for all MSS., and some plan be reflected on for the best manner of republishing Shelley's works, as well as the writings he has left.

"Who will allow money to Ianthe and Charles?*

"As for you, my dear friends, I do not see what you can do for me, except to send me the originals or copies of Shelley's most interesting letters to you. I hope soon to get into my house, where writing, copying Shelley's MSS., walking, and being of some use in the education of Marianne's children, will be my occupations. Where is that letter in verse Shelley once wrote to you? Let me have a copy of it.

"Here is a long letter all about myself; but, though I cannot write, I like to hear of others.

"Adieu, dear friends!
"Your sincerely attached,
"MARY W. SHELLEY."

* Shelley's children by his first wife. — ED.

FROM MRS. SHELLEY TO MRS. GISBORNE.

"*Albeno, near Genoa, Nov. 22d,* 1822.
"MY DEAR FRIEND,

"No one ever writes to me. Each day, one like the other, passes on, and, if I were where I would that I were, methinks I could not be more forgotten. I cannot write myself, only to cast the shadow of my misery on others.

"What I have endured is not to be alleviated by time; for every new event and thought brings more clearly before me the fearful change. My ideas, wanting their support, fall; wanting their mate, they pine; and nothing the earth contains can alleviate that. I see no one who did not know him; and thus I try to patch up the links of a broken chain. I see, consequently, only the Hunts, Lord Byron, and Trelawny; but, although Hunt knew him, he did not know him lately, so my freshest impressions are void for him. Lord Byron reminds me most of Shelley in a certain way, for I always saw them together; and, when Lord Byron speaks, I wait for Shelley's voice in answer as the natural result. But this feeling must wear off; and there is so little resemblance in their minds, that Lord Byron seldom speaks to me of him without unwittingly wounding and torturing me. With Trelawny I can talk, and do talk, for hours unreservedly of him; but he is about to leave us and then I shall be thrown on my own mind, to seek in its frightful depths for memories and eternal sorrow.

"Pardon me, that I still write in this incoherent and unletter like manner; but I strive in vain to do better. My last letter is a proof of how I succeed; for, when I curb myself to the relation of facts alone, or determine so to curb myself, I put off writing from day to day, endeavoring to catch the moment when I shall feel less. But, the pen in my hand, the same spirit guides it, and one only thought swells the torrent of words that is poured out. Perhaps it would be better not to write at all; but the weakness of human nature is to seek for sympathy. I think but of one thing — my past life. While living, (do I live now?) I loved to imagine futurity, and now I strive to do the same; but I have nothing desirable to imagine, save death; and my fancy flags, or sleeps, or wanders, when it endeavors to pursue other thoughts. I imagine my child dead, and what I should do then. I feel that my whole life will be one misery; it will be so — mark me!

"The Hunts are getting on well. Marianne is not better, but she is not worse. We often see Trelawny of an evening. Hunt likes him very much; and, for me, I feel so deep a gratitude to him that my heart is full but to name him. He supported us in our miseries — my poor Jane and me. But for him, menials would have performed the most sacred of offices; and when I shake his hand, I feel to the depth of my soul that those hands collected those ashes. Yes; for I saw them burned and scorched from the office. No fatigue — no sun, or nervous horrors — deterred him, as one or the other of these causes deterred others. He stood on the burning sand for many hours beside the pyre; if he had been permitted by the soldiers, he would have placed him there in his arms. I never, never can forget this; and now he talks of little else save my Shelley and Edward.

"I wish *all* MSS. to be sent, without any exception, and as soon as possible. I have heard from Miss Curran. She is in Paris, and my Shelley's picture is at Rome. Nothing, therefore, can be done with regard to that; so pray let me have the MSS. without any delay — and let me entreat you, as you love me, to wait for nothing, but, the very moment the MSS. are obtained from Peacock, to send them to me. This is of more consequence to me than you think.

"I wish you would enter into an *unbreakable* engagement to me, to write to me once a month. Your letter may be the work of several hours scattered over the month; but put a long letter into the post for me the first of every month. I want some object — some motive, great or small. I should look forward to your letter as a certain thing, and it would be something to expect. Never mind what you write about; let it be about *his* friends — some facts; it would be a great solace to me; indeed it would.

"Well, good night. As usual, all are in bed except me — my restless thoughts homeless in this world, if they do not steal to the bedside of my sleeping babe; and there I tremble. But I think the new soul tries to amalgamate itself with its stubborn shrine, and, if it be too finely tempered, it cannot succeed. Something earthly, though good, seems to announce the decision of nature. So it is with Percy. The crisis was last summer — how I trembled for him then! — and now it is not reason, but habit, that makes me shudder.

"I hear that Peacock has given the *Essay on Poetry* to be published for the *Liberal*, and added that he had other MSS. Now, I am convinced there is nothing *perfect*, and I wish ALL to be sent to me without delay.

"Adieu!
"Affectionately yours,
"MARY W. SHELLEY."

FROM GODWIN TO MRS. SHELLEY.

"*Strand, Feb. 14th*, 1823.

"MY DEAR MARY,

"I HAVE this moment received a copy of Sir Timothy Shelley's letter to Lord Byron, dated February 6th, and which therefore you will have seen long before this reaches you. You will easily imagine how anxious I am to hear from you, and to know the state of your feelings under this, which seems like the last blow of fate.

"I need not of course attempt to assist your judgment upon the proposition of taking the child from you. I am sure your feelings would never allow you to entertain such a proposition.

*   *   *   *   *   *   *

"I requested you to let Lord Byron's letter to Sir Timothy

Shelley pass through my hands, and you did so; but, to my great mortification, it reached me sealed with his Lordship's arms, so that I remain wholly ignorant of its contents. If you could send me a copy, I should then be much better acquainted with your present situation.

"Your novel is now fully printed and ready for publication. I have taken great liberties with it, and I fear your *amour propre* will be proportionably shocked. I need not tell you that all the merit of the book is exclusively your own. Beatrice is the jewel of the book; not but that I greatly admire Euthanasia, and I think the characters of Pepi, Binda, and the witch, decisive efforts of original genius. I am promised a character of the work in the *Morning Chronicle* and the *Herald*, and was in hopes to have sent you the one or the other by this time. I also sent a copy of the book to the *Examiner*, for the same purpose.

"*Tuesday, Feb.* 18*th.*

"Do not, I entreat you, be cast down about your worldly circumstances. You certainly contain within yourself the means of your subsistence. Your talents are truly extraordinary. *Frankenstein* is universally known, and, though it can never be a book for vulgar reading, is everywhere respected. It is the most wonderful work to have been written at twenty years of age [*] that I ever heard of. You are now five-and-twenty, and, most fortunately, you have pursued a course of reading, and cultivated your mind, in a manner the most admirably adapted to make you a great and successful author. If you cannot be independent, who should be?

"Your talents, as far as I can at present discern, are turned for the writing of fictitious adventures.

"If it shall ever happen to you to be placed in sudden and urgent want of a small sum, I entreat you to let me know

---

[*] *Frankenstein* was written by Mrs. Shelley when she was only eighteen, but not published until she was twenty.— ED.

immediately. We must see what I can do. We must help one another.

"Your affectionate father,
"WILLIAM GODWIN."

FROM MRS. SHELLEY TO MRS. GISBORNE.

"*Albaro, May* 3*d*, 1823.

"MY DEAR MRS. GISBORNE,

"YOUR letter was very pleasing to me, since it showed me that it was not want of affection that caused your silence. Utter solitude is delightful to me; but in the midst of the waste, I am much comforted when I hear the quiet voice of friendship telling me that I am still loved by some one, and especially by those who knew my Shelley, and have been his companions. You say well that it is an almost insurmountable difficulty in expressing your thoughts that causes you to be silent; for, though occupation or indolence may often prevent your exerting yourself, yet, when you do write, yours are the best letters I receive, especially as far as clearness and information goes.

"I had a letter to-day from Trelawny at Rome, concerning the disposition of the earthly dress of my lost one. He is in the Protestant burying-ground at that place, which is beside, and not before, the tomb of Cestius. The old wall, with an ancient tower, bounds it on one side, and beneath this tower (a weed-grown and picturesque ruin) the excavation has been made. Trelawny has sent me a drawing of it, and he thus writes: — 'Placed apart, yet in the centre, and the most conspicuous spot in the burying-ground, I have just planted six young cypresses and four laurels, in the front of the recess which you see in the drawing, and which is caused by the projecting part of the old ruin. My own stone (Trelawny, you know, one of the best and most generous of natures, is eccentric in his way), a plain slab, till I can decide upon some fitting inscription, is placed on the left hand. I have likewise dug my grave, so that, when I die, there is only to lift up the coverlet, and roll me into it. You may lie on the other side if you like. It is a lovely spot. The only inscription on Shelley's stone, besides the *Cor cordium* of Hunt, are three lines I have added from Shakspeare: —

> "Nothing of him that doth fade,
> But doth suffer a sea-change
> Into something rich and strange."

This quotation, by its double meaning, alludes both to the manner of his death and his genius; and I think the element on which his soul took wing, and the subtle essence of his being mingled, may still retain him in some other shape. The water may keep the dead, as the earth may, and fire and air. His passionate fondness may have arisen from some sweet sympathy in his nature; thence the fascination which so forcibly attracted him, without fear or caution, to trust an element which almost all others hold in superstitious dread, and venture as cautiously on as they would in a lair of lions.'

"This quotation is pleasing to me also, because, a year ago, Trelawny came one afternoon in high spirits, with news concerning the building of the boat, saying 'Oh, we must all embark, all live aboard; we will all "suffer a sea-change."' And dearest Shelley was delighted with the quotation, saying that he would have it for the motto of his boat.

"Captain Roberts (Jane will tell you who he is) is just come, from Rome. He confirms all that is said in this letter. Roberts has bought the hulk of that miserable boat — new rigged her even with higher masts than before. He has sailed with her at the rate of eight knots an hour, and on such occasions tried various experiments — hazardous ones — to discover how the catastrophe that closed the scene for poor Jane and myself happened. It is plain to every eye. She was run down from behind. On bringing her up from fifteen fathom, all was in her — boots, telescope, ballast — lying on each side of the boat without any appearance of shifting or confusion; the topsails furled, topmast lowered; the false stern (J. can explain) broken to pieces, and a great hole knocked in the stern timbers. When she was brought to Leghorn, every one went to see her, and the same exclamation was uttered by all: 'She was run down'—by that wretched fishing-boat which owned that it had seen them.

"I have written myself into a state of agitation. If I continued my letter, it would only be to pour out the bitterness of my heart. Oh, this spring is so beautiful! The clear sky shines above the calm murderer; the trees are all in leaf, and a soft air is among them; the stars tell of other spheres where I pray to be; for all this beauty, while at times it elevates me, yet in strange words tells me that he, the best and most beautiful, is gone.

'Oh, follow, follow!
*　　*　　*　　*　　*　　*
And on each herb, from which Heaven's dew had fallen,
The like was stamp'd, as with a withering fire.
*　　*　　*　　*　　*　　*
And then,
Low, sweet, faint sounds, like the farewell of ghosts,
Were heard: "Oh, follow, follow, follow me!"'*

"I will finish my letter Monday. God bless you! Good night! I often see him — both he and Edward — in dreams; perhaps I shall to-night. At least, I shall not be in sleep, as I now. The clinging present is so odious.

"*May 6th.*

"I finish my letter. You will soon see me in England. It is not my own desire, or for my own advantage, that I go, but for my boy's; so I am fixed, and enjoy these blue skies, and the sight of vines and olive groves, for the last time. I hope, indeed, to return, if only for repose. The fear of the advanc-

---

Lines from *Prometheus Unbound.*— ED.

ing season will make me begin my journey as quickly as possible. I should in any case have feared an Italian summer for my delicate child. The climate of England will agree with him. Adieu, my dear friend!

"Affectionately yours,
"MARY W. SHELLEY."

FROM GODWIN TO MRS. SHELLEY.

"*No.* 195 *Strand, May* 6*th,* 1823.

"IT certainly is, my dear Mary, with great pleasure that I anticipate that we shall once again meet. It is a long, long time now since you have spent one night under my roof. You are grown a woman, have been a wife, a mother, a widow. You have realized talents which I but faintly and doubtfully anticipated. I am grown an old man, and want a child of my own to smile on and console me.

"When you first set your foot in London, of course I expect that it will be in this house; but the house is smaller, one floor less, than the house in Skinner-street; it will do well enough for you to make shift with for a few days; but it would not do for a permanent residence. But I hope we shall at least have you near us — within a call — how different from your being on the shores of the Mediterranean!

"Your novel has sold five hundred copies — half the impression. I ought to have written to you sooner. Your letter reached me on the 18th ult.; but I have been unusually surrounded with perplexities.

"Your affectionate father,
"WM. GODWIN."

Mrs. Shelley and her child arrived in England early in the autumn of 1823. After an absence in Italy of nearly six years, the climate of this country struck her with a painful sense of gloom and oppression; and she records in her journal her ardent desire to return as soon as possible to the South. She mentions that one word of the Italian language, heard by chance, brings tears into her eyes, though she describes Italy as the murderess of those she loved, and of all her happiness.

For some time after her arrival in London, Mrs. Shelley resided with her father, who was now living in the Strand; but she subsequently removed to Kentish Town, and then to Harrow, in order that she might be near her son, who was being educated at the school there. The expenses incidental to tuition tried her severely; besides which, she contributed towards the support of her aged father; but, with a noble energy of character and entire self-devotion, she worked incessantly with her pen, and met her liabilities by the fruits of her literary industry.

The novels which she published after the death of her husband were — *Valperga*, in 1823; *The Last Man*, 1824; *Perkin Warbeck*, 1830; *Lodore*, 1835; and *Falkner*, 1837. She wrote all the Italian and Spanish lives in *Lardner's Encyclopædia*, with the exception of Tasso and Galileo; and she greatly regretted that the former did not fall to her share. She also wrote two volumes, under the title of *Rambles in Germany and Italy*, giving an account of her travels with her son, his tutor, and some companion, in later years; contributed several short productions to the annuals, and edited (1839–40) Shelley's poetical works, his letters, and his prose writings.

During the earlier days of her return to England,

she had to fight hard against a sense of despondency, which at times almost overcame her. On the 14th of May, 1824, she writes in her journal: —

"Amidst all the depressing circumstances that weigh upon me, none sinks deeper than the failure of my intellectual powers. Nothing I write pleases me. Whether I am just in this, or whether it is the want of Shelley's encouragement, I can hardly tell; but it seems to me as if the lovely and sublime objects of Nature had been my best inspirers, and, wanting these, I am lost. Although so utterly miserable at Genoa, yet what reveries were mine as I looked on the aspect of the ravine — the sunny deep and its boats — the promontories clothed in purple light — the starry heavens — the fire-flies — the uprising of Spring! Then I could think; and my imagination could invent and combine; and self became absorbed in the grandeur of the universe I created. Now, my mind is a blank — a gulf filled with formless mist. 'The Last Man!'* Yes, I may well describe that solitary being's feelings; I feel myself as the last relic of a beloved race, my companions extinct before me.

"Mine own Shelley! what a horror you had of returning to this miserable country! To be here without you, is to be doubly exiled; to be away from Italy, is to lose you twice!"

On the following day, she records the death of Byron, news of which had just reached England. The recollection of his association with her husband, and of his kindness to herself after her great calamity, makes her

* She was at that time writing the novel so called. — ED.

exclaim:—"God grant I may die young! A new race is springing about me. At the age of twenty-six, I am in the condition of an aged person. All my old friends are gone; I have no wish to form new; I cling to the few remaining; but they slide away, and my heart fails when I think by how few ties I hold to the world."

Yet the sight of natural beauty could always soothe her into temporary forgetfulness of grief, and at the same time rouse her intellect into the activity of genius. On the 8th June, 1824, she writes:—

"What a divine night it is! A calm twilight pervades the clear sky; the lamp-like moon is hung out in heaven, and the bright west retains the dye of sunset. If such weather would continue, I should again write; the lamp of thought is again illuminated in my heart, and the fire descends from heaven that kindles it. I feel my powers again; and this is of itself happiness. The eclipse of winter is passing from my mind; I shall again feel the enthusiastic glow of composition — again, as I pour forth my soul upon paper, feel the winged ideas arise, and enjoy the delight of expressing them. Study and occupation will be a pleasure, and not a task; and this I shall owe to the sight and companionship of trees and meadows, flowers and sunshine."

Though in some measure secluded from the world, Mrs. Shelley was remembered by her friends. Charles Lamb, in the course of the year 1827, addressed to her one of his grotesquely humorous and amusing letters:—

"*Enfield, July 26th*, 1827.

"DEAR MRS. SHELLEY,

"AT the risk of throwing away some fine thoughts, I must write to say how pleased we were with your very kind remembering of us (who have unkindly run away from all our friends) before you go. Perhaps you are gone, and then my tropes are wasted. If any piece of better fortune has lighted upon you than you expected, but less than we wish you, we are rejoiced. We are here trying to like solitude, but have scarce enough to justify the experiment. We get some, however. The six days are our Sabbath; the seventh — why, Cockneys will come for a little fresh air, and so ——

"But by *your month*, or October at furthest, we hope to see Islington; I, like a giant refreshed with the leaving off of wine; and Mary pining for Mr. Moxon's books and Mr. Moxon's society. Then we shall meet.

"I am busy with a farce in two acts, the incidents tragi-comic. I can do the dialogue, *commey for;* * but the damn'd plot — I believe I must omit it altogether. The scenes come after one another like geese, not marshalling like cranes, or a Hyde-park review. The story is as simple as G. D.,† and the language plain as his spouse. The characters are three women to one man; which is one more than laid hold on him in the Evangely. I think that prophecy squinted towards my drama.

"I want some Howard Paine to sketch a skeleton of artfully succeeding scenes through a whole play; as the courses are arranged in a cookery-book. I to find wit, passion, sentiment, character, and the like trifles. To lay in the dead colors; I'd Titianesque 'em up. To mark the channel in a

---

* French — *comme il faut.*

† Lamb here refers to an excellent, but single-minded, scholarly friend of his, now dead. Mr. George Dyer, known as the author of many erudite works. He was one of Lamb's stock subjects for joking, and is introduced into the Elia Essays. — ED.

cheek (smooth or furrowed, yours or mine); and, where tears should course, I'd draw the waters down. To say where a joke should come in, or a pun be left out. To bring my personæ on and off like a Beau Nash; and I'd Frankenstein them there. To bring three together on the stage at once; they are so shy with me, that I can get no more than two, and there they stand, till it is the time, without being the season, to withdraw them.

"I am teaching Emma Latin, to qualify her for a superior governesship, which we see no prospect of her getting. 'Tis like feeding a child with chopt hay from a spoon. Sisyphus, his labors were as nothing to it.

"Actives and passives jostle in her nonsense, till a deponent enters, like Chaos, more to embroil the fray. Her prepositions are suppositions; her conjunctions copulative have no connection in them; her concords disagree; her interjections are purely English 'Ah!' and 'Oh!' with a yawn and a gape in the same tongue; and she herself is a lazy, blockheadly supine. As I say to her, *ass in præsenti* rarely makes a wise man *in futuro*.

"But I dare say it was so with you when you began Latin — and a good while after.

"Good bye! Mary's love.

"Yours truly,
"C. LAMB."

It was in 1833 that Mrs. Shelley first went to reside at Harrow. She complains of living very solitarily there, though she was cheered by seeing her son's progress in his studies. All this while she continued to correspond with her old friend, Mrs. Gisborne; and in a letter to her, dated "Harrow, June 11th, 1835," she gossips about her own estimate of her literary powers. She states that when she saw Kean on her return to England, she greatly desired to write for the stage, but that her father earnestly dissuaded her. Nevertheless, she felt persuaded that she could have written a good tragedy; but she adds that she could not do so now, as her feelings are blighted, her ambition gone, and her mind wrecked by loneliness.

"You speak of women's intellect," she continues: "we can scarcely do more than judge by ourselves. I know that, however clever I may be, there is in me a want of eagle-winged resolution, that appertains to my intellect as well as my moral character, and renders me what I am — one of broken purposes, failing thoughts, and a heart all wounds. My mother had more energy of character; still, she had not sufficient fire of imagination. In short, my belief is — whether there be sex in souls or not — that the sex of our material mechanism makes us quite different creatures; better, though weaker, but wanting in the higher grades of intellect. I am almost sorry to send you this letter — it is so querulous and sad; yet, if I write with any effusion, the truth will creep out, and my life since you went has been so strained by sorrows and disappointments, I have no hope. In a few years, when I get over my present feelings, and live wholly in Percy, I shall be happier."

William Godwin died in 1836; an event which, though it could not have been much longer postponed, as the philosopher had reached the age of eighty, was a great grief to Mrs. Shelley, who was tenderly attached to her father.

In the following year, her son went to Cambridge, and

in 1844, on the death of Sir Timothy Shelley, he succeeded to the title.

But, at the same moment that happier and brighter prospects seemed to open to her view, and when she had made arrangements for writing the life of her husband, symptoms of illness, of a threatening character, showed themselves. From time to time they appeared and subsided; but gradually her old energy went, and she died in London on the 21st of February, 1851, in the fifty-fourth year of her age.

The following verses on her death appeared in the *Leader*: —

LINES ON THE DEATH OF MRS. SHELLEY.

Another, yet another, snatch'd away,
By Death's grasp, from among us! Yet one more
Of Heaven's anointed band, — a child of genius, —
A peeress, girt about with magic powers, —
That could at will evoke from her wild thought
Spirits unearthly, monster-shaped, to strike
Terror within us, and strange wonderment, —
Renewing, realizing, once again,
With daring fancy, on her thrilling page,
The fabled story of Prometheus old.

O gifted sister, lovely in thyself,
And claiming from the world the meed of love!
How fondly art thou link'd within our breasts
With his dear memory whose name thou bar'st;
How doubly lov'd because entwined with him!

Mourn her not, Earth! her spirit, disenthrall'd,
No more shall droop in lonely widowhood;
Its happy flight is wing'd to join again

In endless fellowship, 'mid brighter spheres,
The husband of her heart, — the bright-ey'd child
Whom Fate tore from us in his early bloom,
The Poet of the Soul! whose Orphic song,
Steep'd to its depths within the light divine
Of Nature's loveliness, and fraught all o'er
With struggling yearnings for the weal of man,
Descended on each sorrow-canker'd life
Like heaven's dews upon the sunburnt plain.

Mourn her not, Earth! she is at rest with him,
The mighty minstrel of the impassion'd lay, —
The Poet-martyr of a creed too bright,
Whose lofty hymnings were so oft attuned
Unto the music of her own pure name,
The theme and inspiration of his lyre.

Happy departed ones, a brief farewell!
Till friend clasps friend upon the silent shore.

E. W. L.

Edinburgh, February 24th, 1851.

EXTRACTS

FROM

MRS. SHELLEY'S PRIVATE JOURNAL.

Some quotations from this journal have been made in the preceding pages; but further extracts are here appended, for the sake of the interest they possess.

"*October 2d*, 1822. — On the 8th of July I finished my journal. This is a curious coincidence. The date still remains — the fatal 8th — a monument to show that all ended then. And I begin again? Oh, never! But several motives induce me, when the day has gone down, and all is silent around me, steeped in sleep, to pen, as occasion wills, my reflections and feelings. First, I have no friend. For eight years I communicated, with unlimited freedom, with one whose genius far transcending mine, awakened and guided my thoughts. I conversed with him; rectified my errors of judgment; obtained new lights from him; and my mind was satisfied. Now I am alone — oh, how alone. The stars may behold my tears, and the winds drink my sighs; but my thoughts are a sealed treasure, which I can confide to none. But can I express all I feel? Can I give words to thoughts and feelings that as a tempest, hurry me along? Is this the sand that the ever-flowing sea of thought would impress indelibly? Alas! I am alone. No eye answers mine; my voice can with none assume its natural modulation. What a change! Oh, my beloved Shelley! how often during those happy days — happy, though checkered — I thought how superiorly gifted I had been in being united to one to whom I could unveil myself, and who could understand me! Well, then, I am now reduced to these white pages, which I am to blot with dark imagery. As I write, let me think what he would have said if, speaking thus to him, he could have answered me. Yes, my own heart, I would fain know what you think of my desolate state; what you think I ought to do, what to think. I guess you would answer thus: — 'Seek to know your own heart, and, learning what it best loves, try to enjoy that.' Well, I cast my eyes around, and looking forward to the bounded prospect in view, I ask myself what pleases me there. My child; — so many feelings arise when I think of him, that I turn aside to think no more. Those I most loved are gone forever; those who held the second rank are absent; and among those near me as yet, I trust to the disinterested kindness of one alone. Beneath all this, my imagination ever flags. Literary labors, the improvement of my mind, and the enlargement of my ideas, are the only occupations that elevate me from my lethargy; all events seem to lead me to that one point, and the courses of destiny having dragged me to that single resting-place, have left me. Father, mother, friend, husband, children — all made, as it were, the team that conducted me here; and now all except you, my poor boy (and you are necessary to the continuance of my life), all are gone, and I am left to fulfil my task. So be it!

"*October 5th.* — Well, they are come;* and it is all as I said. I awoke as from sleep, and thought how I had vegetated these last days; for feeling leaves little trace on the memory if it be, like mine, unvaried. I had felt for and with myself alone, and I awake now to take a part in life. As far as others are concerned, my sensations have been most painful. I must work hard amidst the vexations that I perceive are preparing for me — to preserve my peace and tranquillity of mind. I must preserve some, if I am to live; for since I bear at the bottom of my heart a fathomless well of bitter waters, the workings of which my philosophy is ever at work to repress, what will be my fate if the petty vexations of life are added to this sense of eternal and infinite misery?

"Oh, my child! what is your fate to be? You alone reach me; you are the only chain that links me to time; but for you I should be free. And yet I cannot be destined to live long! Well, I shall commence my task, commemorate the virtues of the only creature worth loving or living for, and then, may be, I may join him.

* Leigh Hunt and his family. — ED.

Moonshine may be united to her planet, and wander no more, a sad reflection of all she loved on earth:

"*October 7th.* — I have received my desk to-day, and have been reading my letters to mine own Shelley during his absences at Marlow. What a scene to recur to! My William, Clara, Allegra, are all talked of. They lived then, they breathed this air, and their voices struck on my sense; their feet trod the earth beside me, and their hands were warm with blood and life when clasped in mine. Where are they all? This is too great an agony to be written about. I may express my despair, but my thoughts can find no words.

* * * * *

"I would endeavor to consider myself a faint continuation of his being, and, as far as possible, the revelation to the earth of what he was. Yet, to become this, I must change much, and above all I must acquire that knowledge, and drink at those fountains of wisdom and virtue, from which he quenched his thirst. Hitherto I have done nothing; yet I have not been discontented with myself. I speak of the period of my residence here. For, although unoccupied by those studies which I have marked out for myself, my mind has been so active, that its activity, and not its indolence, has made me neglectful. But now the society of others causes this perpetual working of my ideas somewhat to pause; and I must take advantage of this to turn my mind towards its immediate duties, and to determine with firmness to commence the life I have planned. You will be with me in all my studies, dearest love! Your voice will no longer applaud me, but in spirit you will visit and encourage me; I know you will. What were I, if I did not believe that you still exist? It is not with you as with another. I believe that we all live hereafter; but you, my only one, were a spirit caged, an elemental being, enshrined in a frail image, now shattered. Do they not all with one voice assert the same? Trelawny, Hunt, and many others; and so at last you quitted this painful prison, and you are free, my Shelley — while I, your poor chosen one, am left to live as I may.

"What a strange life mine has been! Love, youth, fear, and fearlessness led me early from the regular routine of life, and I united myself to this being, who not one of *us*, though like to us, was pursued by numberless miseries and annoyances, in all which I shared. And then I was the mother of beautiful children; but these stayed not by me. Still he was there; and though, in truth, after my William's death, this world seemed only a quicksand, sinking beneath my feet, yet beside me was this bank of refuge — so tempest-worn and frail, that methought its very weakness was strength — and since Nature had written destruction on its brow, so the Power that rules human affairs had determined, in spite of Nature, that it should endure. But that is gone. His voice can no longer be heard; the earth no longer receives the shadow of his form; annihilation has come over the earthly appearance of the most gentle creature that ever yet breathed this air; and I am still here — still thinking, existing, all but hoping. Well, I will close my book; to-morrow I must begin this new life of mine.

"*October* 19*th.* — How painful all change becomes to one who, entirely and despotically engrossed by their own feelings, leads as it were an *internal* life, quite different from the outward and apparent one. Whilst my life continues its monotonous course within sterile banks, an undercurrent disturbs the smooth face of the waters, distorts all objects reflected in it, and the mind is no longer a mirror in which outward events may reflect themselves but becomes itself the painter and creator. If this perpetual activity has power to vary with endless change the every-day occurrences of a most monotonous life, it appears to be animated with the spirit of tempest and hurricane when any real occurrence diversifies the scene. Thus, to-night, a few bars of a known air seemed to be as a wind to rouse from its depths every deep-seated emotion of my mind. I would have given worlds to have sat, my eyes closed, and listened to them for years. The restraint I was under caused these feelings to vary with rapidity; but the words of the conversation, uninteresting as they might be, seemed all to convey two senses to me, and, touching a chord within me, to form a music of which the speaker was little aware. I do not think that any person's voice has the same power of awakening melancholy in me as Albè's.* I have been accustomed, when hearing it, to listen and to speak little; another voice,

* Lord Byron. — ED.

not mine, ever replied — a voice whose strings are broken. When Albè ceases to speak, I expect to hear *that other* voice, and, when I hear another instead, it jars strangely with every association. I have seen so little of Albè since our residence in Switzerland, and, having seen him there every day, his voice — a peculiar one — is engraved on my memory with other sounds and objects from which it can never disunite itself. I have heard Hunt in company and conversation with many, when my own one was not there. Trelawny, perhaps, is associated in my mind with Edward more than with Shelley. Even our older friends, Peacock and Hogg, might talk together, or with others, and their voices would suggest no change to me. But, since incapacity and timidity always prevented my mingling in the nightly conversations of Diodati, they were, as it were, entirely *tête-à-tête* between my Shelley and Albè; and thus, as I have said, when Albè speaks and Shelley does not answer, it is as thunder without rain — the form of the sun without heat or light — as any familiar object might be shorn of its best attributes; and I listen with an unspeakable melancholy that yet is not all pain.

"The above explains that which would otherwise be an enigma, why Albè, by his mere presence and voice, has the power of exciting such deep and shifting emotions within me. For my feelings have no analogy either with my opinion of him, or the subject of his conversation. With another I might talk, and not for the moment think of Shelley — at least not think of him with the same vividness as if I were alone; but, when in company with Albè, I can never cease for a second to have Shelley in my heart and brain, with a clearness that mocks reality — interfering, even, by its force, with the functions of life — until, if tears do not relieve me, the hysterical feeling, analogous to that which the murmur of the sea gives me, presses painfully upon me.

"Well, for the first time for about a month, I have been in company with Albè for two hours, and, coming home, I write this, so necessary is it for me to express in words the force of my feelings. Shelley, beloved! I look at the stars and at all nature, and it speaks to me of you in the clearest accents. Why cannot you answer me, my own one? Is the instrument so utterly destroyed? I would endure ages of pain to hear one tone of your voice strike on my ear.

"*November* 10*th*. — I have made my first probation in writing, and it has done me much good, and I get more calm; the stream begins to take to its new channel inasmuch as to make me fear change. But people must know little of me who think that, abstractedly, I am content with my present mode of life. Activity of spirit is my sphere. But we cannot be active of mind without an object; and I have none. I am allowed to have some talent — that is sufficient, methinks, to cause my irreparable misery; for, if one has genius, what a delight it is to associate with a superior. Mine own Shelley! the sun knows of none to be likened to you — brave, wise, gentle, noble-hearted, full of learning, tolerance, and love. Love! what a word for me to write!

Yet, my miserable heart, permit me yet to love — to see him in beauty, to feel him in beauty, to be interpenetrated by the sense of his excellence; and thus to love, singly, eternally, ardently, and not fruitlessly; for I am still his — still the chosen one of that blessed spirit — still vowed to him forever and ever!

"*November* 11*th*. — It is better to grieve than not to grieve. Grief at least tells me that I was not always what I am now. I was once selected for happiness; let the memory of that abide by me. You pass by an old ruined house in a desolate lane, and heed it not. But, if you hear that that house is haunted by a wild and beautiful spirit, it acquires an interest and beauty of its own.

"I shall be glad to be more alone again; one ought to see no one, or many; and, confined to one society, I shall lose all energy except that which I possess from my own resources; and I must be alone for these to be put in activity.

"A cold heart! Have I a cold heart? God knows! But none need envy the icy region this heart encircles; and at least the tears are hot which the emotions of this cold heart forces me to shed. A cold heart! Yes, it would be cold enough if all were as I wished it — cold, or burning in that flame for whose sake I forgive this, and would forgive every other imputation — that flame in which your heart, beloved, lay unconsumed. My heart is very full to-night!

"I shall write his life, and thus occupy myself in the

only manner from which I can derive consolation. That will be a task that may convey some balm. What though I weep? All is better than inaction and — not forgetfulness — that never is — but an inactivity of remembrance.

"And you, my own boy! I am about to begin a task which, if you live, will be an invaluable treasure to you in after times. I must collect my materials, and then, in the commemoration of the divine virtues of your father, I shall fulfil the only act of pleasure there remains for me, and be ready to follow you, if you leave me, my task being fulfilled. I have lived; rapture, exultation, content, — all the varied changes of enjoyment, — have been mine. It is all gone; but still, the airy paintings of what it has gone through float by, and distance shall not dim them. If I were alone, I had already begun what I have determined to do; but I must have patience, and for those events my memory is brass, my thoughts a never tired engraver. France — Poverty — A few days of solitude, and some uneasiness — A tranquil residence in a beautiful spot — Switzerland — Bath — Marlow — Milan — The Baths of Lucerne — Este — Venice — Rome — Naples — Rome and misery — Leghorn — Florence — Pisa — Solitude — The Williamses — The Baths — Pisa: these are the heads of chapters, and each containing a tale romantic beyond romance.

I no longer enjoy, but I love! Death cannot deprive me of that living spark which feeds on all given it, and which is now triumphant in sorrow. I love, and shall enjoy happiness again: I do not doubt that, — but when?

"*December* 31*st*. — So, this year has come to an end! Shelley, beloved! the year has a new name from any thou knewest. When spring arrives, leaves you never saw will shadow the ground, and flowers you never beheld will star it; the grass will be of another growth, and the birds sing a new song; the aged earth dates with a new number.

"I trust in a hereafter — I have ever done so. I know that that shall be mine — even with thee, glorious spirit! who surely lookest on, pitiest, and lovest thy Mary.

"I love thee, my only one; I love nature; and I trust that I love all that is good in my fellow-creatures. But how changed I am! Last year, having you, I sought for the affection of others, and loved them even when unjust and cold; but now my heart is truly iced. If they treat me well, I am grateful. Yes, when that is, I call thee to witness in how warm a gush my blood flows to my heart, and tears to my eyes. But I am a lonely, unloved thing, serious and absorbed. None care to read my sorrow.

"Sometimes I thought that fortune had relented towards us — that your health would have improved, and that fame and joy would have been yours; for, when well, you extracted from nature alone an endless delight. The various threads of our existence seemed to be drawing to one point, and there to assume a cheerful hue.

"Again I think that your gentle spirit was too much wounded by the sharpnesses of this world; that your disease was incurable; and that, in a happy time, you became the partaker of cloudless day, ceaseless hours, and infinite love.

"Thy name is added to the list which makes the earth bold in her age, and proud of what has been. Time, with unwearied but slow feet, guides her to the goal that thou hast reached; and I, her unhappy child, am advanced still nearer the hour when my earthly dress shall repose near thine, beneath the tomb of Cestius.

"*February* 2*d*, 1823. — On the 21st of January, those rites were fulfilled. Shelley! my own beloved! You rest beneath the blue sky of Rome; in that, at least, I am satisfied.

"What matters it that they cannot find the grave of my William? That spot is sanctified by the presence of his pure earthly vesture, and that is sufficient — at least, it must be. I am too truly miserable to dwell on what, at another time, might have made me unhappy. He is beneath the tomb of Cestius. I see the spot.

"*February* 3*d*. — A storm has come across me — a slight circumstance has disturbed the deceitful calm of which I boasted. I thought I heard my Shelley call me — not my Shelley in Heaven, — but my Shelley, my companion in my daily tasks. I was reading; I heard a voice say, 'Mary!' 'It is Shelley,' I thought; the revulsion was of agony. Never more ——

"But I have better hopes and other feelings. Your earthly shrine is shattered, but your spirit ever hovers over me, or awaits me, when I shall be worthy to join it. To that spirit, which, when imprisoned here, yet showed by its exalted nature its superior derivation —— *

"*February 24th.* — Evils throng around me, my beloved, and I have indeed lost all in losing thee. Were it not for my child, this would rather be a soothing reflection, and, if starvation were my fate, I should fulfil that fate without a sigh. But our child demands all my care, now that you have left us. I must be all to him: the father, death has deprived him of; the relations, the bad world permits him not to have. What is yet in store for me? Am I to close the eyes of our boy, and then join you?

"The last weeks have been spent in quiet. Study could not give repose to, but somewhat regulated, my thoughts. I said: 'I lead an innocent life, and it may become a useful one. I have talent, I will improve that talent; and if, while meditating on the wisdom of ages, and storing my mind with all that has been recorded of it, any new light bursts upon me, or any discovery occurs that may be useful to my fellows, then the balm of utility may be added to innocence.'

"What is it that moves up and down in my soul, and makes me feel as if my intellect could master all but my fate? I fear it is only youthful ardor — the yet un-

---

* This sentence, like that at the end of the preceding paragraph, appears to have been left incomplete. — ED.

tamed spirit, which, wholly withdrawn from the hopes, and almost from the affections, of life, indulges itself in the only walk free to it, and, mental exertion being all my thought, except regret, would make me place my hopes in that. I am, indeed, become a recluse in thought and act; and my mind, turned Heavenward, would, but for my only tie, lose all commune with what is around me. If I be proud, yet it is with humility that I am so. I am not vain. My heart shakes with its suppressed emotions, and I flag beneath the thoughts that possess me.

"Each day, as I have taken my solitary walk, I have felt myself exalted with the idea of occupation, improvement, knowledge, and peace. Looking back to my past life as a delicious dream, I steeled myself, as well as I could, against such severe regrets as should overthrow my calmness. Once or twice, pausing in my walk, I have exclaimed, in despair — 'Is it even so?' Yet, for the most part resigned, I was occupied by reflection — on those ideas you, my beloved, planted in my mind — and meditated on our nature, our source, and our destination. To-day, melancholy would invade me, and I thought the peace I enjoyed was transient. Then that letter came to place its seal on my prognostications.* Yet it was not the refusal, or the insult heaped upon me, that stung me to tears. It was their bitter words about our

* Mrs. Shelley here alludes to a letter from Sir Timothy to Lord Byron, (who had written to him on the subject,) in which the baronet undertook to support his infant grandson, if the mother would part with him. — ED.

boy. Why, I live only to keep him from their hands. How dared they dream that I held him not far more precious than all, save the hope of again seeing you, my lost one. But for his smiles, where should I now be?

"Stars, that shine unclouded, ye cannot tell me what will be! Yet can I tell *you* a part. I may have misgivings, weaknesses, and momentary lapses into unworthy despondency; but — save in devotion towards my boy — fortune has emptied her quiver, and to all her future shafts I oppose courage, hopelessness of aught on this side, with a firm trust in what is beyond the grave.

"Visit me in my dreams to-night, my beloved Shelley! kind, living, excellent as thou wert! and the event of this day shall be forgotten.

"*March* 19*th*. — As I have until now recurred to this book, to discharge into it the overflowings of a mind too full of the bitterest waters of life, so will I to-night, that I am calm, put down some of my milder reveries; that, when I turn it once, I may not only find a record of the most painful thoughts that ever filled a human heart even to distraction.

"I am beginning seriously to educate myself; and in another place I have marked the scope of this somewhat tardy education, intellectually considered. In a moral point of view, this education is of some years' standing, and it only now takes the form of seeking its food in books. I have long accustomed myself to the study of my own heart, and have sought and found in its recesses that which cannot embody itself in words — hardly in feelings. I have found strength in the conception of its faculties — much native force in the understanding of them — and what appears to me not a contemptible penetration in the subtle divisions of good and evil. But I have found less strength of self-support, of resistance to what is vulgarly called temptation; yet I think, also, that I have found true humility, (for surely no one can be less presumptuous than I,) an ardent love for the immutable laws of right, much native goodness of emotion, and purity of thought.

"Enough, if every day I gain a profounder knowledge of my defects, and a more certain method of turning them to a good direction.

"Study has become to me more necessary than the air I breathe. In the questioning and searching turn it gives to my thoughts, I find some relief to wild reverie; in the self-satisfaction I feel in commanding myself, I find present solace; in the hope that thence arises, that I may become more worthy of my Shelley, I find a consolation that even makes me less wretched in my most wretched moments.

"*March* 30*th*. — I have now finished part of the *Odyssey*. I mark this. I cannot write. Day after day I suffer the most tremendous agitation. I cannot write, or read, or think. Whether it be the anxiety for letters that shakes a frame not so strong as hitherto — whether it be my annoyances here — whether it be my regrets, my sorrow, and despair, or all these — I know not; but I am a wreck.

"*May* 31*st*. — The lanes are filled with fire-flies; they dart between the trunks of the trees, and people the land with earth-stars. I walked among them to-night, and descended towards the sea. I passed by the ruined church, and stood on the platform that overlooks the beach. The black rocks were stretched out among the blue waters, which dashed with no impetuous motion against them. The dark boats, with their white sails, glided gently over its surface, and the star-enlightened promontories closed in the bay; below, amid the crags, I heard the monotonous, but harmonious, voices of the fishermen.

"How beautiful these shores, and this sea! Such is the scene — such the waves within which my beloved vanished from mortality!

"The time is drawing near when I must quit this country. It is true that, in the situation I now am, Italy is but the corpse of the enchantress that she was. Besides, if I had stayed here, the state of things would have been different. The idea of our child's advantage alone enables me to keep fixed in my resolution to return to England. It is best for him — and I go.

"Four years ago, we lost our darling William; four years ago, in excessive agony, I called for death to free me from all I felt that I should suffer here. I continue to live, and *thou* art gone. I leave Italy, and the few that still remain to me. That I regret less; for our intercourse is [so] much checkered with all of dross that this earth so delights to blend with kindness and sympathy, that I long for solitude, with the exercise of such affections as still remain to me. Away, I shall be conscious that these friends love me, and none can then gainsay the pure attachment which chiefly clings to them, because they knew and loved you — because I knew them when with you — and I cannot think of them without feeling your spirit beside me.

"I cannot grieve for you, beloved Shelley! I grieve for thy friends — for the world — for thy child — most for myself, enthroned in thy love, growing wiser and better beneath thy gentle influence, taught by you the highest philosophy — your pupil, friend, lover, wife, mother of your children! The glory of the dream is gone. I am a cloud from which the light of sunset has passed. Give me patience in the present struggle. *Meum cordium cor!* Good night!

> 'I would give
> All that I am to be as thou now art;
> But I am chain'd to time, and cannot thence depart.' *

* * * * * *

"*October* 21*st*, 1838. — I have been so often abused by pretended friends for my lukewarmness in 'the good cause,' that, though I disdain to answer them, I shall put down here a few thoughts on this subject. I am much of a self-examiner. Vanity is not my fault, I think; if it is, it is uncomfortable vanity, for I have none that teaches me to be satisfied with myself; far otherwise, — and if I use the word disdain, it is that I think my qualities (such as they are) not appreciated, from unworthy causes.

* *Adonais.* — ED.

"In the first place, with regard to 'the good cause'— the cause of the advancement of freedom and knowledge, of the rights of women, &c.— I am not a person of opinions. I have said elsewhere that human beings differ greatly in this. Some have a passion for reforming the world; others do not cling to particular opinions. That my parents and Shelley were of the former class, makes me respect it. I respect such when joined to real disinterestedness, toleration, and a clear understanding. My accusers, after such as these, appear to me mere drivellers. For myself, I earnestly desire the good and enlightenment of my fellow-creatures, and see all, in the present course, tending to the same, and rejoice; but I am not for violent extremes, which only bring on an injurious reaction. I have never written a word in disfavor of liberalism; that I have not supported it openly in writing, arises from the following causes, as far as I know:—

"That I have not argumentative powers; I see things pretty clearly, but cannot demonstrate them. Besides, I feel the counter arguments too strongly. I do not feel that I could say aught to support the cause efficiently; besides that, on some topics (especially with regard to my own sex), I am far from making up my mind. I believe we are sent here to educate ourselves, and that self-denial, and disappointment, and self-control, are a part of our education; that it is not by taking away all restraining law that our improvement is to be achieved; and, though many things need great amendment, I can by no means go so far as my friends would have me.

When I feel that I can say what will benefit my fellow-creatures, I will speak; not before.

"Then I recoil from the vulgar abuse of the inimical press; I do more than recoil — proud and sensitive, I act on the defensive — an inglorious position.

"To hang back, as I do, brings a penalty. I was nursed, and fed with a love of glory. To be something great and good was the precept given me by my father; Shelley reiterated it. Alone and poor, I could only be something by joining a party; and there was much in me — the woman's love of looking up and being guided, and being willing to do anything if any one supported and brought me forward, which would have made me a good partisan. But Shelley died, and I was alone. My father, from age and domestic circumstances, could not '*me faire valoir.*' My total friendlessness, my horror of pushing, and inability to put myself forward unless led, cherished, and supported, — all this has sunk me in a state of loneliness no other human being ever before, I believe, endured — except Robinson Crusoe. How many tears and spasms of anguish this solitude has cost me, lies buried in my memory!

"If I had raved and ranted about what I did not understand; had I adopted a set of opinions, and propagated them with enthusiasm; had I been careless of attack, and eager for notoriety: then the party to which I belonged had gathered round me, and I had not been alone.

"It has been the fashion with these same friends to accuse me of worldliness. There, indeed, in my own heart and conscience, I take a high ground. I may distrust my own judgment too much — be too indolent and too timid; but in conduct I am above merited blame.

"I like society; I believe all persons who have any talent (who are in good health) do. The soil that gives forth nothing, may lie ever fallow; but that which produces — however humble its product — needs cultivation, change of harvest, refreshing dews, and ripening sun. Books do much; but the living intercourse is the vital heat. Debarred from that, how have I pined and died!

"My early friends chose the position of enemies. When I first discovered that a trusted friend had acted falsely by me, I was nearly destroyed. My health was shaken. I remember thinking, with a burst of agonizing tears, that I should prefer a bed of torture to the unutterable anguish a friend's falsehood engendered. There is no resentment; but the world can never be to me what it was before. Trust, and confidence, and the heart's sincere devotion, are gone.

"I sought at that time to make acquaintances — to divert my mind from this anguish. I got entangled in various ways through my ready sympathy and too eager heart; but I never crouched to society — never sought it unworthily. If I have never written to vindicate the Rights of Women, I have ever befriended women when oppressed. At every risk, I have befriended and supported victims to the social system; but I make no boast, for in truth it is simple justice I perform; and so I am still reviled for being worldly.

"God grant a happier and a better day is near! Percy

— my all in all — will, I trust, by his excellent understanding, his clear, bright, sincere spirit and affectionate heart, repay me for sad long years of desolation. His career may lead me into the thick of life, or only gild a quiet home. I am content with either, and, as I grow older, I grow more fearless for myself — I become firmer in my opinions. The experienced, the suffering, the thoughtful, may at last speak unrebuked. If it be the will of God that I live, I may ally my name yet to 'the good cause' — though I do not expect to please my accusers.

"Thus have I put down my thoughts. I may have deceived myself; I may be in the wrong; I try to examine myself; and such as I have written appears to me the exact truth.

"Enough of this! The great work of life goes on. Death draws near. To be better after death than in life, is one's hope and endeavor — to be so through self-schooling. If I write the above, it is that those who love me may hereafter know that I am not all to blame, nor merit the heavy accusations cast on me for not putting myself forward. I *cannot* do that; it is against my nature. As well cast me from a precipice, and rail at me for not flying."

ESSAY ON CHRISTIANITY.

BY SHELLEY.

NOW FIRST PRINTED.

ESSAY ON CHRISTIANITY.

The Being who has influenced in the most memorable manner the opinions and the fortunes of the human species is Jesus Christ. At this day his name is connected with the devotional feelings of two hundred millions of the race of man. The institutions of the most civilized portion of the globe derive their authority from the sanction of his doctrines; he is the hero, the God, of our popular religion. His extraordinary genius, the wide and rapid effect of his unexampled doctrines, his invincible gentleness and benignity, the devoted love borne to him by his adherents, suggested a persuasion to them that he was something divine. The supernatural events which the historians of this wonderful man subsequently asserted to have been connected with every gradation of his career, established the opinion.

His death is said to have been accompanied by an accumulation of tremendous prodigies. Utter darkness fell upon the earth, blotting the noonday sun; dead bodies, arising from their graves, walked through the public streets, and an earthquake shook the astonished city, rending the rocks of the surrounding mountains. The philosopher may attribute the application of these events to the death of a reformer, or the events themselves to a visitation of that universal Pan who ——

* * * * * *

The thoughts which the word "God" suggests to the human mind are susceptible of as many variations as human minds themselves. The Stoic, the Platonist, and the Epicurean, the Polytheist, the Dualist, and the Trinitarian, differ infinitely in their conceptions of its meaning. They agree only in considering it the most awful and most venerable of names, as a common term devised to express all of mystery, or majesty, or power, which the invisible world contains. And not only has every sect distinct conceptions of the application of this name, but scarcely two individuals of the same sect, who exercise in any degree the freedom of their judgment, or yield themselves with any candor of feeling to the influences of the visible world, find perfect coincidence of opinion to exist between them. It is [interesting] to inquire in what acceptation Jesus Christ employed this term.

We may conceive his mind to have been predisposed on this subject to adopt the opinions of his countrymen. Every human being is indebted for a multitude of his sentiments to the religion of his early years. Jesus Christ probably [studied] the historians of his country with the ardor of a spirit seeking after truth. They were undoubtedly the companions of his childish years, the food and nutriment and materials of his youthful meditations. The sublime dramatic poem entitled *Job* had familiarized his imagination with the boldest imagery afforded by the human mind and the material world.

Ecclesiastes had diffused a seriousness and solemnity over the frame of his spirit, glowing with youthful hope, and made audible to his listening heart

> "The still, sad music of humanity,
> Not harsh or grating, but of ample power
> To chasten and subdue."

He had contemplated this name as having been profanely perverted to the sanctioning of the most enormous and abominable crimes. We can distinctly trace, in the tissue of his doctrines the persuasion that God is some universal Being, differing from man and the mind of man. According to Jesus Christ, God is neither the Jupiter, who sends rain upon the earth; nor the Venus, through whom all living things are produced; nor the Vulcan, who presides over the terrestrial element of fire; nor the Vesta, that preserves the light which is enshrined in the sun and moon and stars. He is neither the Proteus nor the Pan of the material world. But the word God, according to the acceptation of Jesus Christ, unites all the attributes which these denominations contain, and is the [interpoint] and over-ruling Spirit of all the energy and wisdom included within the circle of existing things. It is important to observe that the author of the Christian system had a conception widely differing from the gross imaginations of the vulgar relative to the ruling Power of the universe. He everywhere represents this Power as something mysteriously and illimitably pervading the frame of things. Nor do his doctrines practically assume any proposition which they theoretically deny. They do not represent God as a limitless and inconceivable mystery; affirming, at the same time, his existence as a Being subject to passion and capable ——

* * * * *

"Blessed are the pure in heart, for they shall see God." Blessed are those who have preserved internal sanctity of soul; who are conscious of no secret deceit; who are the same in act as they are in desire; who conceal no thought, no tendencies of thought, from their own conscience; who are faithful and sincere witnesses, before the tribunal of their own judgments, of all that passes within their mind. Such as these shall see God. What! after death, shall their awakened eyes behold the King of Heaven? Shall they stand in awe before the golden throne on which He sits, and gaze upon the venerable countenance of the paternal Monarch? Is this the reward of the virtuous and the pure? These are the idle dreams of the visionary or the pernicious representations of impostors, who have fabricated from the very materials of wisdom a cloak for their own dwarfish or imbecile conceptions.

Jesus Christ has said no more than the most excellent philosophers have felt and expressed — that virtue is its own reward. It is true that such an expression as he has used was prompted by the energy of genius, and was the overflowing enthusiasm of a poet; but it is not the less literally true [because] clearly repugnant to the mistaken conceptions of the multitude. God, it has been asserted, was contemplated by Jesus Christ, as every poet and every philosopher must have contemplated that mysterious principle. He considered that venerable word to express the overruling Spirit of the collective energy of the moral and material world. He affirms, therefore, no more than that a simple, sincere mind is the indispensable requisite of true science and true happiness. He affirms that a Being of pure and gentle habits will not fail, in every thought, in every object of every thought, to be aware of benignant visitings from the invisible energies by which he is surrounded.

Whosoever is free from the contamination of luxury and license, may go forth to the fields and to the woods, inhaling joyous renovation from the breath of Spring, or catching from the odors and sounds of Autumn some diviner mood of sweetest sadness, which improves the softened heart. Whosoever is no deceiver or destroyer of his fellow-men — no liar, no flatterer, no murderer — may walk among his species, deriving, from the communion with all which they contain of beautiful or of majestic, some intercourse with the Universal God. Whosoever has maintained with his own heart the strictest correspondence of confidence, who dares to examine and to estimate every imagination which suggests itself to his mind — whosoever is that which he designs to become, and only aspires to that which the divinity of his own nature shall consider and approve — he has already seen God.

We live and move and think; but we are not the creators of our own origin and existence. We are not the arbiters of every motion of our own complicated nature; we are not the masters of our own imaginations and moods of mental being. There is a Power by which we are surrounded, like the atmosphere, in which some motionless lyre is suspended, which visits with its breath our silent chords at will.

Our most imperial and stupendous qualities — those on which the majesty and the power of humanity is erected — are, relatively to the inferior portion of its mechanism, active and imperial; but they are the passive slaves of some higher and more omnipotent Power. This power is God; and those who have seen God have, in the period of their purer and more perfect nature, been harmonized by their own will to so exquisite [a] consentaneity of power as to give forth divinest melody, when the breath of universal being sweeps over their frame. That those who are pure in heart shall see God, and that virtue is its own reward, may be considered as equivalent assertions. The former of these propositions is a metaphorical repetition of the latter. The advocates of literal interpretation have been the most efficacious enemies of those doctrines whose nature they profess to venerate. Thucydides, in particular, affords a number of instances calculated ——

* * * * *

Tacitus says, that the Jews held God to be something eternal and supreme, neither subject to change nor to decay; therefore they permit no statues in their cities or their temples. The universal Being can only be described or defined by negatives which deny his subjection to the laws of all inferior existences. Where indefiniteness ends, idolatry and anthropomorphism begin. God is, as Lucan has expressed,

> " Quodcunque vides, quodcunque moveris
> Et cœlum et virtus."

The doctrine of what some fanatics have termed "a peculiar Providence" — that is, of some power beyond and superior to that which ordinarily guides the operations of the Universe, interfering to punish the vicious and reward the virtuous — is explicitly denied by Jesus Christ. The absurd and execrable doctrine of vengeance, in *all its shapes*, seems to have been contemplated by this great moralist with the profoundest disapprobation; nor would he permit the most venerable of names to be perverted into a sanction for the meanest and most contemptible propensities incident to the nature of man. " Love your enemies, bless those who curse you, that ye may be the sons of your Heavenly Father, who makes the sun to shine on the good and on the evil, and the rain to fall on the just and unjust." How monstrous a calumny have not impostors dared to advance against the mild and gentle author of this just sentiment, and against the whole tenor of his doctrines and his life, overflowing with benevolence and forbearance and compassion. They have represented him asserting that the omnipotent God — that merciful and benignant Power who scatters equally upon the beautiful earth all the elements of security and happiness — whose influences are distributed to all whose natures admit of a participation in them — who sends to the weak and vicious creatures of his will all the benefits which they are capable of sharing — that this God has devised a scheme whereby the body shall live after its apparent dissolution, and be rendered capable of indefinite torture. He is said to have compared the agonies which the vicious shall then endure to the excruciations of a living body bound among the flames, and being consumed sinew by sinew, and bone by bone.

And this is to be done, not because it is supposed (and the supposition would be sufficiently detestable) that the moral nature of the sufferer would be improved by his tortures — it is done because it *is just* to be done. My neighbor, or my servant, or my child, has done me an injury, and it is just that he should suffer an injury in return. Such is the doctrine which Jesus Christ summoned his whole resources of persuasion to oppose. "Love your enemy, bless those who curse you:" such, he says, is the practice of God, and such must ye imitate if ye would be the children of God.

Jesus Christ would hardly have cited, as an example of all that is gentle and beneficent and compassionate, a Being who shall deliberately scheme to inflict on a large portion of the human race tortures indescribably intense and indefinitely protracted; who shall inflict them, too, without any mistake as to the true nature of pain — without any view to future good — merely because it is just.

This, and no other, is justice: — to consider, under all

the circumstances and consequences of a particular case, how the greatest quantity and purest quality of happiness will ensue from any action; [this] is to be just, and there is no other justice. The distinction between justice and mercy was first imagined in the courts of tyrants
 to the usurpation of their rulers; mankind receive every relaxation of their tyranny as a circumstance of grace or favor.

Such was the clemency of Julius Cæsar, who, having achieved by a series of treachery and bloodshed the ruin of the liberties of his country, receives the fame of mercy because, possessing the power to slay the noblest men of Rome, he restrained his sanguinary soul, arrogating to himself as a merit an abstinence from actions which, if he had committed, he would only have added one other atrocity to his deeds. His assassins understood justice better. They saw the most virtuous and civilized community of mankind under the insolent dominion of one wicked man, and they murdered him. They destroyed the usurper of the liberties of their countrymen, not because they hated him, not because they would revenge the wrongs which they had sustained. Brutus, it is said, was his most familiar friend. Most of the conspirators were habituated to domestic intercourse with the man whom they destroyed. It was in affection, inextinguishable love for all that is venerable and dear to the human heart, in the names of Country, Liberty, and Virtue; it was in a serious and solemn and reluctant mood, that these holy patriots murdered their father and their friend. They would have spared his violent death, if he could have deposited the rights which he had assumed. His own selfish and narrow nature necessitated the sacrifices they made. They required that he should change all those habits which debauchery and bloodshed had twined around the fibres of his inmost frame of thought; that he should participate with them and with his country those privileges which, having corrupted by assuming to himself, he would no longer value. They would have sacrificed their lives if they could have made him worthy of the sacrifice. Such are the feelings which Jesus Christ asserts to belong to the ruling Power of the world. He desireth not the death of a sinner; he makes the sun to shine upon the just and unjust.

The nature of a narrow and malevolent spirit is so essentially incompatible with happiness as to render it inaccessible to the influences of the benignant God. All that his own perverse propensities will permit him to receive, that God abundantly pours forth upon him. If there is the slightest overbalance of happiness, which can be allotted to the most atrocious offender, consistently with the nature of things, that is rigidly made his portion by the ever-watchful Power of God. In every case, the human mind enjoys the utmost pleasure which it is capable of enjoying. God is represented by Jesus Christ as the Power from which, and through which, the streams of all that is excellent and delightful flow; the Power which models, as they pass, all the elements of this mixed universe to the purest and most perfect shape which it belongs to their nature to assume. Jesus Christ attributes to this Power the faculty of Will. How far such a doctrine, in its ordinary sense, may be philosophically true, or how far Jesus Christ intentionally availed himself of a metaphor easily understood, is foreign to the subject to consider. This much is certain, that Jesus Christ represents God as the fountain of all goodness, the eternal enemy of pain and evil, the uniform and unchanging motive of the salutary operations of the material world. The supposition that this cause is excited to action by some principle analogous to the human will, adds weight to the persuasion that it is foreign to its beneficent nature to inflict the slightest pain. According to Jesus Christ, and according to the indisputable facts of the case, some evil spirit has dominion in this imperfect world. But there will come a time when the human mind shall be visited exclusively by the influences of the benignant Power. Men shall die, and their bodies shall rot under the ground; all the organs through which their knowledge and their feelings have flowed, or in which they have originated, shall assume other forms, and become ministrant to purposes the most foreign from their former tendencies. There is a time when we shall neither be heard or be seen by the multitude of beings like ourselves by whom we have been so long surrounded. They shall go to graves; where then?

It appears that we moulder to a heap of senseless dust; to a few worms, that arise and perish, like ourselves. Jesus Christ asserts that these appearances are fallacious, and that a gloomy and cold imagination alone suggests the conception that thought can cease to be. Another and a more extensive state of being, rather than the complete extinction of being, will follow from that mysterious change which we call Death. There shall be no misery, no pain, no fear. The empire of evil spirits extends not beyond the boundaries of the grave. The unobscured irradiations from the fountain fire of all goodness shall reveal all that is mysterious and unintelligible, until the mutual communications of knowledge and of happiness, throughout all thinking natures, constitute a harmony of good that ever varies and never ends.

This is Heaven, when pain and evil cease, and when the benignant principle, untrammelled and uncontrolled, visits, in the fulness of its power, the universal frame of things. Human life, with all its unreal ills and transitory hopes, is as a dream, which departs before the dawn, leaving no trace of its evanescent hues. All that it contains of pure or of divine, visits the passive mind in some serenest mood. Most holy are the feelings through which our fellow-beings are rendered dear and [venerable] to the heart. The remembrance of their sweetness, and the completion of the hopes which they [excite], constitute, when we awaken from the sleep of life, the fulfilment of the prophecies of its most majestic and beautiful visions.

We die, says Jesus Christ; and when we awaken from the languor of disease, the glories and the happiness of Paradise are around us. All evil and pain have ceased forever. Our happiness, also, corresponds with, and is adapted to, the nature of what is most excellent in our being. We see God, and we see that he is good. How delightful a picture, even if it be not true! How magnificent is the conception which this bold theory suggests to the contemplation, even if it be no more than the imagination of some sublimest and most holy poet, who, impressed with the loveliness and majesty of his own nature, is impatient and discontented with the narrow limits which this imperfect life and the dark grave have assigned forever as his melancholy potion. It is not to be believed that Hell, or punishment, was the conception of this daring mind. It is not to be believed that the most prominent group of this picture, which is framed so heart-moving and lovely — the accomplishment of all human hope, the extinction of all morbid fear and anguish — would consist of millions of sensitive beings, enduring, in every variety of torture which Omniscient vengeance could invent, immortal agony.

Jesus Christ opposed, with earnest eloquence, the panic fears and hateful superstitions which have enslaved mankind for ages. Nations had risen against nations, employing the subtlest devices of mechanism and mind to waste, and excruciate, and overthrow. The great community of mankind had been subdivided into ten thousand communities, each organized for the ruin of the other. Wheel within wheel, the vast machine was instinct with the restless spirit of desolation. Pain had been inflicted, therefore pain should be inflicted in return. Retaliation of injuries is the only remedy which can be applied to violence, because it teaches the injurer the true nature of his own conduct, and operates as a warning against its repetition. Nor must the same measure of calamity be returned as was received. If a man borrows a certain sum from me, he is bound to repay that sum. Shall no more be required of the enemy, who destroys my reputation, or ravages my fields? It is just that he should suffer ten times the loss which he has inflicted, that the legitimate consequences of his deed may never be obliterated from his remembrance, and that others may clearly discern and feel the danger of invading the peace of human society. Such reasonings, and the impetuous feelings arising from them, have armed nation against nation, family against family, man against man.

An Athenian soldier, in the Ionian army which had assembled for the purpose of vindicating the liberty of the Asiatic Greeks, accidentally set fire to Sardis. The city, being composed of combustible materials, was burned to the ground. The Persians believed that this circumstance of aggression made it their duty to retaliate on Athens. They assembled successive expeditions on the most extensive scale. Every nation of the East was united, to ruin the Grecian States. Athens was burned to the ground, the whole territory laid waste, and every living thing which it contained [destroyed]. After suffering and inflicting incalculable mischiefs, they desisted from their purpose only when they became impotent to effect it. The desire of revenge, for the aggression of Persia, outlived, among the Greeks, that love of liberty, which had been their most glorious distinction among the nations of mankind, and Alexander became the instrument of its completion. The mischiefs attendant on this consummation of fruitless ruin are too manifold and too tremendous to be related. If all the thought, which had been expended on the construction of engines of agony and death — the modes of aggression and defence, the raising of armies, and the acquirement of those arts of tyranny and falsehood without which mixed multitudes could neither be led nor governed — had been employed to promote the true welfare and extend the real empire of man, how different would have been the present situation of human society! how different the state of knowledge in physical and moral science, upon which the power and happiness of mankind essentially depend! What nation has the example of the desolation of Attica by Mardonius and Xerxes, or the extinction of the Persian empire by Alexander of Macedon, restrained from outrage? Was not the pretext of this latter system of spoliation derived immediately from the former? Had revenge, in this instance, any other effect than to increase, instead of diminishing, the mass of malice and evil already existing in the world?

The emptiness and folly of retaliation are apparent from every example which can be brought forward. Not only Jesus Christ, but the most eminent professors of every sect of philosophy, have reasoned against this futile superstition. Legislation is, in one point of view, to be considered as an attempt to provide against the excesses of this deplorable mistake. It professes to assign the penalty of all private injuries, and denies to individuals the right of vindicating their proper cause. This end is certainly not attained without some accommodation to the propensities which it desires to destroy. Still, it recognizes no principle but the production of the greatest eventual good with the least immediate injury; and to regard the torture, or the death of any human being as unjust, of whatever mischief he may have been the author, so that the result shall not more than compensate for the immediate pain.

Mankind, transmitting from generation to generation the legacy of accumulated vengeances, and pursuing with the feelings of duty the misery of their fellow-beings, have not failed to attribute to the Universal Cause a character analogous with their own. The image of this invisible, mysterious Being, is more or less excellent and perfect — resembles more or less its original — in proportion to the perfection of the mind on which it is impressed. Thus, that nation which has arrived at the highest step in the scale of moral progression will believe most purely in that God, the knowledge of whose real attributes is considered as the firmest basis of the true religion. The reason of the belief of each individual, also, will be so far regulated by his conceptions of what is good. Thus, the conceptions which any nation or individual entertains of the God of its popular worship may be inferred from their own actions and opinions, which are the subjects of their approbation among their fellow-men. Jesus Christ instructed his disciples to be perfect, as their Father in Heaven is perfect, declaring at the same time his belief that human perfection requires the refraining from revenge and retribution in any of its various shapes.

The perfection of the human and the divine character are thus asserted to be the same. Man, by resembling God, fulfils most accurately the tendencies of his nature; and God comprehends within himself all that constitutes human perfection. Thus, God is a model through which the excellence of man is to be estimated, whilst the *abstract* perfection of the human character is the type of the *actual* perfection of the divine. It is not to be believed that a person of such comprehensive views as Jesus Christ could have fallen into so manifest a contradiction as to assert that men would be tortured after death by that Being whose character is held up as a model to human kind, because he is incapable of malevolence and revenge. All the arguments which have been brought forward to justify retribution fail, when retribution is destined neither to operate as an example to other agents nor to the offender himself. How feeble such reasoning is to be considered has been already shown; but it is the character of an evil Dæmon to consign the beings whom he has endowed with sensation to unprofitable anguish. The peculiar circumstances attendant on the conception of God casting sinners to burn in Hell forever, combine to render that conception the most perfect specimen of the greatest imaginable crime. Jesus Christ represented God as the principle of all good, the source of all happiness, the wise and benevolent Creator and Preserver of all living things. But the interpreters of his doctrines have confounded the good and the evil principle. They observed the emanations of their universal natures to be inextricably entangled in the world, and, trembling before the power of the cause of all things, addressed to it such flattery as is acceptable to the ministers of human tyranny, attributing love and wisdom to those energies which they felt to be exerted indifferently for the purposes of benefit and calamity.

Jesus Christ expressly asserts that distinction between the good and evil principle which it has been the practice of all theologians to confound. How far his doctrines, or their interpretation, may be true, it would scarcely have been worth while to inquire, if the one did not afford an example and an incentive to the attainment of true virtue, whilst the other holds out a sanction and apology for every species of mean and cruel vice.

It cannot be precisely ascertained in what degree Jesus Christ accommodated his doctrines to the opinions of his auditors; or in what degree he really said all that he is related to have said. He has left no written record of himself, and we are compelled to judge from the imperfect and obscure information which his biographers (persons certainly of very undisciplined and undiscriminating minds) have transmitted to posterity. These writers (our only guides) impute sentiments to Jesus Christ which flatly contradict each other. They represent him as narrow, superstitious, and exquisitely vindictive and malicious. They insert, in the midst of a strain of impassioned eloquence or sagest exhortation, a sentiment only remarkable for its naked and drivelling folly. But it is not difficult to distinguish the inventions by which these historians have filled up the interstices of tradition, or corrupted the simplicity of truth from the real character of their rude amazement. They have left sufficiently clear indications of the genuine character of Jesus Christ to rescue it forever from the imputations cast upon it by their ignorance and fanaticism. We discover that he is the enemy of oppression and of falsehood; that he is the advocate of equal justice; that he is neither disposed to sanction bloodshed or deceit, under whatsoever pretences their practice may be vindicated. We discover that he was a man of meek and majestic demeanor, calm in danger; of natural and simple thought and habits; beloved to adoration by his adherents; unmoved, solemn, and severe.

It is utterly incredible that this man said, that if you hate your enemy you would find it to your account to return him good for evil; since, by such a temporary oblivion of vengeance, you would heap coals of fire on his head. Where such contradictions occur, a favorable construction is warranted by the general innocence of manners and comprehensiveness of views which he is represented to possess. The rule of criticism to be adopted in judging of the life, actions, and words of a man who has acted any conspicuous part in the revolutions of the world, should not be narrow. We ought to form a general image of his character and of his doctrines, and refer to this whole the distinct portions of actions and speech by which they are diversified. It is not here asserted that no contradictions are to be admitted to have taken place in the system of Jesus Christ between doctrines promulgated in different states of feeling or information, or even such as are implied in the enunciation of a scheme of thought, various and obscure through its immensity and depth. It is not asserted that no degree of human indignation ever hurried him, beyond the limits which his calmer mood had placed, to disapprobation against vice and folly. Those deviations from the history of his life are alone to be vindicated which represent his own essential character in contradiction with itself.

Every human mind has what Bacon calls its "*idola specûs*"—peculiar images which reside in the inner cave of thought. These constitute the essential and distinctive character of every human being; to which every action and every word have intimate relation; and by which, in depicting a character, the genuineness and meaning of these words and actions are to be determined. Every fanatic or enemy of virtue is not at liberty to misrepresent the greatest geniuses and most heroic defenders of all that is valuable in this mortal world. History, to gain any credit, must contain some truth, and that truth shall thus be made a sufficient indication of prejudice and deceit.

With respect to the miracles which these biographers have related, I have already declined to enter into any discussion on their nature or their existence. The supposition of their falsehood or their truth would modify in no degree the hues of the picture which is attempted to be delineated. To judge truly of the moral and philosophical character of Socrates, it is not necessary to determine the question of the familiar Spirit which [it] is supposed that he believed to attend on him. The power of the human mind, relatively to intercourse with, or dominion over, the invisible world, is doubtless an interesting theme of discussion; but the connection of the instance of Jesus Christ with the established religion of the country in which I write, renders it dangerous to subject one's self to the imputation of introducing new Gods or abolishing old ones; nor is the duty of mutual forbearance sufficiently understood to render it certain that the metaphysician and the moralist, even though he carefully sacrifice a cock to Esculapius, may not receive something analogous to the bowl of hemlock for the reward of his labors. Much, however, of what his [Christ's] biographers have asserted, is not to be rejected merely because inferences, inconsistent with the general spirit of his system, are to be adduced from its admission. Jesus Christ did what every other reformer who has produced any considerable effect upon the world has done. He accommodated his doctrines to the prepossessions of those whom he addressed. He used a language for this view sufficiently familiar to our comprehensions. He said, — However new or strange my doctrines may appear to you, they are in fact only the restoration and reëstablishment of those original institutions and ancient customs of your own law and religion. The constitutions of your faith and policy, although perfect in their origin, have become corrupt and altered, and have fallen into decay. I profess to restore them to their pristine authority and splendor. "Think not that I am come to destroy the Law and the Prophets. I am come not to destroy, but to fulfil. Till heaven and earth pass away, one jot or one tittle shall in nowise pass away from the Law, till all be fulfilled." Thus, like a skilful orator (see Cicero, *De Oratore*), he secures the prejudices of his auditors, and induces them, by his professions of sympathy with their feelings, to enter with a willing mind into the exposition of his own. The art of persuasion differs from that of reasoning; and it is of no small moment, to the success even of a true cause, that the judges who are to determine on its merits should be free from those national and religious predilections which render the multitude both deaf and blind.

Let not this practice be considered as an unworthy artifice. It were best for the cause of reason that mankind should acknowledge no authority but its own; but it is useful to a certain extent, that they should not consider those institutions which they have been habituated to reverence as opposing an obstacle to its admission. All reformers have been compelled to practice this misrepresentation of their own true feelings and opinions. It is deeply to be lamented that a word should ever issue from human lips which contains the minutest alloy of dissimulation, or simulation, or hypocrisy, or exaggeration, or anything but the precise and rigid image which is present to the mind, and which ought to dictate the expression. But the practice of utter sincerity towards other men would avail to no good end, if they were incapable of practising it towards their own minds. In fact, truth cannot be communicated until it is perceived.

The interests, therefore, of truth require that an orator should, as far as possible, produce in his hearers that state of mind on which alone his exhortations could fairly be contemplated and examined.

Having produced this favorable disposition of mind, Jesus Christ proceeds to qualify, and finally to abrogate, the system of the Jewish law. He descants upon its insufficiency as a code of moral conduct, which it professed to be, and absolutely selects the law of retaliation as an instance of the absurdity and immorality of its institutions. The conclusion of the speech is in a strain of the most daring and most impassioned speculation. He seems emboldened by the success of his exculpation to the multitude, to declare in public the utmost singularity of his faith. He tramples upon all received opinions, on all the cherished luxuries and superstitions of mankind. He bids them cast aside the claims of custom and blind faith, by which they have been encompassed from the very cradle of their being, and receive the imitator and minister of the Universal God.

EQUALITY OF MANKIND.

"The spirit of the Lord is upon me, because he hath chosen me to preach the gospel to the poor; He hath sent me to heal the broken-hearted, to preach deliverance to the captives, and recovery of sight to the blind, and to set at liberty them that are bruised." (Luke, ch. iv., v. 18.) This is an enunciation of all that Plato and Diogenes have speculated upon the equality of mankind. They saw that the great majority of the human species were reduced to the situation of squalid ignorance and moral imbecility, for the purpose of purveying for the luxury of a few, and contributing to the satisfaction of their thirst for power. Too mean-spirited and too feeble in resolve to attempt the conquest of their own evil passions, and of the difficulties of the material world, men sought dominion over their fellow-men, as an easy method to gain that apparent majesty and power which the instinct of their nature requires. Plato wrote the scheme of a republic, in which law should watch over the equal distribution of the external instruments of unequal power — honors, property, &c. Diogenes devised a nobler and a more worthy system of opposition to the system of the slave and tyrant. He said: "It is in the power of each individual to level the inequality which is the topic of the complaint of mankind. Let him be aware of his own worth, and the station which he occupies in the scale of moral beings. Diamonds and gold, palaces and sceptres, derive their value from the opinion of mankind. The only sumptuary law which can be imposed on the use and fabrication of these instruments of mischief and deceit, these symbols of successful injustice, is the law of opinion. Every man possesses the power in this respect, to legislate for himself. Let him be well aware of his own worth and moral dignity. Let him yield in meek reverence to any wiser or worthier than he, so long as he accords no veneration to the splendor of his apparel, the luxury of his food, the multitude of his flatterers and slaves. It is because, mankind, ye value and seek the empty pageantry of wealth and social power, that ye are enslaved to its possessions. Decrease your physical wants; learn to live, so far as nourishment and shelter are concerned, like the beast of the forest and the birds of the air; ye will need not to complain, that other individuals of your species are surrounded by the diseases of luxury and the vices of subserviency and oppression." With all those who are truly wise, there will be an entire community, not only of thoughts and feelings, but also of external possessions. Insomuch, therefore, as ye live [wisely], ye may enjoy the community of whatsoever benefits arise from the inventions of civilized life. They are of value only for purposes of mental power; they are of value only as they are capable of being shared and applied to the common advantage of philosophy: and, if there be no love among men, whatever institutions they may frame must be subservient to the same purpose — to the continuance of inequality. If there be no love among men, it is best that he who sees through the hollowness of their professions should fly from their society, and suffice to his own soul. In wisdom, he will thus lose nothing; in power, he will gain everything. In proportion to the love existing among men, so will be the community of property and power. Among true and real friends, all is common; and, were ignorance and envy and superstition banished from the world, all mankind would be friends. The only perfect and genuine republic is that which comprehends every living being. Those distinctions which have been artificially set up, of nations, societies, families, and religions, are only general names, expressing the abhorrence and contempt with which men blindly consider their fellow-men. I love my country; I love the city in which I was born; my parents, my wife, and the children of my care; and to this city, this woman, and this nation, it is incumbent on me to do all the benefit in my power. To what do these distinctions point, but to an evident denial of the Unity which humanity imposes on you of doing every possible good to every individual, under whatever denomination he may be comprehended, to whom you have the power of doing it? You ought to love all mankind; nay, every individual of mankind. You ought not to love the individuals of your domestic circle less, but to love those who exist beyond it more. Once make the feelings of confidence and of affection universal, and the distinctions of property and power will vanish; nor are they to be abolished without substituting something equivalent in mischief to them, until all mankind shall acknowledge an entire community of rights.

But, as the shades of night are dispelled by the faintest glimmerings of dawn, so shall the minutest progress of the benevolent feelings disperse, in some degree, the gloom of tyranny, and [curb the] ministers of mutual suspicion and abhorrence. Your physical wants are few, whilst those of your mind and heart cannot be numbered or described, from their multitude and complication. To secure the gratification of the former, you have made yourselves the bondslaves of each other.

They have cultivated these meaner wants to so great an excess as to judge nothing so valuable or desirable

[as] what relates to their gratification. Hence has arisen a system of passions which loses sight of the end they were originally awakened to attain. Fame, power, and gold, are loved for their own sakes — are worshipped with a blind, habitual idolatry. The pageantry of empire, and the fame of irresistible might, are contemplated by the possessor with unmeaning complacency, without a retrospect to the prosperities which first made him consider them of value. It is from the cultivation of the most contemptible properties of human nature that discord and torpor and indifference, by which the moral universe is disordered, essentially depend. So long as these are the ties by which human society is connected, let it not be admitted that they are fragile.

Before man can be free, and equal, and truly wise, he must cast aside the chains of habit and superstition; he must strip sensuality of its pomp, and selfishness of its excuses, and contemplate actions and objects as they really are. He will discover the wisdom of universal love; he will feel the meanness and the injustice of sacrificing the reason and the liberty of his fellow-men to the indulgence of his physical appetites, and becoming a party to their degradation by the consummation of his own. He will consider, εὐγέναιας δέκαι.

Such, with those differences only incidental to the age and state of society in which they were promulgated, appear to have been the doctrines of Jesus Christ. It is not too much to assert that they have been the doctrines of every just and compassionate mind that ever speculated on the social nature of man. The dogma of the equality of mankind has been advocated with various success, in different ages of the world. It was imperfectly understood, but a kind of instinct in its favor influenced considerably the practice of ancient Greece and Rome. Attempts to establish usages, founded on this dogma, have been made in modern Europe, in several instances, since the revival of literature and the arts. Rousseau has vindicated this opinion with all the eloquence of sincere and earnest faith; and is, perhaps, the philospher among the moderns who, in the structure of his feelings and understanding, resembles most nearly the mysterious sage of Judea. It is impossible to read those passionate words in which Jesus Christ upbraids the pusillanimity and sensuality of mankind, without being strongly reminded of the more connected and systematic enthusiasm of Rousseau. "No man," says Jesus Christ, "can serve two masters. Take, therefore, no thought for to-morrow, for the morrow shall take thought for the things of itself. Sufficient unto the day is the evil thereof." If we would profit by the wisdom of a sublime and poetical mind, we must beware of the vulgar error of interpreting literally every expression it employs. Nothing can well be more remote from truth than the literal and strict construction of such expressions as Jesus Christ delivers, or than [to imagine that] it were best for man that he should abandon all his acquirements in physical and intellectual science, and depend on the spontaneous productions of nature for his subsistence. Nothing is more obviously false than that the remedy for the inequality among men consists in their return to the condition of savages and beasts. Philosophy will never be understood if we approach the study of its mysteries with so narrow and illiberal conceptions of its universality. Rousseau certainly did not mean to persuade the immense population of his country to abandon all the arts of life, destroy their habitations and their temples, and become the inhabitants of the woods. He addressed the most enlightened of his compatriots, and endeavored to persuade them to set the example of a pure and simple life, by placing in the strongest point of view his conceptions of the calamitous and diseased aspect which, overgrown as it is with the vices of sensuality and selfishness, is exhibited by civilized society. Nor can it be believed that Jesus Christ endeavored to prevail on the inhabitants of Jerusalem neither to till their fields, nor to frame a shelter against the sky, nor to provide food for the morrow. He simply exposes, with the passionate rhetoric of enthusiastic love towards all human beings, the miseries and mischiefs of that system which makes all things subservient to the subsistence of the material frame of man. He warns them that no man can serve two masters — God and Mammon; that it is impossible at once to be high-minded and just and wise, and to comply with the accustomed forms of human society, seek power, wealth, or empire, either from the idolatry of habit, or as the direct instruments of sensual gratification. He instructs them that clothing and food and shelter are not, as they suppose, the true end of human life, but only certain means, to be valued in proportion to their subserviency to that end. These means it is the right of every human being to possess, and that in the same degree. In this respect the fowls of the air and the lilies of the field are examples for the imitation of mankind. They are clothed and fed by the Universal God. Permit, therefore, the Spirit of this benignant Principle to visit your intellectual frame, or, in other words, become just and pure. When you understand the degree of attention which the requisitions of your physical nature demand, you will perceive how little labor suffices for their satisfaction. Your Heavenly Father knoweth you have need of these things. The universal Harmony, or Reason, which makes your passive frame of thought its dwelling, in proportion to the purity and majesty of its nature will instruct you, if ye are willing to attain that exalted condition, in what manner to possess all the objects necessary for your material subsistence. All men are [impelled] to become thus pure and happy. All men are called to participate in the community of Nature's gifts. The man who has fewest bodily wants approaches nearest to the Divine Nature. Satisfy these wants at the cheapest rate, and expend the remaining energies of your nature in the attainment of virtue and knowledge. The mighty frame of the wonderful and lovely world is the food of your contemplation, and living beings who resemble your own nature, and are bound to you by similarity of sensations, are destined to be the nutriment of your affection; united, they are the consummation of the widest hopes your mind can contain. Ye can expend thus no labor on mechanism consecrated to luxury and pride. How abundant will not be your progress in all that truly ennobles and extends human nature! By rendering yourselves thus worthy, ye will be as free in your imaginations as the swift and many-colored fowls of the air, and as beautiful in pure simplicity as the lilies of the field. In proportion as mankind becomes wise — yes, in exact proportion to that wisdom — should be the extinction of the unequal system under which they now subsist. Government is, in fact, the mere badge of their depravity. They are so little aware of the inestimable benefits of mutual love as to indulge, without thought, and almost without motive, in the worst excesses of selfishness and malice. Hence, without graduating human society into a scale of empire and subjection, its very existence has become impossible. It is necessary that universal benevolence should supersede the regulations of precedent and prescription, before these regulations can safely be abolished. Meanwhile, their very subsistence depends on the system of injustice and violence which they have been devised to palliate. They suppose men endowed with the power of deliberating and determining for their equals; whilst these men, as frail and as ignorant as the multitude whom they rule, possess, as a practical consequence of this power, the right which they of necessity exercise to prevent, (together with their own), the physical and moral and intellectual nature of all mankind.

It is the object of wisdom to equalize the distinctions on which this power depends, by exhibiting in their proper worthlessness the objects, a contention concerning which renders its existence a necessary evil. The evil, in fact, is virtually abolished wherever *justice* is practised; and it is abolished in precise proportion to the prevalence of true virtue.

The whole frame of human things is infected by an insidious poison. Hence it is that man is blind in his understanding, corrupt in his moral sense, and diseased in his physical functions. The wisest and most sublime of the ancient poets saw this truth, and embodied their conception of its value in retrospect to the earliest ages of mankind. They represented equality as the reign of Saturn, and taught that mankind had gradually degenerated from the virtue which enabled them to enjoy or maintain this happy state. Their doctrine was philosophically false. Later and more correct observations have instructed us that uncivilized man is the most pernicious and miserable of beings, and that the violence and injustice, which are the genuine indications of real inequality, obtain in the society of these beings without palliation. Their imaginations of a happier state of human society were referred, in truth, to the Saturnian period; they ministered, indeed, to thoughts of despondency and sorrow. But they were the children of airy hope — the prophets and parents of man's futurity. Man was once as a wild beast; he has become a moralist, a metaphysican, a poet, and an astronomer. Lucretius or Virgil might have referred the comparison to themselves; and, as a proof of the progress of the nature of man, challenged a comparison with the cannibals of Scythia.*

* Jesus Christ foresaw wnat the poets retrospectively imagined.

The experience of the ages which have intervened between the present period and that in which Jesus Christ taught, tends to prove his doctrine, and to illustrate theirs. There is more equality because there is more justice, and there is more justice because there is more universal knowledge.

To the accomplishment of such mighty hopes were the views of Jesus Christ extended; such did he believe to be the tendency of his doctrines — the abolition of artificial distinctions among mankind, so far as the love which it becomes all human beings to bear towards each other, and the knowledge of truth from which that love will never fail to be produced, avail to their destruction. A young man came to Jesus Christ, struck by the miraculous dignity and simplicity of his character, and attracted by the words of power which he uttered. He demanded to be considered as one of the followers of his creed. "Sell all that thou hast," replied the philosopher; "give it to the poor, and follow me." But the young man had large possessions, and he went away sorrowing.

The system of equality was attempted, after Jesus Christ's death, to be carried into effect by his followers. "They that believed had all things in common; they sold their possessions and goods, and parted them to all men, as every man had need; and they continued daily with one accord in the temple, and, breaking bread from house to house, did eat their meat with gladness and singleness of heart." (Acts, ch. 2.)

The practical application of the doctrines of strict

justice to a state of society established in its contempt, was such as might have been expected. After the transitory glow of enthusiasm had faded from the minds of men, precedent and habit resumed their empire; they broke like an universal deluge on one shrinking and solitary island. Men to whom birth had allotted ample possession, looked with complacency on sumptuous apartments and luxurious food, and those ceremonials of delusive majesty which surround the throne of power and the court of wealth. Men from whom these things were withheld by their condition, began again to gaze with stupid envy on pernicious splendor; and, by desiring the false greatness of another's state, to sacrifice the intrinsic dignity of their own. The demagogues of the infant republic of the Christian sect, attaining, through eloquence or artifice, to influence amongst its members, first violated (under the pretence of watching over their integrity) the institutions established for the common and equal benefit of all. These demagogues artfully silenced the voice of the moral sense among them by engaging them to attend, not so much to the cultivation of a virtuous and happy life in this mortal scene, as to the attainment of a fortunate condition after death; not so much to the consideration of those means, by which the state of man is adorned and improved, as an inquiry into the secrets of the connection between God and the world — things which, they well knew, were not to be explained, or even to be conceived. The system of equality which they established, necessarily fell to the ground, because it is a system that must result from, rather than precede, the moral improvement of human kind. It was a circumstance of no moment that the first adherents of the system of Jesus Christ cast their property into a common stock. The same degree of real community of property could have subsisted without this formality, which served only to extend a temptation of dishonesty to the treasurers of so considerable a patrimony. Every man, in proportion to his virtue, considers himself, with respect to the great community of mankind, as the steward and guardian of their interests in the property which he chances to possess. Every man, in proportion to his wisdom, sees the manner in which it is his duty to employ the resources which the consent of mankind has intrusted to his discretion. Such is the [annihilation] of the unjust inequality of powers and conditions existing in the world, and so gradually and inevitably is the progress of equality accommodated to the progress of wisdom and of virtue among mankind.

Meanwhile, some benefit has not failed to flow from the imperfect attempts which have been made, to erect a system of equal rights to property and power, upon the basis of arbitrary institutions. They have undoubtedly, in every case, from the instability of their formation, failed. Still, they constitute a record of those epochs at which a true sense of justice suggested itself to the understandings of men, so that they consented to forego all the cherished delights of luxury, all the habitual gratifications arising out of the possession or the expectations of power, all the superstitions with which the accumulated authority of ages had made them dear and venerable. They are so many trophies erected in the enemy's land, to mark the limits of the victorious progress of truth and justice.

Jesus Christ did not fail to advert to the

[THE REST IS WANTING.]

THE END.